Vaughn Joy
Selling Out Santa

Pop Culture in Context

Edited by
Liz W. Faber, Emily Hamilton-Honey,
and Judith Rauscher

Volume 1

Vaughn Joy

Selling Out Santa

—

Hollywood Christmas Films in the Age of McCarthy

DE GRUYTER

ISBN 978-3-11-162416-7
e-ISBN (PDF) 978-3-11-163142-4
e-ISBN (EPUB) 978-3-11-163153-0
DOI https://doi.org/10.1515/9783111631424

Library of Congress Control Number: 2025939182

Bibliographic information published by the Deutsche Nationalbibliothek
The Deutsche Nationalbibliothek lists this publication in the Deutsche Nationalbibliografie;
detailed bibliographic data are available on the Internet at http://dnb.dnb.de.

© 2026 the author(s), published by Walter de Gruyter GmbH, Berlin/Boston, Genthiner Str. 13, 10785
Berlin, Germany.
This book is published with open access at www.degruyterbrill.com.

Cover image: duckycards / E+ / Getty Images

www.degruyterbrill.com
Questions about General Product Safety Regulation:
productsafety@degruyterbrill.com

Acknowledgements

As will be seen in this book, Christmas is not just a day; it is a frame of mind. Kris Kringle (Edmund Gwenn) expresses this sentiment in the now-classic American Christmas film *Miracle on 34th Street* (1947). These words echo throughout the following pages as a reminder that at Christmas, we are our best selves, we project a vision of the people we wish we always were with the hope that, as Scrooge reminds us in Charles Dickens's *A Christmas Carol*, we might carry Christmas with us in our hearts all the year. I have been fortunate enough to have found a collection of loving individuals, my very own Bob Cratchits, who carry the Christmas spirit in them, extending goodwill, generosity, and random acts of kindness just to make others' lives a little bit brighter, lighter, and lovelier.

Firstly, I would like to thank my dissertation committee Melvyn Stokes, Alex Goodall, Nick Witham, Thomas Doherty for their guidance, suggestions, and support throughout the writing and publishing process.

Special thanks to everyone at De Gruyter Brill including Stella Diedrich for her keen editing skills, Ulla Schmidt for her patience, and especially David Eisler for his immense faith in my work. Likewise, my gratitude goes out to UCL for providing the funding to publish this book as an Open Access e-book. Education and knowledge should be accessible to all.

I would also like to thank the staff of the Reuben Library at the British Film Institute and Joan Miller, archivist of The Ogden and Mary Louise Reid Cinema Archives at Wesleyan University. The sources in each of these archives proved invaluable to the research and the conclusions drawn in this book.

Countless individuals deserve recognition and gratitude for their roles in my academic career, but none more than George B. Stow whose genuine faith in me – and tough love mentoring – inspired me to have faith in myself as a researcher, as a historian, as a writer, and as a person from a similar background. This book and a glass of blackberry brandy are offered in his memory.

Alongside Dr. Stow, I'd like to thank Charles Desnoyers for his friendship in mentorship, Andrew Dolan for his classical kindness, and Francis Ryan for opening up the world of cultural histories and introducing me to some of the authors quoted in these pages. A massive thank you as well to Jon Chandler for his support in every aspect of my academics and future.

Secondly, I would be remiss if my main Cratchits were not named. To my brother, Teagan Patrick Joy, for his love, guidance, and strength over the last 30 years: thank you for loving me. To my oldest friends, Regan Moran, Alison Ryan, and Dominic Tunney, for being my constants: thank you for always, always being there and for being my sunshine. To Susie Ashton for her emotional range: thank you for making me laugh as I cry (and until I cry again). To Dr. Genny for her fast friendship: thank you for becoming one of my newest oldest friends. To Dr. Andrzej Stuart-Thompson for reinvigorating my intellectual passions: thank you for being brilliant and for being in my life. To Dara Howley for her warmth and hospitality: thank you for giving me a home. To Robert Camaj, Cait Moser, Marie Wheatley, Paul Fitzpatrick, Dominic Steele, Jeff Lucia, Holly Causer, James Worth, Shane Howley, Kelly Demjanick, Simon Heptinstall, Tobi Olowe, and so many other wonderful people whom I am lucky enough to call my friends and family: thank you.

To Mr. Cary Grant himself, my husband Benjamin Railton: thank you. Thank you for your love, your gentleness, your hours upon hours of emotional and mental support, your editing prowess, and your good influence on my life (read: introducing me to the American Studies treasure of Bruce Springsteen). I am so happy I married you.

I dedicate this book to my three grandfathers:

My Poppop, David, aka Kris Kringle himself.

My Papa, Bill, for teaching me that Santa is a Teamster.

My Pappy, Bernie, my Jewish Santa à la Danny Kaye, who embodied the Christmas spirit every day of his life and whose selflessness inspires me every day of mine.

Contents

Introduction

Christmas isn't just a day. It's a frame of mind. That's what's been changing.
- Kris Kringle, *Miracle on 34th Street* (1947)

American Christmas is and has always been a frame of mind, not only for the individual but for the national audience as well. In the holiday classic *Miracle on 34th Street* (1947), the heartwarming Santa Claus figure Kris Kringle (Edmund Gwenn) voices concern for the ways in which Christmas has been changing in his contemporary 1947 world. Little did Kringle know, he had already been bought and sold not only by R.H. Macy who hired him to sell overstock toys in the Manhattan department store as the face of Christmas, but also by Hollywood where Christmas was increasingly being seen as a marketable, lucrative frame of a uniquely American post-war mind. Through this festive frame, a post-war, early Cold War Hollywood deconstructed and reconstructed deeply American ideas and traditions, selling Santa out to prevailing ideas of commercialism, dispelling Dickens's collectivist spirit in favor of individualist seclusion, and condemning Capra's populist hallmarks to a fate worse than a stocking full of coal.

Kringle's fear that both he and his beloved holiday had been rebranded into something unfamiliar by unknown economic forces echoes a social and political fear of widespread change and also carries the implication that the Christmas he had known and loved before had always been a stable, consistent American tradition. While Kringle's concerns of social change are entirely accurate to the post-war moment, the idea of the holiday's consistency is a misconception and a crucial one to understanding how the frame of mind that is Christmas is so intimately bound with dominant American narratives and attitudes of any given era. Particularly, in Hollywood's polished portrayals of an already idealized version of Americana, Christmas reflects America's contemporary proclaimed values wrapped in tinsel and bows for an audience willing and eager to retreat into an escapist fantasy of ostensible goodwill despite any major challenges of their times. In 1947, this was never truer nor more accurate, though *Miracle*'s Kringle could not have known how drastically American Christmas as a mentality was about to change as a direct result of the political, cultural, economic, and social moment imminently bearing down on Hollywood.

* * *

Never a singular thing in itself, Christmas in America has always been an amalgamation of various traditions that bring together communities of immigrants with different customs, religions, and beliefs in the natural world. As a combination of winter celebrations, Saturnalia, and Christian holy days, the "American" Christmas developed alongside American identities and what emerged was a holiday so closely linked with the social, cultural, and political conditions of any given era. In the nineteenth century, as Penne L. Restad argues, media capabilities, commercial opportunities, and the marketplace of ideas expanded nationally as byproducts of the goal of a reunified and expanded national identity that emerged in the years following the American Civil War.[1] Christmas became a significant national holiday to express these idealized American values of community, unification, and goodwill with a profound connection between that holiday tradition and American patriotism itself.[2]

American Christmas traditions thus developed as a reflection of the needs of the moment. In each era of American history, Christmas has served a political, social, economic, and cultural purpose that ultimately exhibits an idealized version of the values for which Americans espouse themselves to stand. Stephen Nissenbaum, in his definitive book on the origins of American Christmas traditions through the nineteenth century, summarizes the significance of Christmas to American identity as follows:

> Christmas rituals—whether in the form of the rowdy excesses of carnival or the more tender excesses that surround the Christmas tree—have long served to transfigure our ordinary behavior in an almost magical fashion, in ways that reveal something of what we would like to be, what we once were, or what we are becoming despite ourselves. It is because the celebration of Christmas always illuminates these underlying features of the social landscape—and sometimes the very 'fault lines' which threaten to divide it—that the content of the holiday, its timing, and even the matter of whether to celebrate it at all, have often been hotly contested.[3]

Christmas as an illumination of the social landscape is the guiding principle of this book. As this landscape changes, perceptions of Christmas change in tandem. These changes have been visible in mass media since the nineteenth century with illustrations, literature, and physical representations of Christmas iconography updated and adapted for the periods in which they are invoked. As an annual celebration with such wide-reaching cultural coverage and implications, the American Christmas tradition is forever evolving, expanding, and encapsulating all that has come before, building on centuries of traditions while also being distilled into a seemingly singular celebration. It is both plural in its make-up and singular

---

1 Penne L. Restad, *Christmas in America: A History* (New York: Oxford University Press, 1995), 91.
2 Karal Ann Marling, *Merry Christmas!: Celebrating America's Greatest Holiday* (Cambridge, MA: Harvard University Press, 2001), 83.
3 Stephen Nissenbaum, *The Battle for Christmas: A Cultural History of America's Most Cherished Holiday*, 1st ed. (New York: Vintage Books, 1996), xii.

in its common portrayals, especially in the media and in its most glamourized form in Hollywood films.

Selling Out Santa offers several multi-layered arguments and perspectives that each carry at their core the necessity of connecting the content of films to the political, cultural, social, and economic moments in which they are made. The primary theory within this book is that each of these aspects of the wider world beyond a film have significant impacts on the practicalities of its production, the means of its marketing, and the realities of its reception in which the audiences will meet the film with their own experiential understanding of their times and react to the filmic rendering of that cultural messaging on screen whether that messaging is overtly political or not. Ultimately, the interconnectivity between the political, cultural, social, and economic realms is all present in the content of films depicting a vision of the real world and therefore make a statement about the real-world moment in which the film is made. This book demonstrates how the Christmas films studied fit into their appropriate historical contexts by analyzing a vast cross-section of sources including manuscript collections from federal agencies, memoirs and autobiographies, social surveys, reception materials, promotional materials, contemporary scholarly works and studies, and analysis of the films themselves.

Perhaps the most prominent film historian bringing these strands of life in American society together as a particular lens through which to view American cinema as a cultural artifact in itself, was Robert Sklar with his seminal 1975 book *Movie-Made America: A Cultural History of American Movies.* In the preface, Sklar writes, "One of the tasks of cultural historians is to elucidate the nature of cultural power in the modern United States, and more important, its connections with economic, social, and political power."[4] In the mid-century in particular, film began to be seen as a productive tool for bringing together these aspects of life – political, social, and economic – on screen as a space to construct and exert that cultural power. As film and propaganda scholar Jonathan Auerbach wrote, "film

4 Robert Sklar, *Movie-Made America: A Cultural History of American Movies*, rev. ed. (New York: Vintage Books, 1994), x. Other such ideas about the prominence of film to cultural histories of the US and the relationship between them and the political, social, and economic moments which they are both reflecting and reacting to have been wide-ranging in historical scholarship for decades. In 1974, Peter C. Rollins wrote a bibliographic essay capturing scholars' analyses of how "films inevitably register the feelings and attitudes of the periods in which they are made." Similarly, [replace capital I] In 1980, Vivian Sobchack's bibliographic essay explored Film Studies as integral to American Studies and cultural history, writing "Movies are a continuous inscription and interpretation of American experience through time and in the world." Peter C. Rollins, "Film and American Studies: Questions, Activities, Guides", *American Quarterly* 26, no. 3 (1974): 249; Vivian C. Sobchack, "Beyond Visual Aids: American Film as American Culture", *American Quarterly* 32, no. 3 (1980): 293.

could so fluently articulate as well as mold mass desires". This fluency and command of the audience is on display in the post-war moment in which the US government, fresh from their development of cinematic propaganda for the war effort, turned their sights to how film could potentially be used against US interests if communist propaganda supplanted that on behalf of the military.[5]

This study takes the 15 years encapsulating this post-war period and the early Cold War between 1946 and 1961 as the setting to argue that the contexts outside of the Christmas films analyzed here impacted those films. This 15-year period is significant for several reasons. Firstly, as Gary W. Reichard argues, these years encapsulating the Harry S. Truman and Dwight D. Eisenhower presidential administrations were the last period of "politics as usual" in modern American history.[6] For Reichard, both before and after these 15 years were eras of extremes with the New Deal era and World War II leading up to 1946 and the intensification of the Cold War and ensuing Vietnam conflict beyond 1961 drastically altering politics for the rest of the twentieth century. These post-war years prior to the Cold War's more heated extremes offered a brief reprieve in which Reichard reads a relatively stable equilibrium within US politics. This book generally agrees with that assessment relative to World War II and the very real threats of nuclear annihilation peaking in 1962 and beyond, but it will explore how even these post-war years of relative stability were tumultuous in themselves filled with the torment of psychological pressures and weaponized fear that impacted the cultural sector, specifically through Hollywood films.

Secondly, this era is defined by Peter Kuznick and James Gilbert as the first wave of the Cold War. As Kuznick and Gilbert write, "Historians debate the date of [the Cold War's] inception but, for our purposes, August 6, 1945, the day the United States dropped the first atomic bomb on Japan and introduced nuclear terror to the world, is as good a starting point as any."[7] So too for the purposes of this book, the Cold War's first phase began in the summer of 1945 and ushered in an age of grappling with the knowledge that, for an American, their nation not only had the capabilities to commit an atrocity, but also the willingness to do so twice. This climate of fear of course escalated in 1949 when it became clear that other nations had begun developing atomic technologies – such as when the USSR tested its

---

5 Jonathan Auerbach, "American Studies and Film, Blindness and Insight", *American Quarterly* 58, no. 1 (2006): 37.
6 Gary W. Reichard, *Politics as Usual: The Age of Truman and Eisenhower* (Arlington Heights, IL: Harlan Davidson, 1988), xv.
7 Peter J. Kuznick and James Burkhart Gilbert, eds., *Rethinking Cold War Culture* (Washington DC: Smithsonian Institution Press, 2001), 1.

first atomic bomb in October 1949 – but it began when the US first used their bombs in 1945.

Throughout this project, the term "post-war" will be used more regularly in conversation with the cultural developments in this 15-year period than the term "Cold War". While both are used, it should be noted that the term "Cold War" as used here is not synonymous with the culture, but rather connotes and imports the nuclear fears, military industrial complex, anti-communism, and general atmosphere of suspicion and angst it created in the US. These aspects of course had an impact on the broader culture, but this book will make a point to emphasize that the "post-war culture" as a generalizing term carries less militaristic connotations than the use of "Cold War culture". As Kuznick and Gilbert write about their similar distinctions, "It is the interaction between these unique elements of Cold War culture and the long-standing trends that existed independently and in large part antedated the Cold War that created American civilization in this age."[8] Emphasizing that the post-war period is a continuation or reinvention of established American cultural trends up to the mid-century allows for this disambiguation and more precise invocation of the fears associated with the Cold War without implying a discontinuity from earlier periods, such as with the discussions of Dickensian tropes in Chapter 2 or dating and marriage trends in Chapter 3.

Thirdly, when looking at Hollywood specifically, the political, cultural, economic, and social reality of this 15-year period was one of tremendous upset and change in the motion picture industry's business practices. In the late 1940s and early 1950s, multiple branches of the US federal government had an overwhelming presence in Hollywood pressuring the industry's executives to make cultural changes within its business practices – including enacting the Hollywood blacklist –, altering those practices' financial practicalities via antitrust regulation, and exerting their political stances in the cultural sector. This book studies the cultural ramifications of those specific pressures in these years starting in 1946 to understand the filmic standards for Christmas films prior to the overt presence and actions of the House Committee on Un-American Activities (HUAC) regarding Hollywood in 1947, the first popular awareness of federal intervention in the motion picture industry. It then analyses the growing federal presence – by way of covert Federal Bureau of Investigation (FBI) investigations and a decision by the Supreme Court of the United States (SCOTUS) – and the simultaneous cultural changes occurring in Hollywood outputs throughout the 1950s observing that, through the films studied, presentations of Christmas were shifting into vehicles of more socially conservative messaging than those prior. This book finishes its examination of

---

8 Kuznick and Gilbert, 10.

these cultural ramifications in 1961, one year after significant public stands against the Hollywood blacklist that had been imposed by studio executives in response to HUAC's first hearings in 1947.

In understanding these cultural ramifications, it is important to caution intent. While there is evidence explored in Chapters 1 and 3 of the desires for pro-American propaganda in films, this book is not attempting to ascribe to the federal government the intention of drastically altering filmic content. Instead, it explores the consequences of the federal presence within – and cultural and political atmospheres outside of – Hollywood in this period. Some historians of this period do argue that there was a federal intention to censor, influence, and dictate the cultural content of films out of Hollywood. John Sbardellati, for instance, in his book *J. Edgar Hoover Goes to the Movies: The FBI and the Origins of Hollywood's Cold War* clearly states, "Hoover and his allies aimed not merely to harass their political foes but to reshape American culture by fostering a Cold War consensus particularly attuned to the red peril at home."[9] However, establishing such an intention is not the central focus of this book.

Alternatively, in his *Hollywood's Censor: Joseph I. Breen & the Production Code Administration,* Thomas Doherty ascribes changes in the post-war period not to the intentional, malevolent designs of an individual or a singular organization. Rather, he points to myriad "post-war plagues", the responses to which changed cultural content. Specifically, Doherty highlights President of the Motion Picture Association of America (MPAA) Eric Johnston's responses which he describes as "craven, stoic, and sluggish", such as the establishment of the blacklist under the pressure of "panicky moguls".[10] This book largely agrees with Doherty's assessment while focusing primarily on federal pressures on the industry and adding to the atmosphere around the wider "plagues" – such as the growing social and political conservative ideological movements – as layers to the cultural ramifications of said "plagues".

To analyze these cultural ramifications of the federal presence as well as situating the films studied into their wider cultural moments beyond the direct actions within Hollywood itself, this book uses a single genre as a case study: Christmas films. Using a single genre allows for a means of control in examining various established tropes and themes within a set of films to mark changes in their portrayal over time. For instance, Christmas films, as argued in Chapter 4, offer a unique perspective to analyze portrayals of commercialism and consumption

---

9 John Sbardellati, *J. Edgar Hoover Goes to the Movies: The FBI and the Origins of Hollywood's Cold War* (Ithaca, NY: Cornell University Press, 2012), 4.
10 Thomas Doherty, *Hollywood's Censor: Joseph I. Breen & the Production Code Administration* (New York: Columbia University Press, 2007), 228.

across a 15-year period in which the economy is changing considerably and the modern middle class is emerging as a stable social class in itself. Viewing these Christmas films as a source base for the cultural messaging about the consistent concept of commercialism and how it is portrayed at Christmas – an increasingly materialistic holiday – allows for a controlled comparison throughout the 15-year period as social and economic variables changed.

As for the films themselves, this study examines 12 family-oriented Christmas films released by major studios and/or directors between 1946 and 1961. This period begins with Frank Capra's post-war release *It's a Wonderful Life* (1946) – the first Hollywood film to fully engage with the American Christmas tradition – which ushers in a 15-year period of Christmas releases in its wake. The films examined in this book are: *It's a Wonderful Life*, *It Happened on 5th Avenue* (1947), *Miracle on 34th Street* (1947), *Christmas Eve* (1947), *The Bishop's Wife* (1947), *Holiday Affair* (1949), *The Lemon Drop Kid* (1951), *Susan Slept Here* (1954), *White Christmas* (1954), *The Apartment* (1960), *Babes in Toyland* (1961), and *Pocketful of Miracles* (1961). While this is not an exhaustive list of the films that could be considered "Christmas films" in this period, these 12 all exhibit multiple hallmarks of the holiday. For instance, Christmas is integral to the plot of each film, meaning that the plot either could not happen at another time of year or that the plot relies heavily on and is strengthened emotionally by the sentimentality always already imported by the American Christmas tradition. Christmas as a frame of mind, as *Miracle*'s Kringle terms it, is used to imbue the films with connotations of Christmases past for the audience familiar with the holiday's tropes. In some, Christmas might be used to justify morally positive decisions that go against the moral character of the protagonist, as in *The Lemon Drop Kid*; it might be the setting of a traumatic incident made even more difficult due to the kindness, generosity, and prosperity entangled with the season, as in *The Apartment*; or it might be employed as an opportunity for reconciliation with and goodwill towards loved ones as in nearly all of the studied films.

This use of Christmas to import sentiment, goodwill, and a sense of positive communalism is not coincidentally aligned with visions of American ideals. As Restad writes in her comprehensive history of Christmas in America, Hollywood's Christmas films use the genre and its visual and audio cues as directed by the historical American traditions of the holiday – Santa Claus figures, Christmas trees, decorations, classic Christmas music, etc. – to "circumscribe Christmas in order to convey a potent, highly condensed expression of American faith and values."[11] Likewise, in the introduction to his edited volume on Christmas movies, Mark Con-

11 Restad, *Christmas in America*, 171.

nelly writes, "Christmas is important for the conventions it places in the viewer's mind. Such is the significance of Christmas to movies in general."[12] Each of these 12 films uses the sentimentality of its Christmas setting or invocation of icons within the American Christmas tradition, e.g. the "Christmas spirit", as a way to signal American values in an idealized world. For instance, as explored in Chapter 1, *It's a Wonderful Life* employs Dickensian tropes to address the social problems of the post-war period and inspire hope in Americans after multiple decades of nationally traumatic events.

It should also be noted that these 12 Christmas films are stories about white characters in heteronormative relationships from a cross section of social classes across the 15 years. While this is obviously not a true reflection of the American population's actual demographic diversity, it is representative of the vast majority of the filmic outputs from the major Hollywood studios in the post-war period. As cultural texts of this holiday that historically have been used to express an idealized vision of America, it is significant to note that the Christmas films released between 1946 and 1961 feature almost entirely white Americans.

As this project will argue in analyzing these 12 films over this 15-year period, the use of Christmas begins to change in the 1950s for myriad reasons in the wider world. Economically, many Americans were enjoying more financial security than the nation had seen in several decades. Socially, classes were transforming with this increasing economic affluence and the prevailing social attitude was veering towards individualistic conservatism due to the fear and suspicions encouraged by the political situation. Politically, that situation reflected the gradual heating up of the Cold War and the shift to a more conservative government in reaction to the decades of Democratic administrations led predominantly by New Deal policies. Culturally, therefore, the films in this study reflect that growing social conservatism and some of the political conservatism, but more than anything they reflect the tension of the moment by deflecting emotionally into escapism.

There is a tendency in modern parlance to think of "conservative" as a purely political adjective, but I want to resist this inclination. "Conservative" in this book is used in many ways, some of which are political but many of which are social and cultural, by which I mean a literal conservation of social values and resistance to overwhelming cultural change. This social conservatism manifests in the 1950s, as will be seen throughout this book but largely in Chapter 3, as a resounding shift inward, from collectivist to individualist, from robust community to insular family units, from meaningful, cooperative connections to disparate domestic contain-

---

12 Mark Connelly, ed., *Christmas at the Movies: Images of Christmas in American, British and European Cinema*, Cinema and Society Series (London: I.B. Tauris Publishers, 2000), 7.

ment.[13] Social conservatism and its cultural portrayals are always in conversation with the predominant political leanings of a period, but they are also distinct in themselves.

In resisting the inclination to reduce "conservative" to one political definition, I want to similarly make the case for nuance when discussing these topics. The 1950s and Hollywood are two massive topics with innumerable entry points and moving parts. In this book, I hope to make my arguments for the changes of the Hollywood Christmas over time – from Dickensian collectivism through individualist farces into complex expressions of escapist cynicism – with the appropriate nuance and acknowledgement that the trend is not absolute. Instead, this book offers the argument that, in a broad sense, Christmas films were changing and becoming more socially conservative in their presentations of every day American livelihoods.

While this study spans the post-war, early Cold War period in which there were both liberal and conservative presidential administrations, I want to emphasize that the trend I am identifying speaks to a largely fiscally liberal political landscape with a rapidly growing socially conservative consolidation sweeping the cultural sphere, and especially Hollywood. For instance, in Chapter 3, Elaine Tyler May's idea of "domestic containment" frames my argument about the socially conservative presentation of families while Chapter 4 delves into the subtle changes in Hollywood's portrayal of Christmas's commodities during the rebounding of the economy that then thrived under Eisenhower throughout the 1950s in large part due to his liberally high taxes on the wealthy.[14] Both movements are at play and are present in these Christmas films as they reflect the wider changes in society throughout the 1946 to 1961 period.

Further, the Christmas films released in the 1950s are reacting to the similar social and political pressures directly levied on Hollywood by the federal institutions named above. As HUAC carried out the second round of hearings in 1951–52, the motion picture industry was steeped in the anti-communist and anti-labor blacklist, reminding filmmakers that their roles, careers, and livelihoods were under incessant surveillance and threat should they defy the Hollywood ex-

---

13 The phrasing "domestic containment" comes from Elaine Tyler May who argued a domestic counterpart to the US Cold War foreign policy of containment of Communism abroad. Elaine Tyler May, *Homeward Bound: American Families in the Cold War Era*, 3rd ed. (New York: Basic Books, 2017), 16.

14 For more on the complexities of conservatism during the period of the so-called Liberal Consensus, see the historiographical essay, Jennifer Delton, "Politics of Liberal and Conservatism," in *The Routledge History of the Twentieth-Century United States*, ed. by Jerald Podair and Darren Dochuk (New York: Routledge, 2018), 127–137.

ecutives who made the blacklist and were themselves reacting to the pressures placed on them. This trickle-down effect of the political pressures from the power of the state to individual filmmakers had significant ramifications for the cultural outputs of the 1950s and beyond.

This confluence of the economic, social, political, and cultural on multiple levels, from filmmakers to industry heads to the powers of the state to the nation as a whole, and the role that not only the media but also Christmas would come to play in all of this in the 1950s, is best summarized by Christmas historian Karal Ann Marling. Marling writes, "A major reconsideration of Christmas began in the 1950s, a movement toward a holiday whose meaning would be profoundly influenced by the media".[15] As part of this major reconsideration of how the holiday embodied and reflected the nation, sociologist and anthropologist James H. Barnett wrote a survey interpreting the contemporary cultural celebration of Christmas in the US in 1954 entitled *The American Christmas: A Study in National Culture.* This post-war, early Cold War period in itself is significant not only for the US and the world but also for Hollywood specifically, and the use of Christmas as a lens offers a unique chance to look at an established genre consisting almost wholly of particularly idealized American values.

Connelly agrees with this perception of the post-war, early Cold War period as especially important for the development of the modern American Christmas tradition. Connelly writes, "Christmas was, no doubt, more like Christmas in the 1950s."[16] Similarly, as Restad writes, "The film industry streamlined, consolidated, and revised the holiday to match modern American life."[17] As this book argues in agreement with both Connelly and Restad, the holiday was ever-consolidating and adapting to reflect its contemporary contexts in terms of American identity and values, and Hollywood particularly made efforts in this period to establish a universally American aesthetic, tone, and generic expectation of an American Christmas. Restad continues, "In its reach for bigger audiences, media recreated Christmas in the language of the twentieth century. It introduced new stories based on old themes and simplified further the complex issues of Christmas materialism and Christmas spirit."[18] Christmas had been an ever-evolving holiday as an amalgamation of different religions, immigrant traditions, and regionally specific customs that was streamlined into a consistent cache of tropes and themes identifiable by and accessible to a twentieth-century audience.

---

15 Marling, *Merry Christmas!*, 335.
16 Connelly, *Christmas at the Movies*, 7.
17 Restad, *Christmas in America*, 165.
18 Restad, 164.

Significantly, however, Restad also emphasizes this reciprocal relationship between cultural media and Christmas as they acted on each other. She writes, "media did no more than the culture that it spoke to allowed. Its portrayals of Christmas in the twentieth century sketched a familiar outline of modern life that sharpened the dialectic between the spiritual and the material, and ultimately located in the holiday a commentary on American life."[19] The reciprocity between the American cultural moment and the established Christmas traditions thus far worked together to invent a contemporary, new American Christmas on screen. This book argues that the cultural, social, economic, and political contexts of the 1950s – both in the wider country and within Hollywood itself – constitute the period when this shift occurs and observes the films released between 1946 and 1961, as the necessary context to support the argument for that immense cultural change from antiquated Victorian Santa and Dickensian tropes to the modern American embrace of commercialist escapism. As Connelly writes, "The values of Christmas have become those of America, or vice versa, and Hollywood has thrown its weight behind them."[20]

Chapter 1 explores a microcosmic example of how the political pressures on the motion picture industry starting in 1947 introduced a convoluted and ultimately doomed crusade against communists in which established American traditions were deemed un-American by radical conservative thinkers and organizations. Specifically, the chapter introduces these pressures and the historical context of Hollywood's business practices and working political culture. In this post-war era of Hollywood, political factions began to split based on ideological extremes as led by players within the industry, such as Ronald Reagan and Ayn Rand, who not only welcomed the presence of HUAC and increased social conservatism but also actively facilitated it with their roles in the industry. Next, this chapter turns to the FBI's investigation of one of the most iconic American Christmas films of all time, Frank Capra's *It's a Wonderful Life* (1946).

Chapter 2 expands away from this analysis of a single film to look at four Christmas films released in the following year as they relate not only to other Hollywood releases, namely William Wyler's *The Best Years of Our Lives* (1946), but also to social problems and psychological issues in the post-war period. Examining the four Christmas films – *It Happened on 5th Avenue* (1947), *Miracle on 34th Street* (1947), *Christmas Eve* (1947), and *The Bishop's Wife* (1947) – in their contextual social moment serves two purposes. Firstly, it establishes the significance of the connection between Christmas and contemporary American values and culture in a

---

19 Restad, 164.
20 Connelly, *Christmas at the Movies*, 3.

given period. Secondly, these four films support the argument that, up to 1947, Christmas films were closely linked with both Dickensian traditions and Santa Claus mythologies that necessitated social ills be resolved with goodwill by the film's end. This trend was about to change due to the cultural, political, economic, and social changes in wider society, and especially those directly pressuring Hollywood, to produce cinema less critical of American society than these earlier ones highlighting social problems.

Chapter 3 ties the previous two chapters together by looking at the drastic decline of social problem and psychological films released in the 1950s as a byproduct of both federal political pressures on the industry and the decade's changing culture. This chapter analyses in detail the work of contemporary film analyst Dorothy Jones whose research into HUAC's allegations of communist propaganda in Hollywood films concluded not only that was there no such propaganda, but also that film outputs tended to be reactive to those allegations. In light of the decline of social problem and psychological films, Jones found that films largely conformed to generally lighter fare that resisted critical commentaries on life in the US. This chapter examines four films released between 1949 and 1954 – *Holiday Affair, The Lemon Drop Kid* (1951), *Susan Slept Here* (1954), and *White Christmas* (1954) – to illuminate how Christmas films reflected these changes. Having been associated with the communalist themes of Dickens and Santa Claus for over a century, Christmas on film in this period abruptly becomes much more focused on the individual, the family unit, and the escapist power of romantic comedies.

Chapter 4 diverges from the chronological pattern established in the first three chapters to examine the intimate connection between the contemporary moment and a consistent theme in Christmas narratives for over a century: commercialization. The commercialization of Christmas is analyzed in films from the entire 15-year period with particular focus on *Miracle on 34th Street* and *Holiday Affair* (1949) for how each portrays the post-war economy in department stores at Christmas. Continuing with a close analysis of the period's shopping trends and their reflections on screen as the American economy grew in the 1950s, the chapter finishes with a case study on one particular item mentioned in many of the films in this study: a mink coat. The case study on mink illuminates the drastic changes in economic stability for the white Americans on screen and in society throughout this period as many entered the middle class in the 1950s and items that were once necessities became increasingly affordable luxuries.

Chapter 5 likewise examines the full 15-year period concerned in this book as it offers a comparative study of two filmmakers and their careers as they develop over time. Walt Disney and Frank Capra, two iconic marquee names in mid-century Hollywood, had opposite experiences in this politically intensive post-war period. While Disney cooperated with investigations, named names to HUAC, and remained entirely focused on building his brand by amassing a multi-media empire, Capra became disillusioned with the American values that he spent much of the 1930s and 40s extolling on film. After his services to the American culture in those decades and to the American military during World War II, Capra was rewarded with allegations of communist sentiments in his films and the spiral downwards for his career culminated in the ill-advised and ill-received realist Christmas film *Pocketful of Miracles* (1961). The same week, Disney's far more successful escapist Christmas film *Babes in Toyland* (1961) established a new market for Christmas entertainments in the industry by releasing the first Christmas film specifically marketed toward children. Despite being for children, *Babes in Toyland* matched the tone of the moment by capturing a darker edge and grittier undercurrent that echoed the previous year's Best Picture winner, William Wyler's 1960 Christmas film *The Apartment*.

Ultimately, this book suggests that Christmas films, through their unique perspective offering a pure distillation of secular, idealized visions of Americana, reflected a prominent change over time to what that idealistic America looks like. Hollywood Christmas films are the summation of centuries' worth of amalgamation of various traditions and icons and cultural touchstones that became embedded with each period's contemporary ideas of American identity. The Christmas films released between 1946 and 1961 are no different from this trend but do encapsulate a profound development of the Christmas holiday that occurred in response to the cultural, social, economic, and political contexts of their releases, imbued with all the fear, tension, affluence, social conservatism, familial ideals, gender conventions, and nuclear threats of the post-war, early Cold War period.

Chapter 1
American Archetypes and Un-American Committees: Anti-Communism, the FBI, and *It's a Wonderful Life* (1946)

> This town needs this measly one-horse institution if only to have some place where people can come without crawling to Potter.
> - George Bailey, *It's a Wonderful Life* (1946)

George Bailey, portrayed evocatively by James Stewart in Frank Capra's 1946 *It's a Wonderful Life*, sneers this as a last remark in a confrontation with the corrupt, monopolizing local town banker, Mr. Potter (Lionel Barrymore). This emotional scene between the two is set in 1919 amid a meeting to decide the fate of the Bailey Brothers' Building & Loan Association after the death of its co-founder, George's father, Peter Bailey (Samuel S. Hinds). George sacrificed his college education to stay and help settle his father's estate and run the Building & Loan in the face of its primary adversary and board member, Potter, who motioned that "this measly one-horse institution" be dissolved with all assets turned over to the receiver. George's remark ending his impassioned speech about the value of supporting a hardworking citizenry with a communal banking system in order to provide them housing echoes a set of deep-seated, traditional American values.

For a 1946 audience, George's speech capturing an antipathy to monopolistic financial institutions and belief in the need to protect citizens' capital from being centralized into one man's pocket would almost certainly have tapped into memories of the Great Depression and the distrust many Americans still held for big banks.[1] The nuanced critique of how the free market should be managed and regulated within these words and many other similar speeches delivered by George Bailey in the film, is evidence of his positive portrayal of many American traditional, patriotic values including one most integral: the ability, and indeed the necessity, of critiquing American institutions.[2] Yet, in the following year, the FBI's Los Angeles office drew up an internal memo in which an informant condemned *It's a Wonderful Life* for its unfair representation of bankers, glorification of the

---

1 Jeanine Basinger, *The "It's a Wonderful Life" Book* (New York: Knopf, 1986), 52.
2 Merle Curti, *The Roots of American Loyalty* (New York: Columbia University Press, 1946), 6.

common man, and a perceived connection to communist subversion in Holly-wood.[3]

This memo was one of a series of reports drawn up by the LA office document-ing the FBI's ongoing surveillance of potential communist threats in Hollywood be-tween 1943 and 1958. Among other things, these reports – discussed further below – identified films with content that could be construed theoretically as ideological-ly subversive communist propaganda. Looking more deeply at this memo and the FBI's claims of subversive material in this film, as well as the broader history of anti-communism in Hollywood, this chapter will explore how the FBI came to cri-tique Capra's now-Christmas classic at all.

This chapter also uses *It's a Wonderful Life* and the contextual history of Hol-lywood in this immediate post-war period as a microcosm of the larger debates that will be explored in this book. Capra's film, as will be argued, is a deeply Amer-ican film that not only reflects the current moment as a response to the national traumas Americans endured in the first half of the twentieth century, but also broadens what it is to be an American at Christmas in the mid-century. As a Christ-mas film that has come to be regarded as a classic, *It's a Wonderful Life* is Capra's take on Charles Dickens's 1843 novel *A Christmas Carol* with an American twist and contemporary updates for a post-war audience. Exploring how this film – that depicts such American qualities and values, promotes the tenets of the "Amer-ican Dream", and models a critically patriotic view of the United States – was named in an FBI file as potentially un-American exposes the jarring disconnect be-tween Hollywood filmmakers such as Capra and the politics of the moment in which they were working.[4] By the end of 1947, that disconnect was made even more evident within the motion picture industry as Hollywood executives, who were receiving increasing federal pressure to restrict filmic content in this post-war, early Cold War period reacted to those pressures and established the Holly-wood blacklist.

---

3 This memo is one entry in a series of reports explored more fully on pages 39 and 40. All versions of FBI reports from this series on Communist infiltration in the motion picture industry that have been released via Freedom of Information Act requests are available as downloadable pdfs from a central webpage accessible here: http://web.archive.org/web/20050309061626/http://foia.fbi.gov/foiaindex/compic.htm. As shorthand, in the citations, only the specific location of refer-enced material accessible at that link will be cited, and further details on the dates of each file will be available in the Appendix. This *It's a Wonderful Life* analysis is in the report dated October 2, 1947: Federal Bureau of Investigation, "Communist Infiltration – Motion Picture Industry (COMPIC) (Excerpts)", file 100–138754, serial 251x1, Federal Bureau of Investigation, 159–160.
4 This idea of critical patriotism is defined as a "perspective that highlights the nation's short-comings in order to move it closer to its ideals" from: Ben Railton, *Of Thee I Sing: The Contested History of American Patriotism*, American Ways (Lanham, MD: Rowman & Littlefield, 2021), xiv.

In analyzing *It's a Wonderful Life*, it is clear that George Bailey's character and the film's message as a whole are far from propagators of communist ideology as the FBI concluded. Instead, George Bailey offers a different version of capitalism personified: the common man's capitalist to compete with the FBI's fears of the common man's communist. The subtle difference is in the reminder that George Bailey is quite literally also a capitalist, a banker, and a loud proponent of the free market while the film's villain, Potter, is an active threat to that free market. In condemning the film as portraying bankers negatively, the FBI report betrays their own ideology by aligning itself with the most extreme type of capitalism, that of the monopolistic Scrooge-like character, Potter.

Helpfully, the FBI notes early in section four of the report, "Communist Influence in Motion Pictures", that their agents were not trained to analyze films for propaganda concerns. The section reads "it was not believed that the Bureau's representatives are experts in this field, nor was it believed that censorship of motion pictures was within the purview of the activities of the Bureau." Instead, film analysis was carried out by "Confidential Informants" familiar with "the tactics used by the Communists in their attempt to influence motion pictures and actual examples of Communist propaganda in motion picture films."[5] While the informants' names are redacted in the files, the section goes on to identify individuals such as screenwriters James K. McGuinness and Ayn Rand as arbiters of how to spot communist subversion in films. Notably, the section quotes directly from Ayn Rand's 1947 pamphlet "Screen Guide for Americans", which offered guidelines for filmmakers from a conservative perspective to protect them from any suspicion of being communist sympathizers.[6]

This chapter provides a microcosmic example of the profound shift that was taking place in Hollywood in 1947. After Capra's *It's a Wonderful Life*, broader political and cultural post-war pressures converged on and in Hollywood by way of the FBI, HUAC, the Motion Picture Alliance for the Preservation of American Ideals (MPAPAI), and the executives who would meet in November 1947 and establish the Hollywood blacklist. These post-war intrusions into and reactions within the motion picture industry caused cultural ramifications that would ripple throughout the 1950s and beyond as strikingly evidenced in the emerging Christmas film genre.

---

5 FBI, "COMPIC", file 100–138754, serial 251x1, 148.
6 FBI, 150.

Foreign, Domestic, & Hollywood Affairs, 1930s to 1947

Hollywood was a particular target for anti-communist investigations in the 1940s but was certainly not the only one. Prior to the 1950 rise and 1954 fall of Senator Joseph R. McCarthy after whom the era of extreme anti-communist fervor came to be named, the Second Red Scare was well underway with a multi-pronged federal approach and as a "staple of post-war Republican campaign oratory".[7] HUAC was a Congressional watchdog allegedly fighting for American values. The FBI, under J. Edgar Hoover, had been virulently investigating organizations and individuals with alleged ties to communists and barring them from federal employment for years prior to taking keen interest in the film industry.[8] The mounting pressures of concerns over communist ideologies spreading around the world prompted demands for domestic responses to keep the US federal government – as well as the cultural and public sectors – free of communist sympathizers. As histories of J. Edgar Hoover's FBI and its struggles with the Roosevelt and Truman administrations as well as HUAC are well documented, this section will offer a brief introduction to the period's significant political and cultural developments including the organizations concerned and their relevance to the mounting federal pressures on Hollywood to react to potential communist subversion on screen.[9]

As the Great Depression ravaged the country in the 1930s, many Americans suffered under the severity of failures in the capitalist system. The Depression, for some, seemed to have "signaled the final collapse of capitalism that Marx had predicted" and, for this reason, saw some Americans turning to communism as a potential alternative.[10] However, historian of the era Richard Fried describes membership of the Communist Party of the United States of America (CPUSA) in the 1930s as a having a "revolving door" effect with many signing up but only engaging or maintaining membership for a short period.[11] These brief interludes

---

7 Robert Griffith, *The Politics of Fear: Joseph R. McCarthy and the Senate*, 2nd ed. (Amherst: University of Massachusetts Press, 1987), 52.

8 Stephen M. Underhill, *The Manufacture of Consent: J. Edgar Hoover and the Rhetorical Rise of the FBI* (East Lansing: Michigan State University Press, 2020), 128.

9 For more on the FBI, HUAC, and the Second Red Scare, see: Richard M. Fried, *Nightmare in Red: The McCarthy Era in Perspective* (Oxford: Oxford University Press, 1991); Rhodri Jeffreys-Jones, *The FBI: A History* (New Haven, CT: Yale University Press, 2007); Kenneth O'Reilly, *Hoover and the Un-Americans: The FBI, HUAC, and the Red Menace* (Philadelphia: Temple University Press, 1983); Sbardellati, *J. Edgar Hoover Goes to the Movies*; Athan G. Theoharis, *Chasing Spies: How the FBI Failed in Counterintelligence But Promoted the Politics of McCarthyism in the Cold War Years* (Chicago: Ivan R. Dee, 2002); Underhill, *The Manufacture of Consent*.

10 Fried, *Nightmare in Red*, 10.

11 Fried, 12.

with the CPUSA proved disastrous a decade or so later for many in teaching, entertainment, or governmental professions.

Chronologically, the timeline of events over that next decade leading to the FBI and HUAC's presence in Hollywood in the post-war period is generally agreed by many historians of the era as Jeff Smith helpfully lays out.[12] Smith's timeline is as follows: Labor unions increased in popularity during the Great Depression while many artists and filmmakers joined together to form an American cinematic arm of the international Popular Front movement in the 1930s, an entertainment industry coalition of antifascist organizations dedicated to cinematic realism in Hollywood and sharing the plight of Americans on screen.[13] Meanwhile, HUAC was established in 1938 and the Nazi-Soviet Nonaggression Pact of 1939 caused mass disaffection from communist membership. As World War II raged on, Congressional committees took private testimonies on potential communist influence in Hollywood and radio in 1940 and 1941, and studios produced both pro-American propaganda and pro-Soviet films while the US and USSR were allies. Labor strikes within Hollywood mounted in 1945 just before Winston Churchill delivered his "Iron Curtain" speech in 1946 in which he warned about the satellite countries adopting communism in Eastern Europe, and by 1947, anti-communism and the policy of containment were both established in US foreign and domestic policy.[14] This condensed timeline of events derived from Smith is widely accepted by other scholars – and so will be here too – as the lead-up to this post-war period, though expansion on some Hollywood links within it is necessary.

HUAC was initially formed in 1938 when a fear of fascism in Europe and of communism spreading throughout the world drove some Americans to the view that basic American values, or "Americanism", needed defending. Many prominent members of the Hollywood elite sympathized with the Committee's underlying purpose and over the years promoted their own view of Americanness. For instance, actors such as Gary Cooper and British-born Victor McLaglen were loud proponents of their American identities. After officially becoming an American citizen in 1935, McLaglen said, "We consider an enemy anything opposed to the American ideal, whether it's an enemy outside or inside these boarders. If that includes the Communists in this country, why, we're organized to fight them too."[15]

12 Jeff Smith, *Film Criticism, the Cold War, and the Blacklist: Reading the Hollywood Reds* (Berkeley: University of California Press, 2014), 3.
13 For more on the Popular Front, see: Ronald Radosh and Allis Radosh, *Red Star Over Hollywood: The Film Colony's Long Romance with the Left* (San Francisco: Encounter Books, 2005); Sbardellati, *J. Edgar Hoover Goes to the Movies.*
14 Smith, *Film Criticism, the Cold War, and the Blacklist*, 3.
15 Anthony Slide, "Hollywood's Fascist Follies," *Film Comment*, July 1991, 63, ProQuest.

American domestic anti-communism was more muted after Pearl Harbor, with the United States and Soviet Union finding themselves unlikely allies in the fight against the Axis powers. This also had its effects in Hollywood, where the efforts of government propagandists, especially from June 1942 in the Office of War Information (OWI), led to the production of a group of pro-Russian films, including *Mission to Moscow* (1943) and *Song of Russia* (1944).[16] *Mission to Moscow* in particular is commonly identified as the worst offender in terms of sympathizing with the Soviets and therefore communism. The film represented what Hoover feared most during the war, as historian John Sbardellati explains using some of the FBI's own language from the Communist Influence in the Motion Picture Industry reports:

> The Communists could now pose as "ardent patriots," merging their organizations "with all legitimate efforts" in Hollywood and across the nation. Thus, "by deception and patriotic subterfuge," the Communists were, according to the FBI, exploiting the war effort. Contact with Communists could not go untainted. The G-men believed that the Reds used insidious methods in "hiding the communist apparatus in the regular activities of the country [so] that it is extremely difficult for the unsuspecting citizen to distinguish them."[17]

While Hoover was already turning his sights towards Hollywood, *Mission to Moscow* solidified his concerns about the potential for communist influences in entertainment media and the ways in which the US and USSR alliance could subvert the Hollywood audience.

During World War II and Hoover's increasing insistence on covert investigations into Hollywood as well as other cultural and intellectual organizations, the power of Hoover and his organization expanded greatly. Under the Roosevelt administration, the FBI expanded from 713 special agents and $6.6 million in annual appropriations in 1939 to 4,370 special agents and $44.2 million in 1945.[18] This dramatic expansion of resource allocation for internal domestic surveillance is rooted

16 Reynold Humphries, *Hollywood's Blacklists: A Political and Cultural History* (Edinburgh: Edinburgh University Press, 2010), 92. For a fuller historiography on the anti-communist sentiments of the early twentieth century, see: Daniel Bell, *The New American Right* (New York: Criterion Books, 1955); Richard Hofstadter, "The Pseudo-Conservative Revolt", in *The New American Right* (New York: Criterion Books, 1955); Michael J. Heale, *American Anticommunism: Combating the Enemy Within, 1830–1970* (Baltimore, MD: Johns Hopkins University Press, 1990); Joel Kovel, *Red Hunting in the Promised Land: Anticommunism and the Making of America* (New York: Basic Books, 1994); Ellen Schrecker, *Many Are the Crimes: McCarthyism in America* (London: Little, Brown and Company, 1998); Alex Goodall, *Loyalty and Liberty – American Countersubversion from World War I to the McCarthy Era* (Chicago: University of Illinois Press, 2013).
17 Sbardellati, *J. Edgar Hoover Goes to the Movies*, 16.
18 Underhill, *The Manufacture of Consent*, 78–79.

in Hoover's obsession with the potential threat of communist ideology spreading within the US and his equation of the US-USSR allyship with sympathy for communism.

Encouraged by the grand alliance between the US and Soviet Union, the official foreign relationship between the two was one of mutual aid during the war under Roosevelt and at the start of Truman's administration. Despite this mutual aid, Truman was growing increasingly upset by communist activities in Eastern Europe.[19] Truman's accession to power in April 1945 brought into office a president more inclined to a stricter anti-communist position, who would ultimately take a firmer stance on what he saw as the growing communist threat both abroad and at home.[20] This can best be seen through actions he took both internationally and domestically in 1947.

In what came to be known as the "Truman Doctrine," announced in March 1947 and amended on July 4th, Truman pledged economic and military aid to Greece and Turkey to assist in fighting the perceived threat of Soviet-supported communist insurgencies in regions of the two countries.[21] Also in July, the president signed the National Security Act to go into effect on September 18, 1947, creating the Central Intelligence Agency (CIA) and beginning the centralization of the American military that would eventually lead to the creation of the Department of Defense in 1949.[22] The US was then moving, in terms of foreign policy, towards a policy of containment of communism internationally by aiding nations in their fights against communist revolutionaries and ideologies.

The Truman Administration was simultaneously adopting a policy of greater hostility towards communists and communist sympathizers within the United States. On March 21, 1947, the president issued Executive Order 9835 – better known as the Loyalty Order – which allowed for the investigations and termination of federal employees if suspected of communist activity.[23] After the Republicans won control of Congress in November 1946, the legislative branch soon went even further than the executive. In June, the Taft-Hartley Act was passed into law

---

19 Schrecker, *Many Are the Crimes*, 19.
20 Humphries, *Hollywood's Blacklists*, 93.
21 Humphries, 105.
22 Charles A. Stevenson, "The Story Behind the National Security Act of 1947", *Military Review* 88, no. 3 (June 2008): 13.
23 This Executive Order was not universally well received. See The Board of Directors of the American Psychological Association, "Across the Secretary's Desk: Board of Directors' Letter to President Truman Concerning Loyalty Investigations", for a condemnation of the approaches of the Employee Loyalty Program and subsequent plea for greater care to be taken in the execution of further investigations.

when Congress overrode President Truman's veto. The Act required that all labor union officers sign affidavits proclaiming no connection to communist activities in order to preserve their union's certification rights with the National Labor Relations Board.[24] These 1947 actions encouraged the growing anti-communist sentiment in the United States and would set the federal precedent for HUAC's public introduction to Hollywood and subsequent hearings.

Within Hollywood itself during the 1940s, the working culture was starting to split quite extremely. In 1944, Hollywood established its own organization to police Americanism within the film industry.[25] The MPAPAI was made up of famously politically conservative members of the Hollywood elite including stars John Wayne, Gary Cooper, James K. McGuinness, and Adolphe Menjou, director Sam Woods, and studio head Walt Disney.[26] The MPAPAI was originally criticized by many in Hollywood, especially union leaders who saw the alliance as a far-right watchdog aligned with infamously pro-fascist, anti-Semitic politicians such as Senator Robert Rice Reynolds, whom the MPAPAI had specifically contacted for his endorsement.[27] In 1945 and 1946 while the MPAPAI was gaining prominence in Hollywood, the film industry itself experienced a number of strikes that, after eighteen months, had the effect of breaking apart leftist, independent unions, most notably the Conference of Studio Unions (CSU). Ultimately, these strikes played into the hands of studio heads and the MPAPAI, weakening several unions and much of left-wing solidarity in Hollywood, creating resentment across broken union lines, and playing a part in persuading some to be "friendly witnesses" in HUAC's ensuing investigations into Hollywood.[28]

Simultaneously, outside of the unions there were other concerns between independent filmmakers and the major studio heads. Frank Capra was one such filmmaker who returned from wartime service to a divided Hollywood with studio heads enjoying consolidated power as the strikes drove further wedges between the workers. Capra took to *The New York Times* and published an article entitled "Breaking Hollywood's 'Pattern of Sameness'" on May 5, 1946 in which he con-

---

24 Thom Andersen, "Red Hollywood", in *'Un-American' Hollywood: Politics and Film in the Blacklist Era*, ed. Frank Krutnik et al. (New Brunswick, NJ: Rutgers University Press, 2007), 227.
25 HUAC, in the years between 1938 and 1944, was chaired by the conservative Democratic representative from Texas, Martin Dies, and more commonly referred to as the Dies Committee. The Dies Committee was also critical of Hollywood in the war years, investigating communist affiliations in Hollywood as early at 1940. Humphries, *Hollywood's Blacklists*, 77.
26 Paul Buhle and David Wagner, *Radical Hollywood: The Untold Story Behind America's Favorite Movies* (New York: New Press, 2002), 62.
27 Humphries, *Hollywood's Blacklists*, 62–64.
28 Humphries, 65–67.

demned the studios for their actions and encouragement of bland films rushed through production creating what he termed a "pattern of sameness" in cultural outputs. He also took umbrage with what he perceived to be a lack of risks taken in the artform and the development of what he identifies as an "aspirational" quality to films rather than a "realistic" quality. Capra wrote that "Hollywood became increasingly self-satisfied, snug, complacent, and the characteristics became evident on screen. Life as portrayed on the screen became a Hollywood version of how life should be lived, whether in poverty or luxury, rather than how it was actually being lived."[29] At the end of this article lambasting the studio heads and their lack of creative ambition, Capra announced that he, together with directors William Wyler and George Stevens and producer Samuel J. Briskin, was starting a production company for independents: Liberty Films. The new company would go on to release only two films – both from Capra, *It's a Wonderful Life* and *State of the Union* (1948) – as other concerns in Hollywood made its success as an independent production company even more difficult. This tumultuous moment in Hollywood that Capra is criticizing as well as all of the labor divisions inspiring it constituted the context into which HUAC was soon introduced.

On September 23, 1947, HUAC, invited by the MPAPAI into Hollywood, issued its first subpoenas to members of Hollywood accused of affiliation with the Communist party.[30] The hearings following these subpoenas were held in October 1947, when eleven of nineteen subpoenaed unfriendly witnesses were called to testify before Congress. One of the eleven, Bertolt Brecht, broke from the rest of the group and complied with the committee's questioning, leaving the others to become famous (or notorious) as the "Hollywood Ten" for defying the committee. The Hollywood Ten refused to answer the committee's questions which they deemed a violation of their First Amendment rights. The most iconic question of these early Cold War hearings – "are you now or have you ever been a member of the Communist Party of the United States?" – defined an era as the glitz and glam of Hollywood brought it to the homes of every cinema-going American.

The cultural split in Hollywood widened even further in response to HUAC's first hearings. Coming to the defense of the Hollywood Ten was the Committee for the First Amendment (CFA). The CFA was created by Philip Dunne, John Huston, and William Wyler and composed of Hollywood personalities who opposed what they deemed HUAC's unconstitutional investigations into private beliefs. Members

---

29 Frank Capra, "Breaking Hollywood's 'Pattern of Sameness'", *The New York Times*, May 5, 1946, *The New York Times* Archive.
30 Gordon Kahn, *Hollywood on Trial: The Story of the 10 Who Were Indicted* (New York: Boni & Gaer, 1948), 5.

of the CFA who flew from Hollywood to Washington DC to defend their colleagues included big names such as Humphrey Bogart, Lauren Bacall, Gene Kelly, and Danny Kaye.[31] Wyler himself wrote in an open forum published in *The Hollywood Reporter* on November 7, 1947 that the CFA was not comprised of communists or communist sympathizers, but rather "spoke up and will continue to speak up in defense of our industry as a whole and in defense of the basis [*sic*] civil rights of all American citizens."[32]

In support of HUAC's presence and in addition to the MPAPAI were several organizations and individuals. On November 17, 1947, future US president Ronald Reagan became president of the Screen Actors Guild (SAG), establishing a moderate stance against Hollywood left radicalism that would last through his tenure to 1952.[33] One week later, Congress voted to hold the Hollywood Ten in contempt, prompting fifty Hollywood executives to meet at the Waldorf-Astoria Hotel in New York to decide the Ten's professional fates. This meeting resulted in the foundations of the blacklist, with Eric Johnston, president of the MPAA, announcing that the Hollywood Ten would be suspended without pay and that "no Communists or subversives would 'knowingly' be employed in Hollywood" thereafter.[34] Johnston's direct response to the federal pressures thus far, as well as pressures from private groups including the American Legion, on the motion picture industry instigated the Hollywood blacklist. As a result of the executive leadership in Hollywood establishing the blacklist, factions formerly in support of those defying HUAC began to falter. Together with most of Hollywood, most members of the CFA began to distance themselves from the Hollywood Ten out of fear of both the blacklist and any further federal or Hollywood backlash.

As the blacklist would ravage the careers of suspected communists over the next decade and beyond due to the unlikely potentiality for them to inject communist propaganda in Hollywood films, the MPAPAI was considering the exact same issue but with pro-American propaganda instead. During the 1947 HUAC hearings, friendly witness and MPAPAI co-founder James K. McGuinness argued that Hollywood itself should be actively making anti-communist films as a "necessity of doing a patriotic and public duty."[35] Despite the Committee's allegations that Hol-

31 Victor Navasky, *Naming Names*, 1st ed. (New York: Hill and Wang, 1999), 80.

32 William Wyler, "Open Forum", *The Hollywood Reporter*, November 7, 1947, 11, ProQuest.

33 David Haven Blake, *Liking Ike: Eisenhower, Advertising, and the Rise of Celebrity Politics* (Oxford: Oxford University Press, 2016), 153.

34 Navasky, *Naming Names*, 83.

35 *Hearings Regarding the Communist Infiltration of the Motion Picture Industry, Before the Committee on Un-American Activities, House of Representatives*, 80th Cong. 146 (1947) http://archive.org/details/hearingsregardin1947aunit.

lywood leftists were subverting films for their own gains, Committee Chair J. Parnell Thomas had asked whether HUAC could influence Hollywood into creating such pictures filled with anti-communist propaganda. McGuinness agreed that it could and further suggested that this propaganda should be made for public distribution in schools and churches as well as played for free in cinemas.[36] McGuinness's ideas on propaganda were not only supported here by Thomas and the House Committee members but also by Hoover's FBI when they cited him, as stated above, in the reports at the heart of this chapter.

This brief history of the many influences of the US anti-communist political and cultural movements both foreign and domestic as well as within Hollywood specifically provides context for both HUAC's involvement in Hollywood in 1947 and the FBI's continuous observation of Hollywood throughout the 1940s and 1950s. The context of the Truman Administration's anti-communist actions, as well as the beginnings of HUAC's involvement with Hollywood and its connection to the MPAPAI, provides the immediate backcloth to the publication of Ayn Rand's pamphlet "Screen Guide for Americans" in 1947 and the FBI's subsequent use of it in their reports.[37] The turbulent history of Hollywood strikes, which largely destroyed left-wing unions such as the CSU, ultimately weakened solidarity among left-wing members of the motion picture industry and led to the consolidation of power and influence by more conservative, independent organizations in line with the MPAPAI. It was in this context of Hollywood in shambolic disarray of warring political factions, continuous labor strife, and federal threats pressuring Hollywood's executive leadership that Ayn Rand's MPAPAI pamphlet was foregrounded by the FBI and used to condemn *It's a Wonderful Life.*

Ayn Rand, the Conservative Right, and the "Screen Guide for Americans"

The FBI report dated August 7, 1947, according to historian John Noakes, identifies eight films released between 1943 and 1948 as potentially subversive for mass American audiences.[38] At the beginning of the report, Rand's "Screen Guide for

---

36 Humphries, *Hollywood's Blacklists*, 92–93.

37 Barbara Branden, *The Passion of Ayn Rand* (London: W.H. Allen, 1987), 199.

38 John A. Noakes, "Bankers and Common Men in Bedford Falls: How the FBI Determined That 'It's a Wonderful Life' Was a Subversive Movie," *Film History* 10, no. 3 (1998): 311. It should be noted that this August 7, 1947, version of the report is not in the FBI Freedom of Information Act release discussed in more detail below. Access to scans of several pages of this early version of the report were provided by Noakes directly to this researcher.

Americans" is quoted and used as a reference for a concise breakdown of communist propaganda tactics that Hollywood producers and writers should endeavor to avoid. This pamphlet also bears the imprint of the MPAPAI, of which Rand was a board member, and was printed in both the MPAPAI's own publication *The Vigil* and the conservative magazine *Plain Talk*.[39]

Rand's connection with the MPAPAI and her subsequent pamphlet on the film industry were not her first dealings with Hollywood. Having fallen in love with a vision of America portrayed in Hollywood films as a young adult in Soviet Russia, Rand immigrated to Chicago in 1926 before shortly thereafter moving to Hollywood. With grand ambitions to become a screenwriter, Rand visited early studio lots where a chance encounter with Cecil B. DeMille himself secured her a job as a junior writer for his studio.[40] Rand's immediate opportunities in the US offered her a stark juxtaposition with her previous life in Russia until the following year when DeMille shuttered his studio in response to the industry's shift into talking pictures. Her career in Hollywood saw a number of ups and downs and branched into a more prominent literary career as a playwright and novelist by the mid-1930s. As a self-proclaimed expert on political propaganda after studying and living under a Communist regime, Rand imbued her works with her Nietzsche-inspired philosophical ideals and political views developed from her earlier experiences in both Russia and the US. As biographer Jennifer Burns writes of Rand's first book *We the Living*, her "anti-Communism is woven into every scene in the novel and its overall structure."[41]

Simultaneously, with the Great Depression ravaging on, communist sympathies and party membership began to rise, and Rand became disgusted with any "collective solution" provided by the New Deal and embraced by Americans in need.[42] Despite her career's start being a chance encounter with a generous studio head, Rand turned deeper into her individualist ideology and belief in selfishness as a virtue. A then-established novelist and political writer, Rand returned to Hollywood in 1943 to produce a film adaptation of her latest novel, *The Fountainhead*. By 1945, already an industry celebrity, Rand joined the MPAPAI with the likes of *The Fountainhead* director King Vidor, McGuinness, Disney, and other film professionals obstinately opposed to Communism.[43] With this platform and coalition of powerful cultural figures, Rand was able to draw on her earlier ideas on propa-

---

39 Jennifer Burns, *Goddess of the Market: Ayn Rand and the American Right* (Oxford: Oxford University Press, 2009), 118.
40 Burns, 17–21.
41 Burns, 30.
42 Burns, 35.
43 Burns, 100.

ganda and turn from philosophical fiction writing to more fully political non-fiction outputs putting the MPAPAI's political leanings to paper.

In 1946, one year prior to her "Screen Guide for Americans", Rand published her first piece in the MPAPAI's magazine *The Vigil:* an unfinished treatise entitled "Textbook of Americanism".[44] This essay comprising ten questions was promised in *The Vigil* as the first part of a longer series by "distinguished American author" Ayn Rand. The "Textbook of Americanism" sought to simplify the questions of the "basic issue of the world" into an "objective" dichotomy between individualism – represented by the US – and collectivism – represented by the Soviet Union and Nazi Germany.[45] The short essay published by the MPAPAI does little more than offer Rand a platform for her philosophical stances on political morality and does not reference at all the motion picture industry, its role in society, or how it can present these "objective" realities. Rand's "Textbook of Americanism" was also a platform for her personal politics and suffered similar criticism from members of the conservative Foundation for Economic Education as "illogical" in its assertions about the unalienable rights of man and the nature of governments.[46]

Despite such criticisms, Rand's overt political treatise was not a complete aberration for the late 1940s during which time a number of European intellectuals were influencing American conservative thought. As an immigrant to the US from Soviet Russia, Rand's political views were influenced by her earlier life in Communist Russia and studies at the University of Leningrad. As Rand was publishing her political musings, the Austrian economist Friedrich Augustus von Hayek's 1944 book *The Road to Serfdom* was gaining an American audience for its potential to be "revolutionary in academic circles".[47] In these immediate post-war years, the conservative Right underwent an intellectual reimagining in which American philosophers and political thinkers began to build on the foundations laid by earlier and contemporary European philosophers reacting to their first-hand accounts of the political chaos of the first half of the twentieth century. Concerning the late 1940s coalition of American and European conservatives at the annual Mont Pélerin Society meeting in the Swiss Alps, historian of conservative intellectualism George Nash writes: "For the American Right, already indebted to Europeans for help in its resuscitation during the 1940s, this exposure to

---

44 Burns, 118.
45 Ayn Rand, "Textbook of Americanism" (The Motion Picture Alliance for the Preservation of American Ideals, 1946), Foundation for Economic Education, https://fee.org/resources/textbook-of-americanism/.
46 Burns, *Goddess of the Market*, 119.
47 Gregory L. Schneider, *The Conservative Century: From Reaction to Revolution* (Lanham, MD: Rowman & Littlefield Publishers, 2009), 41.

wider currents was, one suspects, particularly important; it stretched the web of influence and tended to make American conservative thought more cosmopolitan."[48]

This budding resuscitation of the American Right and the realignment of its policy concerns with social, moral, and religious traditions provided the context in which Rand published and conservative pressures on Hollywood flourished throughout the early Cold War.[49] In 1948, University of Chicago professor Richard Weaver published his *Ideas Have Consequences*, drawing the conclusion that Western civilization had been in decline since a rejection of philosophical realism in the fourteenth century.[50] The following year, Mount Holyoke College professor Peter Viereck's *Conservatism Revisited: The Revolt against Revolt* made the moralistic case for Conservatism as a Christian-based, individualist, humanist philosophy. Viereck drew an intellectual lineage from Hellenic thinkers through the Roman Empire's "exaltation of the law" to Aristotelianism and other traditions in the Middle Ages.[51] Other European thinkers inspiring the American Right included Alexis de Tocqueville and Edmund Burke as the Conservative intellectual movement began to grow well into the 1950s.

Beyond drawing intellectual lineages from Western civilizations, the post-war period also saw new renderings and interpretations of American history produced for the general public. Popular histories transcended traditional books and were also disseminated in more popular media such as magazines, radio programs, television, and, as historian Nick Witham writes, film.[52] Historians and intellectuals

---

48 George H. Nash, *The Conservative Intellectual Movement in America Since 1945*, 30th anniversary edition (1976; reis. Wilmington, DE.: ISI Books, 2008), 22.

49 For more on the American Right during the Cold War and foundations of modern social conservatism, see: Bell, *The New American Right*; Donald F. Crosby, *God, Church, and Flag: Senator Joseph R. McCarthy and the Catholic Church, 1950–1957* (Chapel Hill: University of North Carolina Press, 1978); Lewis L. Gould, *The Republicans: A History of the Grand Old Party* (2003; reis. Oxford: Oxford University Press, 2014); Griffith, *The Politics of Fear*; Heale, *American Anticommunism*; Michael Kazin, *The Populist Persuasion: An American History*, 2nd rev. ed. (1995; revised New York: Cornell University Press, 2017); Nash, *The Conservative Intellectual Movement in America Since 1945*; Robert Mason, *The Republican Party and American Politics from Hoover to Reagan* (Cambridge: Cambridge University Press, 2012); Lisa McGirr, *Suburban Warriors: The Origins of the New American Right*, Politics and Society in Twentieth-Century America (Princeton: Princeton University Press, 2001); Kim Phillips-Fein, *Invisible Hands: The Making of the Conservative Movement from the New Deal to Reagan* (New York: W. W. Norton & Company, 2009).

50 Donald T. Critchlow, *The Conservative Ascendancy: How the GOP Right Made Political History* (Cambridge, MA: Harvard University Press, 2007), 18.

51 Nash, *The Conservative Intellectual Movement*, 65–66.

52 Nick Witham, *Popularizing the Past: Historians, Publishers, and Readers in Postwar America* (Chicago: University of Chicago Press, 2023), 7.

across the political spectrum were writing their own popular histories imbued with their political leanings. According to Witham in his history of five post-war historians, "while the national past was regularly molded into a form of propaganda, the Cold War also provided an opportunity for historians to reframe American history to suit a range of dissenting political perspectives."[53] In this time, Conservative histories emphasized cultural traditions as central to a society's stability and the obligation to maintain a consistent stand against liberalism, progressivism, and most especially, Communism.[54] This connection between cultural, social conservatism and the revival of the American Right's intellectual political ideology is particularly evident in Rand's dealings with Hollywood through the MPAPAI.

The MPAPAI, through Ayn Rand's pamphlet, made clear that their purpose was not to stifle or extinguish the rights of creativity and expression among artists, but rather to provide clear guidelines for what could or could not be done in films to avoid arousing federal attentions through FBI and, in time, HUAC investigations. Rand wrote, "We are unalterably opposed to any political 'industry code,' [...] forbidding any political opinion to anyone by any form of collective force or pressure." She also claimed the pamphlet was "merely offer[ed] [...]to the independent judgment and for the voluntary action of every honest man in the motion picture industry."[55]

Rand's insistence that the decision was up to artists' judgement was not completely unfamiliar to Hollywood. Long before the MPAPAI was formed, the Production Code – often referred to colloquially as the "Hays Code" after Will H. Hays, president of the Motion Picture Producers and Distributors of America since 1922 – had been adopted by the movie industry in 1930. The Production Code was a self-policing policy within Hollywood to ensure all films submitted to it were up to a certain level of moral conduct, based mostly on Catholic and conservative views.[56]

---

53 Witham, 7.
54 Charles W. Dunn and J. David Woodard, *The Conservative Tradition in America*, 2nd ed. (1996; revised, Lanham, MD: Rowman & Littlefield, 2003), 4. Some titles in this cultural revolution of the American Right as provided by Dunn and Woodard include: Eric Voegelin's *The New Science of Politics*; William F. Buckley, Jr.'s *God and Man at Yale*; Gertrude Himmelfarb's *Lord Acton*; Leo Strauss's *Natural Right and History*; John Hallowell's *The Moral Foundations of Democracy*; Whittaker Chambers's *Witness*; and Robert Nisbet's *Quest for Community*.
55 Ayn Rand, "Screen Guide for Americans" (The Motion Picture Alliance for the Preservation of American Ideals, 1947), 1, MSU Archive.
56 For more on the Production Code, see: *Doherty, Hollywood's Censor*.

Rand positioned herself as obstinately opposed to any such industrial code, which she regarded as an expression of threat or force. The notion that her own "screen guide" was any different, however, was easily undermined by her scathing suggestion that not to follow these guidelines would be to out oneself as a dishonest man, and worse, a communist sympathizer. Yet her own rules were highly simplistic, assuming that whether one followed the rules or not determined whether one was a communist or communist sympathizer. She also paid particular attention to producers, assuming that the producer had the ability to stop a film from coming under suspicion as communist propaganda. In reality, films are complex cultural products, produced by many hands – a view shared by studio-heads and friendly HUAC witnesses Louis B. Mayer and Jack L. Warner in their testimonies.[57]

Ultimately, it should be clear that while Rand held an important position in the MPAPAI and wrote as a spokesperson for their anti-communist rhetoric, she was also one voice of many in both Hollywood and the cultural conservative movement. Her contributions are significant as the "Screen Guide for Americans" was not only cited but also quoted by the FBI in their reports on communist infiltration of the motion picture industry, yet also significant is the fact that she willingly gave friendly testimony at HUAC and was not asked to return a second time. Rand's misinterpretation of *Song of Russia* while testifying added an additional blow, exposing her misunderstanding of how cinematic propaganda works and encouraging the committee to reject hearing her interpretations of William Wyler's *The Best Years of Our Lives*.[58] However, despite this embarrassment before the committee, the criticism of her "Textbook for Americanism" for being ideologically incoherent, and her failure to accurately understand the need for earlier pro-Soviet propaganda during the wartime alliance, Rand's "Screen Guide for Americans" deserves to be examined. Her place in the Hollywood Right, her celebrity as an acclaimed political writer, and her insistence on her ability to recognize communist propaganda led the FBI to use her "Screen Guide for Americans" to further an investigation into the political ideology in Hollywood films with Rand named as an industry expert. Rand's pamphlet will be analyzed in more depth below with a view to understanding how her guidelines relate to earlier traditions both in Hollywood and American history, as well as how the FBI used them in their observations of Hollywood.

---

57 Humphries, *Hollywood's Blacklists*, 92. The views of Mayer and Warner are of particular interest since, in their testimony, they admitted that their studios respectively had produced the pro-Soviet propaganda films *Mission to Moscow* (1943) and *Song of Russia* (1944).
58 Burns, *Goddess of the Market*, 125.

The List of (Un-)American Sensibilities

Rand's pamphlet argues that Hollywood should conform to a list of "don'ts" in its approach to filmmaking.[59] She references each of these in a list of bold headings together with a brief explication of how each is a tool of communist propaganda. Her points are:

1. Don't Take Politics Lightly
2. Don't Smear the Free Enterprise System
3. Don't Smear Industrialists
4. Don't Smear Wealth
5. Don't Smear the Profit Motive
6. Don't Smear Success
7. Don't Glorify Failure
8. Don't Glorify Depravity
9. Don't Deify "The Common Man"
10. Don't Glorify the Collective
11. Don't Smear an Independent Man
12. Don't Use Current Events Carelessly
13. Don't Smear American Political Institutions

Rand stressed that following these tenets would distinguish all who did as noncommunist patriots upholding traditional American values. Yet her idea that unthinking adherence to a particular code of values was the best defense of patriotism had already been challenged. In 1946, the year before her pamphlet was issued, historian Merle Curti had argued in *The Roots of American Loyalty* that:

> Whether America will provide an even larger freedom at home, an even stronger hope for the world, depends upon what citizens make of our country – depends not only upon the strength of our devotion to it, but also upon the character of that devotion. In a democracy blind, unthinking love of country must presumably give way more and more to intelligent and understanding patriotism, if that democracy as such is to survive. That being so, an examination of the sources and nature of American patriotism may be more than an academic exercise; and he who reads it thoughtfully may be helped toward more enlightened citizenship.[60]

---

59 Rand's list echoes the some of the language of the 1927 list of "Don'ts and Be Carefuls" enacted to be followed by members of the Motion Picture Association Producers and Distributors of America and later replaced by the Hays Code. For more on the Influence of the 1927 list, see: Gerald Mast, *The Movies in Our Midst: Documents in the Cultural History of Film in America* (Chicago: University of Chicago Press, 1982).
60 Curti, *The Roots of American Loyalty*, vii.

Curti emphasized that Americans' patriotic duty was to question American political institutions and to maintain the perspective that what the common citizen makes of the country is the true meaning of the nation's success in preserving the freedoms it holds dear both domestically and abroad. Rand's list fundamentally goes against this idea of patriotic duty, and in its insistence that patriotism is compliance to it, it suggests that the "blind" loyalty Curti condemns, is rather more American than questioning the government's actions.

Curti's idea of the strength of the American union being dependent on what the citizenry make of it was not a new idea in 1946. In Carl Russell Fish's 1927 book *The Rise of the Common Man*, he catalogued the history of the common man in American life between 1830 and 1850. In explaining what liberty meant to that generation of Americans he wrote that, to the previous generation, liberty had been a goal to be won and subsequently defended in the early years of the United States. To the generation that begot President Andrew Jackson, the iconic common American man who rose to prominence defending the rights and lives of other common men across the nation, liberty was already a natural-born right for Americans.[61] Andrew Jackson, for many Americans was and still is portrayed as "a man of the people" and as "the people's champion against the power-lusting aristocracy of wealth."[62] The idea of the common man as *the* American man is consequently a long-held tradition. It implies that every man, no matter how ordinary, has the potential to achieve greatness due to his personal qualities and the liberties afforded him as an American.[63] Ayn Rand's assertion that filmmakers should not deify the common man was in direct opposition to this whole image of America as exceptional because of its demographic make-up of common men who are capable of exceptional feats.

Rand's second, third, fourth, and fifth points – not smearing the free enterprise system, industrialists, wealth, or the profit motive – also challenged what might be perceived as traditional American values. The term "millionaires" was first used in 1840 when leading New York merchants, still reeling from the 1837 financial panic, drew up a list of the wealthiest businessmen in New York and their estimated net worth.[64] The term was later used by scholars and businessmen alike to throw light on the growing divide between the classes. William Miller wrote, "With the shocking discovery of overbearing wealth came the even more

---

61 Carl Russell Fish, *The Rise of the Common Man: 1830–1850*, vol. VI (New York: Macmillan Company, 1927), 7.

62 Jeffrey Richards, "Frank Capra and the Cinema of Populism", *Cinema*, no. 5 (1972): 23.

63 Fish, *The Rise of the Common Man*, 7.

64 William Miller, "The Realm of Wealth", in *The Reconstruction of American History*, ed. John Higham (London: Hutchinson, 1962), 137.

shocking disclosure of endemic poverty ... As wealth and population grew, the number of the poor seemed to have grown faster."[65] This business class emerging as millionaires and helping to deepen the economic divides between classes was perceived by many as divisive and un-American. Over time, the emerging million-aires in the 1840s gave way to the monopolies and trusts that followed towards the end of the nineteenth century. Fish's earlier perception of the greatness of the common American man, and the liberties innately granted him as an American, would be threatened by the later rise of monopolies. Monopolistic corruption was seen as a direct threat to the potential of common men to fulfil American promises of exceptionalism, whether they were based on unfair competition or government-chartered monopolies such as the second Bank of the United States that common man hero Andrew Jackson had fought against and ultimately destroyed.[66]

Rand's second point (not smearing the free enterprise system) tried hard to discredit those who did as un-American in her paragraph of explanation – "*Don't* pretend that Americanism and the Free Enterprise System are two different things," she insisted. "They are inseparable, like body and soul. The basic principle of inalienable individual rights, which is Americanism, can be translated into practical reality *only* in the form of the economic system of Free Enterprise."[67] This equation of the free enterprise system to Americanism is not necessarily accurate and opens Rand up to problematic interpretations of capitalism, specifically in terms of monopolism, an inherently extreme manipulation of the free enterprise system that many have traditionally regarded as un-American. As Daniel T. Rodgers wrote, early twentieth-century "progressive" reformers attempted to regulate and dismantle large business corporations that were concentrating wealth and ruthlessly destroying their competitors. Such reform efforts were justified by those involved in terms of a traditional American discourse of "anti-monopolism" that stretched back to the presidency of Andrew Jackson.[68]

Rand's pamphlet also stipulated what not to do with respect to presenting economics in film: "*Don't* attack individual rights, individual freedom, private action, private initiative, and private property ... *Don't* preach the superiority of public

---

65 Miller, 149.

66 See Elizabeth A. Laughlin, "The Rise of American Industrial and Financial Corporations", *Gettysburg Economic Review* 6, no. 5 (2012): 42–57; Robert V. Remini, *Andrew Jackson and the Bank War: A Study in the Growth of Presidential Power* (New York: W. W. Norton, 1967).

67 Rand, "Screen Guide for Americans", 2. Emphasis by author.

68 Daniel T. Rodgers, "In Search of Progressivism", *Reviews in American History* 10, no. 4 (1982): 123.

ownership as such over private ownership."[69] It was very much in keeping with the thrust of her argument here that the FBI would use her pamphlet to critique *It's a Wonderful Life*, arguing that the portrayal of the villainous banker, Potter, was an "attempt to show that people who had money were mean and despicable characters."[70] Disregarding the fact that, to George Bailey, Potter is a monopolizing villain, challenging traditional American values, the FBI file reflects Rand's insistence that private actions, initiatives, or property must not be maligned.

Starting and ending her pamphlet with a promise that the corrupt communists in Hollywood are using highly advanced propaganda tactics, Rand assured her readers of the Communists' purpose in Hollywood. This section is also quoted in full in the FBI files under the section "Communist Influence in Motion Pictures" – in which Rand is specifically named – as the agents writing the file attempt to justify investigations into and observations of Hollywood:

> The purpose of the Communists in Hollywood is *not* the production of political movies openly advocating Communism. Their purpose is *to corrupt our moral premises by corrupting non-political movies* – by introducing small, casual bits of propaganda into innocent stories – thus making people absorb the basic premises of Collectivism *by indirection and implication.*
>
> Few people would take Communism straight. But a constant stream of hints, lines, touches and suggestions battering the public from the screen will act like the drops of water that split a rock if continued long enough. The rock they are trying to split is Americanism.[71]

Each of Rand's points from the "Screen Guide for Americans" are then summarized in the FBI file as alleged devices used by communists in the film industry to further their ideological agenda and split the proverbial rock of Americanism. The message of Rand's pamphlet can thus be pared down to three essential guidelines for keeping communist propaganda out of films: 1) it is necessary to acknowledge that capitalism's free enterprise is invariably equal to American traditional values; 2) it is anti-American to glorify commonality, averageness, and failure of any kind; and 3) acquiring independent wealth and financial success are typically American goals and ideals.

Rand's tripartite critique of what she perceived as communist identifiers is contrary to the traditional American values explored above of lauding the common, working man and ardently fighting against monopolism. Within the motion picture industry itself, Rand's views can be seen as a direct attack on the populist

---

69 Rand, "Screen Guide for Americans", 2. Emphasis Rand's.
70 FBI, "COMPIC", file 100–138754, serial 251x1, 159.
71 Rand, "Screen Guide for Americans", 1. Emphases Rand's. This section can also be found without emphases in FBI, "COMPIC", file 100–138754, serial 251x1, 150.

tradition in American films – an approach which will be explored more fully below. Capra is often heralded as Hollywood's most influential and enduring populist director. In conventional populist films, the main character is a common, working man from a small town, fighting against a big business complex or political machine – the staples of many Frank Capra films.[72] Wes D. Gehring defines populism on film as "a basic belief held by many people that the superior and majority will of the common man is forever threatened by the usurping, sophisticated, evil few."[73] Films in this tradition often incorporated Presidents Andrew Jackson and Abraham Lincoln as populist hallmarks to solidify the importance of the common man in this vision of traditional American values.[74] As will be noted below, this populist view was one that dominated films of the 1930s and into the 1940s, but lost favor in Hollywood in the mid- to late-1940s.

This decline in the populist film tradition may be related to the growing prominence of the views of Rand and the other conservatives within Hollywood in the later 1940s. Rand – like the MPAPAI, FBI, and HUAC – was intent on challenging and discrediting populist-style ideas that grew out of traditional American ideas and values by reinterpreting them as communist propaganda. As will be seen, by the end of the 1940s, populist elements in Hollywood films would be severely diminished as a consequence of these conservative attacks on the values inherent in populist cinema. Therefore, in her strategy to discredit allegedly communist propaganda in Hollywood, Rand tarred some deeply American ideas and values during the early stages of the Cold War by associating them with communism.

"Corrupting Non-Political Movies by Indirection and Implication"
If much of Rand's "Screen Guide for Americans" is read in reverse, as a list of things that should be done – e.g. *"do glorify* wealth" and *"do smear* the collective" – it becomes a guide to subverting cinema successfully with a conservative, pro-capitalist, ostensibly pro-American ideology. In Rand's view, the correct representations of Americanism are ardent and bold proclamations of her three pared down points identified above: 1) an acknowledgement of the free enterprise system as typically American; 2) an unfavorable perception of commonality and averageness; 3) a favorable view of the acquisition of wealth. Those who criticized or offered alternative views of these things stood accused of communist sympathies.

72 Richards, "Frank Capra", 23.
73 Wes D. Gehring, *Populism and the Capra Legacy* (Westport, CT: Greenwood Press, 1995), 1.
74 Richards, "Frank Capra", 23.

Throughout her pamphlet and boldly at the end, Rand wrote that, "These are the things which Communists and their sympathizers try to sneak into pictures intended as non-political – and these are the things which you must keep out of your scripts, if your intention is to make non-political movies."[75] By encouraging filmmakers to actively suppress any communist rhetoric, Rand was effectively taking a political stand on the same non-political films she was writing about. Moreover, Rand highlights that one "cannot expect Communists to remain 'neutral' and not to insert their own ideas into their work."[76] Reading these 13 points in reverse offers a checklist of how to insert anti-communist or pro-capitalist propaganda into an allegedly non-political film. By glorifying the profit motive and free enterprise system, and by smearing the common man, failure, and the collective, a filmmaker can take a pro-American stance and please the FBI's informants through a supposedly non-political film, therefore making any film a potential medium for political subversion on either side of the perceived dichotomy of communist and capitalist. As mentioned above, co-founder of the MPAPAI, friendly witness to HUAC, and FBI-named expert in analyzing communist propaganda in films, James K. McGuinness shared his interest in Hollywood films making this precise type of pro-American propaganda during his HUAC testimony.

"Communist Infiltration of the Motion Picture Industry"

Rand's "Screen Guide for Americans" MPAPAI pamphlet might have just been another attempt at internal censorship in Hollywood if it weren't for the FBI. Rand, on her own as an influential intellectual and a public voice in opposition to communism, was an effective tool in mid-century public discourse, but when legitimized as a source for the federal government, her words promptly become immensely more significant in this historical moment.

The FBI memo from the Los Angeles office in which *It's a Wonderful Life* is mentioned is one of a series under the names "Communist Infiltration of the Motion Picture Industry" or "Summary on the Communist Infiltration into the Motion Picture Industry" and eventually shortened to "COMPIC". According to the Freedom of Information Act release made public on the FBI's website in 2005, there were at least ten versions of the report between February 18, 1943 and November 14, 1958 while Hollywood was under FBI observation and investigation.[77] The 1943

---

75 Rand, "Screen Guide for Americans", 11.
76 Rand, 12.
77 See page 17, note 22 and Appendix for more details.

version is solely concerned with communist infiltration of labor unions in the motion picture industry. The next five reports – written between May 24, 1947 and January 3, 1956 – are more specifically concerned with communist ideology and propaganda in films released in this period as well as communist influence on labor unions, intellectual groups, and the hearings, testimonies, associations, and movements of individuals identified as either "friendly" or "unfriendly" witnesses by HUAC. The subsequent four – written between May 15, 1956 and November 14, 1958 – concern the HUAC hearings and subpoenas for the music side of the motion picture industry as well as tracking the downfall of the industry's blacklist and the Academy Award indirectly awarded to Hollywood Ten member Dalton Trumbo in 1957 for *The Brave One.*

These reports quote directly from the "Screen Guide for Americans" and emphasize the internal struggles within Hollywood as the division between political factions worsened in the film industry. As the report named *It's a Wonderful Life*, an ostensibly non-political film from the innocuous Christmas film genre, using Rand's guide and the notes from the informant, the next section will analyze whether Capra's Christmas classic is a propagator of communist propaganda as the FBI suspected or if it is a populist film in a deeply American tradition.

George Bailey as the Enduring Populist

Using this framework of Rand's guidelines for suppressing communist sympathies in non-political films, it is possible to read *It's a Wonderful Life* through the FBI's concerns and assess why a film that is ultimately critically approving of capitalism was not a strong enough stance to hold in the post-war period without provoking anti-communist suspicions. Further, in reading Capra's *It's a Wonderful Life* as a populist fantasy, it can be better understood how the film's anti-monopolistic sentiment stands apart from the rest of the films in this chapter as being critical of capitalism in a patriotic tradition rather than blindly and only pro-capitalist or anti-communist.

It's a Wonderful Life was released in December 1946 by Liberty Films. The story follows hero George Bailey butting heads with the Scrooge-like banker Henry F. Potter. Their dichotomy is very much that of a neighborly sweetheart in George versus a monopolistic miser in Mr. Potter. Set in the fictional town of Bedford Falls, New York, the story, narrated by a trio of angels, runs from 1909 when George heroically saves his brother's life, to Christmas Eve 1945 when George's own life is saved both by divine intervention and the kindness of his community. In the first hour and twenty minutes of the two-hour, 10-minute film, George performs a series of selfless deeds for his friends, neighbors, and family both through the independent, family-owned lending association the Building & Loan, and through his personal relationships. More than halfway through the film, his uncle misplaces $8000, enough to cause scandal, fraud, and threaten the closure of the Building & Loan for good. George begs Potter for help to which he responds by calling the papers and local authorities to alert them of the scandal, adding with a snide laugh to George, "you're worth more dead than alive."

George takes this remark as advice and contemplates suicide on a bridge to secure his $15,000 life-insurance to save the Building & Loan and, by extension, the townspeople it serves, from financial ruin. Clarence (Henry Travers), his guardian angel, jumps from the bridge instead, knowing George will follow to save his life, and in turn save his own. George mutters a wish that he had never been born, prompting Clarence to lead him through an alternate sequence in which this is true allowing Potter to have taken over the entire town – renaming it egregiously and narcissistically as Pottersville. Without George to stop Potter's monopolistic takeover of the town, George's loved ones are condemned to slums, brothels, strip clubs, jail, and in some cases an early grave. George then realizes his own intangible value and returns to his own timeline and to his wife who has saved the day by contacting friends and family, near and far to donate towards George and the Building & Loan. The film ends with a hearty rendition of "Auld Lang Syne", George kissing his wife and youngest daughter, and a note from Clarence reading "Remember no man is a failure who has friends."

In the August 7, 1947 memo, the FBI highlights concerns with the writers involved with the film, as well as Frank Capra himself, identifying his earlier 1939 populist film, *Mr. Smith Goes to Washington,* as "decidedly Socialist in nature."[78] Capra's signature style – "Capracorn" as it came to be known – was populist cinema that, as mentioned above, employed specific American iconography, themes, and storylines to speak to the common working man. *Mr. Smith Goes to Washington* is a purely populist film that uses these generic hallmarks to prop up the common man against the large obstacle of corruption in the US government, similarly to how *It's a Wonderful Life* empowers the common man against a monopolizing power. Looking more at populist cinema, and specifically these two films, further exposes these American values that were deemed "decidedly Socialist in nature" by the FBI.

---

78 Federal Bureau of Investigation, "Communist Infiltration into the Motion Picture Industry" Report LA 100–15732 (Los Angeles: FBI, August 7, 1947), pdf scan acquired by this researcher.

Populist Cinema

The 1930s witnessed the emergence of populist cinema, largely dominated by Frank Capra. The films focused in essence on the common man working for the good of his neighbors. Jeffrey Richards notes that a populist film is one in which the protagonist is a small-town, good neighborly, decent man set in opposition to a "Big Business complex or Political Machine."[79] Wes D. Gehring, similarly, claims that populism is "a basic belief held by many people that the superior and majority will of the common man is forever threatened by the usurping, sophisticated, evil few."[80] In the face of the Great Depression, a declining faith in individualism, and the acknowledgement that the government was failing society's lowest classes, populist cinema geared towards the middle class held that "there was nothing basically wrong with the country and that if friends rallied round and people loved and helped one another, everything could be solved without government interference."[81] The inherent belief behind populist cinema was that returning to original American populist ideas of equality of opportunity for every common man would resurrect the traditional American feel-good spirit and rekindle the hope that can be seen at the end of populist films. Hallmarks of populist cinema, therefore, were: 1) depictions of the common man working for the common good; 2) a good-neighborly aspect of rallying around a small community against a large political or industrial opponent; 3) aforementioned depictions of earlier American populist figures such as Andrew Jackson and Abraham Lincoln, and 4) a message of hope to leave the audience with at the film's end.

Capra's 1939 *Mr. Smith Goes to Washington* is interpreted in the August 1947 FBI report as "decidedly Socialist." However, the true spirit of the film is decidedly populist. The protagonist, Jefferson Smith (James Stewart) – named after Thomas Jefferson and the most common surname possible – is a midwestern scout leader who gives Washington DC his all, literally sacrificing his physical well-being in the name of populist, traditional American values. Despite some criticisms that the young, idealistic politician receives "at best, a personal victory," the allure of *Mr. Smith*, and Capra's other populistic films, is in the feeling of hope rendered at the film's end. As Gehring writes, "Political machines have much to fear from societies that are still capable of producing idealistic young men while simultaneously maintaining old cracker-barrel shrines," such as the imagery of Smith dejectedly exploring Washington in search of a deeper meaning for why he is there fighting

79 Richards, "Frank Capra", 23.
80 Gehring, *Populism and the Capra Legacy*, 1.
81 Richards, "Frank Capra", 22.

against the corrupt politicians and media.[82] Ultimately, Smith regains his conviction when stood before the Lincoln Memorial, the symbol of the American "whose legend stands at the heart of populism."[83]

It's a Wonderful Life follows a similar pathway to *Mr. Smith*, but with one key difference: the divine intervention of Clarence. George Bailey and Jefferson Smith are American archetypes and typical populist characters, mirroring almost every trait in each other including having both been played by James Stewart. For a brief moment even, when George is at his most frantic before begging Potter for help, a portrait of Abraham Lincoln can be seen in the den of his family home, symbolizing the traditional values inherent in George's character. The difference between George and Jefferson Smith is that George is not emboldened by being in the presence of the Lincoln portrait but is driven to the brink of suicide before Clarence appears to help him.

This diversion from Capra's classic populist film formula shifts his story into populist fantasy, taking the former "fantasy of good-will" and making it palatable for a 1946 audience that had diminished hope for a happy-ending, politically populist film, such as *Mr. Smith*.[84] Gehring notes that, "the 1940s and 1950s would find the populist increasingly out of favor, though the character would still occasionally surface, often with a provocative twist."[85] The provocative twist in *It's a Wonderful Life* is the inclusion of divine intervention. In showing the audience that populist, common man hero George Bailey needs the help of the supernatural to achieve his feel-good, good-neighborly ending, Capra is softening the delivery of the populist tradition for an audience that is no longer willing to have such blind faith in the "good-will of man" storyline.

This decline in the production of and desire for populist films can be seen in the treatment of *It's a Wonderful Life*. As evidenced above, Rand, the MPAPAI, and HUAC were determined to challenge and discredit the populist tradition by equating it to communism; however, the populist tradition was already diminishing by 1946. *It's a Wonderful Life*'s populist message centers on the small-town, good-neighbor, big-hearted, common American man, George Bailey. With divine intervention, George is able to overcome his personal qualms with his own perceived lack of success, when he is reminded that to be a successful American, all one needs to do is be a good, moralistic person. This message was also encouraged in the publicity pressbook for the film, with one slogan reading, "You don't have

---

82 Gehring, *Populism and the Capra Legacy*, 9.
83 Jeffrey Richards, *Visions of Yesterday* (London: Routledge, 1973), 234.
84 Gehring, *Populism and the Capra Legacy*, 15.
85 Gehring, 9.

to go places, do things, and see people to achieve success."[86] While these sentiments about interpersonal, non-economic success among the good-neighborly common men of America offer a very traditionally American image in line with populist cinema's established hallmarks, it did not fit with Rand's, and therefore the
FBI's, views of Americanism.

George Bailey as a Common Man's Capitalist

The report itself claimed that, in *It's a Wonderful Life*, "a subtle attempt was made to
magnify the problems of the so-called 'common man' in society," and that in one informant's opinion, "this picture deliberately maligned the upper class attempting to
show the people who had money were mean despicable characters."[87] A redacted informant declared, "in substance [*It's a Wonderful Life*] represented a rather obvious
attempt to discredit bankers by casting Lionel Barrymore as a 'scrooge-type' so that
he would be the most hated man in the picture ... a common trick used by the Communists."[88] One informant also remarked that the film would not have "suffered at
all" in portraying Potter as "a man who was protecting funds put in his care by private individuals and adhering to rules governing the loan of that money rather than
portraying the part as it was shown." This informant went on to state, "It was not
necessary to make him such a mean character and 'I would never have done it
that way.'"[89] In other words, if Potter were not shown as merciless, but rather as following the rules, the film would not have suffered and would not have been condemned for showing a capitalist as such an evil man.

In one sense, all three principal arguments from Rand – capitalism's free enterprise is invariably equal to American traditional values; glorifying commonality,
averageness, and failure are anti-American; and acquiring independent wealth and
financial success are typically American goals and ideals – are applicable to *It's a
Wonderful Life*. The film does portray an emotionless, evil, greedy, and monopolistic banker attacking the seemingly common man protagonist until the latter fails,
but still ultimately comes out on top with some spiritual help. However, the film
itself, and George Bailey more directly, are also subtle critiques of merciless, monopolistic capitalism, and staunchly in favor of a more compassionate economy.
Potter may be portrayed as a "scrooge-type," to evoke hatred from the audience,

86 *It's a Wonderful Life* Pressbook, Liberty Films, 1946, microform, Reuben Library, British Film
Institute.
87 FBI, "COMPIC", file 100–138754, serial 251x1, 160.
88 FBI, 160.
89 FBI, 160. Informant is paraphrased and quoted in this sentence.

but George is also a banker, allowing for a possible good-hearted presentation of bankers to also exist in the film. Rand and the FBI had left very little room for nuanced critique, despite the nature of the filmmaking art. This lack of room for nuance within a critical appraisal of capitalism began a trend observable over the 15-year period until 1961. By not allowing any room for nuance, the films studied in this book began to safeguard against further conservative attentions by conforming to the pressures placed on the industry.

It's a Wonderful Life creates an anti-monopolistic message through George Bailey's portrayal of a good banker. The premise of the film pits a compassionate banker of the people against a monopolizing big business banker.[90] Rand warns in her pamphlet against defaming the profit motive and wealth, fearing that the presentation of bankers as wholly evil would poison the audience against capitalism. However, it is precisely the fact that George Bailey offers a foil to Potter that immediately soothes those qualms and at the same time offers a different approach to capitalism that inherently is not communist in nature.

Early in the film, George speaks to his father Peter about his future prospects. This conversation sets up the struggle between two forms of American idealism that will distinguish the rest of the film.[91] George is a restless young man who wants to travel, see the world, have adventures, and make a great impact. He tells his father he wants to do "something big and something important," implying he cannot do those things if he stays in Bedford Falls like his father. Peter retorts that with the Building & Loan he is doing something important in a small way, and "satisfying a fundamental urge" of man by helping him acquire "his own roof and walls and fireplace." The film sets up a dichotomy between two opposing but equally valid versions of American values: in one, there is the drive George Bailey feels to impact the whole world in a big way, through urban development and innovation; while in the other, his father is committed to making small fundamental changes in a small town that impact the lives of every citizen, ultimately creating a happier populace and, through implied ripple effects, impacting the nation as a whole.

In this conversation, Capra is setting up a dialogue between the old views of the populist tradition and the new. For Peter Bailey, the older and wiser populist hero in the film, the primary goal in his life was to be the decent, common, good-neighborly man who provides for his small community at a time when this was a possible goal. George, on the other hand, comes into adulthood in 1919 and will see the Great Depression and the Second World War first-hand as a banker. Like the

---

90 Noakes, "Bankers and Common Men in Bedford Falls", 311.
91 Another hallmark of populist films is a strong, morally-guiding father figure, such as Peter Bailey in *It's a Wonderful Life*. Gehring, *Populism and the Capra Legacy*, 24.

audience viewing *It's a Wonderful Life* in cinemas in 1946, George has a diminished hope in the populist tradition as portrayed in Peter Bailey; however, he is intent on preserving his father's legacy as an enduring populist. Capra will deliver George as a populist hero in the legacy of the populists who came before him, even if that means – in terms of the plot – using divine intervention.

This is the final conversation George and Peter have before Peter passes away and George takes over the Building & Loan in his stead. The foundations of George's faith in humanity and populist character are derived from his father, in whose memory he works the rest of his life to provide for and aid others in any way he can. He becomes the ethical, alternative financial solution for the townspeople; a loving husband and father; an air raid warden in wartime; even a self-sacrificing martyr if need be to preserve the Building & Loan as an institution of hope and salvation in contrast to Potter's monopolizing bank.

At many moments in the film, George and Potter square off against each other, each presenting his own outlook on the place of bankers in society. Potter sees the townspeople as "a discontented, lazy rabble" and labels the Baileys as "starry-eyed dreamers." He uses ethnic-slurs to refer to the immigrants in town, and he is pictured during the war assigning every military service-member application invariably to 1-A, eligible for service. George, on the other hand, is friends with the townspeople he serves, having grown up alongside them, married locally, and settled to raise his family in Bedford Falls. George contradicts Potter's idea that men should wait and save money before investing in a home with a long, emotional speech, claiming ultimately that the "rabble" he referred to, the ordinary people of the town, "do most of the working and paying and living and dying in this community."

George begs the board of trustees deciding the fate of the Building & Loan to think harder about the decision they have been asked to make from an economic perspective. He appeals to the businessmen by asking, "Doesn't it make them better citizens? Doesn't it make them better customers?" These words stand out in the film as a confrontation on behalf of basic American traditional values, questioning the extent to which the economy should take the interests of private citizens into account. At one extreme, high prices and mortgages look good on paper, but without thinking of the human aspect behind those numbers, they will ultimately turn customers against landlords and bankers, breeding resentment, fear, and hatred of the economic system. Instead of condemning capitalism, George Bailey critiques it and offers a solution through maintaining human interest rather than treating the common man as a faceless service-member application sent to die on the front lines without a second thought.

At a crucial point, Potter begins to correctly fear that he is losing to George's compassionate, common man's capitalism, and in an attempt to preserve his wealth and bury the Building & Loan for good, offers George a job. In George's hesitation to accept, Potter asks him if he is afraid of success. Rand's pamphlet warns producers not to smear success stating, "It is the Communists' intention to make people think that personal success is somehow achieved at the expense of others and that every successful man has hurt somebody by becoming successful," adding, "when you defame success, you defame human dignity." By having Potter ask if George is afraid of success, the film forces the question of what success even is. In Rand's view, success is inherently financial, but *It's a Wonderful Life* offers the idea that success is defined by the individual and whatever endeavors he undertakes. Potter did acquire his financial success at the expense of others' emotional, physical, and mental wellbeing as seen in the alternate reality sequence in Pottersville.

Again, in questioning the values within *It's a Wonderful Life*, the FBI report sides with the monopolistic view of capitalism as the obvious and correct version of it. Potter's success is maligned because it was inherently exploitative in nature. The report ignores any other interpretation of success, however. George's success in emotional depth and meaningful relationships with his friends, family, and acquaintances that are a direct result of the reciprocated hard-work each party puts into those relationships is disregarded. In this way – but with a different definition of success – the film nearly agrees with Rand's pamphlet, that virtuous success for Americans is only possible with dignity, self-respect, and respect for others, all qualities that Potter lacks. The question of whether George fears success sets him up to redefine success for himself and the audience, ultimately concluding that success is for the individual to define for themselves.

In many ways, George Bailey is a common man's capitalist. Instead of advocating the strict, emotionless extreme of capitalism portrayed by Potter, George makes room for sentiment, compassion, and humanity in his version of the capitalist banking system embodied by the Building & Loan. This type of nuanced critique of capitalism and the values inherent in it was judged in the harsh philosophy of Rand, the MPAPAI, and the FBI to be communist subversion, and therefore un-American in nature. However, these arbitrary and fear-mongered suspicions were not necessarily shared across Hollywood. In October 1947, director and screenwriter John Charles Moffitt testified before HUAC in favor of the nuanced critique of capitalism set forth in *It's a Wonderful Life*, claiming the film certainly portrayed an evil banker in Potter, but also introduced two positive businessmen in George Bailey and his father, who used "money as a benevolent influence."[92] Moffitt's friendly testimony and the nature of film itself suggest that forcing an

---

92 *Hearings Regarding the Communist Infiltration of the Motion Picture Industry,* 120–121.

artistic representation into a pre-determined list of dos and don'ts in order to label that art as one extreme or another is highly arbitrary.

The FBI's struggle in identifying communist subversion in non-political films was at best misguided and betrayed both the nature of art and the coveted, traditional American patriotic trait of critiquing American political institutions and systems. If anything, *It's a Wonderful Life* is a pro-American, pro-capitalist, populist film, advocating the survival of compassionate financial institutions and an economy more virtuously rooted in American values as shown through the common man's capitalist, George Bailey.

Conclusion

Within the cultural and political shift happening in foreign, domestic, and Hollywood spaces in this post-war period, the FBI's use of Rand's MPAPAI pamphlet to accuse a Christmas film of potential communist subversion is a perfect microcosm. Capra's *It's a Wonderful Life* offers a nuanced critique of capitalism while holding up deeply entrenched American values and iconography indicative of America's mythic history of exceptional common men. For such a nuanced challenge to American financial institutions to be a concern to the FBI is indicative of a much wider problem encroaching on Hollywood in 1947.

The federal pressures threatening the motion picture industry – namely the FBI and HUAC – in 1947 effectively forced the leaders of the industry to comply with content control in films when they enacted the blacklist. This endorsement of self-censorship led to a fundamental shift in Hollywood's products that is particularly evident in how the Christmas films in this study reflect the cultural, political, economic, and social aspects of the years in which they were released during this 15-year period between 1946 and 1961. Christmas films allow for a unique analysis of this particularly influential cultural moment as the mainstream American Christmas tradition up to this point generally followed similar trends of Dickensian or nostalgic tropes, as *It's a Wonderful Life* does. The Dickensian tropes of this and other Christmas films will be explored more fully in Chapter 2. Just as *It's a Wonderful Life* was examined here for its reflections of traditional American values in George's own character and its nuanced approach to financial institutions and critical views of monopolistic capitalists, the next chapter will explore Christmas films released in 1947 and how they reflect specifically the social and psychological problems many Americans lived with in the post-war moment.

Chapter 2
Reflections of Reality: Social Problem and Psychological Films, 1947

> Henry, I've changed my mind about the cathedral. I'm going to give my money to those who need it. To the poor and the homeless and the unappreciated people in the city and all over the world. And I want you to direct the spending of the money.
> - Agnes Hamilton, *The Bishop's Wife* (1947)

At the climax of Henry Koster's 1947 film *The Bishop's Wife*, wealthy widow Agnes Hamilton (Gladys Cooper) is influenced by divine intervention to donate her money to "the poor and the homeless and the unappreciated people in the city and all over the world." Having been persuaded by the angel Dudley (Cary Grant) to consider the social problems affecting their community, this charitable donation is in place of Agnes's previous promise to donate that money to the titular bishop, Henry (David Niven), for his planned grandiose cathedral. The emphasis on the social problems in the community situate *The Bishop's Wife* in its historical moment, having been released in 1947. Not only does the film lean into the economic issues and housing crisis of the post-war period, but *The Bishop's Wife* also takes a moral stance calling for aid to the impoverished and homeless.

Each of the four Christmas films released in 1947 – *The Bishop's Wife*, *Christmas Eve*, *Miracle on 34th Street*, and *It Happened on 5th Avenue* – reflect aspects of America's social and/or psychological problems in the immediate post-war period. More importantly, these films are not standouts from Hollywood's other outputs in the two years following World War II: namely, *It's a Wonderful Life* (1946), as discussed in Chapter 1, addresses the period's social problems, as does the 1947 winner of the Academy Award for Best Picture, William Wyler's *The Best Years of Our Lives* (1946). These films identified social problems that demanded the nation's attention including not only the housing crisis, but also its intersections with the veterans themselves who had returned from WWII, the social implications of their reintegration into American life, and the realities of a wartime returning to a peacetime economy with an influx of working-age adults back into the social order after four years of robust social and economic change at home.

Each of these four Christmas films released in 1947 speaks directly to the particular moment in which they were made, a moment that was soon to change. As discussed in Chapter 1, the latter half of 1947 witnessed the intersection and escalation of many key events in the wider world and within Hollywood. These events included: the reintroduction of conservative ideologies into intellectual circles and Hollywood including Ayn Rand's *Screen Guide for Americans*; the FBI's usage of

Rand's pamphlet in their reports on Communism in the motion picture industry; HUAC beginning its investigations into communist subversion in the motion picture industry followed by the prosecution and subsequent sentencing of the Hollywood Ten for their defiance of the Committee; and the ultimate creation of the blacklist as a measure of control over creatives in Hollywood. These disruptions in the movie industry had a marked influence on the films produced during this period as reported on at the time by film analyst Dorothy Jones. Jones and her findings will be explored more fully in Chapter 3. However, it is important to note here that, when searching for communist subversion in films released in the seven years between the second half of 1947 and 1954, Jones found not only no actual communist propaganda but also a dramatic decline in the production of social problem and psychological films over the same period from 28% of Hollywood's total films to a low of 9.2%.[93]

Acknowledging that this decline in social problem and psychological films is imminent, this chapter will analyze the four films released in the immediate post-war year of 1947 and how they reflected real social issues faced by Americans. Beginning with a discussion of *It's a Wonderful Life* and *The Best Years of Our Lives* to situate these four films in the appropriate Hollywood context, the chapter will then explore some of the real-life social issues depicted in *The Bishop's Wife*, *It Happened on 5th Avenue*, *Miracle on 34th Street*, and *Christmas Eve*.

Social Problem and Psychological Films

Taking as a given the idea that Hollywood films generally reflected the moment in which they were made in some way, it follows that certain genres may be more popular in some eras than in others. Because Hollywood and cultural production more generally are complex systems with myriad influences, the prevailing influences on each period are different. Films in one period may be more influenced by the economics of the audience while in another the predominant political ideology may have a more prominent impact on the types of films being made. Peter Roffman and Jim Purdy suggest, for example, that the 1920s saw a significant decline in films critiquing American society and the American Dream because, as they write, "an audience which now hungered after the symbols of wealth would no longer respond to the films depicting a corrupt and exploitative ruling class."[94] If films

---

[93] Dorothy Jones, "Communism and the Movies: A Study of Film Content", in *Report on Blacklisting*, ed. John Cogley (Fund for the Republic, 1956), 219–221.

[94] Peter Roffman and Jim Purdy, *The Hollywood Social Problem Film: Madness, Despair, and Politics from the Depression to the Fifties* (Bloomington: Indiana University Press, 1981), 10–11.

are a reflection of society, they conclude, the growing affluence among the majority of the 1920s audience then demands a more sympathetic portrayal of that majority and its values on screen.

Roffman and Purdy further suggest that as the Great Depression began and the disparity between classes widened considerably, the social problem film returned to Hollywood:

> A hungry and insecure audience needed the psychic relief and rejuvenation of entertainment films but also demanded that filmmakers give at least token recognition to the ever-pressing social realities of the time. The result was a move toward greater realism in style and subject matter which allowed for a substantial body of socially oriented films.[95]

The idea of "greater realism" present in many films from the Great Depression through World War II and into the immediate post-war period studied in this chapter is of primary interest here. The social problems within these films could be on any scale from the realities of individual families struggling to provide for their children to the international threats of fascism distilled into accessible microcosms for an American audience. These social realities continued on screens into the post-war period up to 1947 before the sudden and extreme decrease after the federal interventions in Hollywood referenced above.

Not every Hollywood film engages directly or in the same way with salient cinematic trends or with the same contemporary issues. For instance, *Crossfire* (1947) directed and produced by future members of the Hollywood Ten Edward Dmytryk and Adrian Scott, concerned both antisemitism and veteran's affairs in the post-war period, while future HUAC-informer Elia Kazan's *Gentleman's Agreement* (1947) shed light on social antisemitism.[96] Both of these films were firmly under the social problems category of films in the post-war period, filling a hole for American filmmakers who, in "seeking a more intelligent and sophisticated audience, undertook substantial, important themes that dealt with the social fabric of American life."[97] Among the films that spoke to that social fabric are *It's a Wonderful Life* and *The Best Years of Our Lives.* These two films both reflect social issues in their moments but from opposite philosophical leanings: *Wonderful Life* being an optimistic film with supernatural elements while *Best Years* taps into the sober realism Roffman and Purdy identified.

---

95 Roffman and Purdy, 11.
96 For a fuller history of how the federal pressures on Hollywood impacted the production of both *Crossfire* and *Gentleman's Agreement*, see Eric A. Goldman, *The American Jewish Story through Cinema* (Austin: University of Texas Press, 2013).
97 Goldman, 51.

Case Study: Optimism vs. Realism in *It's a Wonderful Life* and *The Best Years of Our Lives*

It's a Wonderful Life and *The Best Years of Our Lives* each depict to some degree the immediate aftermath of World War II. The former also depicts the long-term build up to that post-war moment, portraying the ravages of the Spanish Influenza, the Great Depression, and WWII on the fictional small American town of Bedford Falls. In effect, both films are responses to national traumas that end with a similar moral message of allowing one's loved ones to help them in times of need, being open to the love and support of those loved ones, and reviving the actual communal spirit of a small-town community after more than a decade of social upheaval and challenges. Yet, the approaches each film takes in getting to that point offer divergent philosophies for addressing harsh social conditions.

It's *a Wonderful Life* is Frank Capra's American twist on the classic Dickensian elements of *A Christmas Carol*. Originally written in 1843, *A Christmas Carol* soon became a foundational aspect of the American Christmas tradition as it developed throughout the nineteenth century. In 1867, Dickens travelled to the US to perform a three-month tour of dramatic readings from the novella, popularizing elements of the story for an American audience with whom it seemed to resonate at the same time as the holiday was coming to be redefined around the country, both in stores and by popular cultural figures.[98] Among the many influences using Dickensian elements as signifiers of an American Christmas was Norman Rockwell with his Dickensian illustrations for *The Saturday Evening Post* throughout the 1920s and 30s. As historian Karal Ann Marling writes:

> The enormous popularity of Rockwell's Dickensian illustrations (which later became best-selling greetings cards) surely rests on their fidelity to the spirit of the Olde English Christmas that Dickens helped to enshrine in the American psyche – a spirit of adult nostalgia for one's childhood, for home, for bygone times, and a universal good cheer, benevolence, and simplicity that stood in strong contrast to the commercial bustle of the modern, Santa Claus holiday.[99]

This emphasis on nostalgia, childhood, home, bygone times, and the benevolence and kindness inspired by those Dickensian visual cues and literary themes is embedded both in the American Christmas tradition and Capra's *It's a Wonderful Life*.

What Capra does in *It's a Wonderful Life* is show the past 30 years of national hardships Americans in 1946 might have had some memory of and then use super-

---

98 Marling, *Merry Christmas!*, 137.
99 Marling, 137.

natural intervention to help George Bailey (James Stewart) reframe his own retrospection into optimism for the future. For approximately an hour and twenty minutes, *It's a Wonderful Life* follows George through those previous national moments, depicting his individual experiences throughout them and capturing a sense of nostalgia, building a home in Bedford Falls, and showing both George's kindness and that of the townspeople helping him throughout his life. George's perspective is quite egocentric, however, and he fails to fully acknowledge the instances of community and selfless giving from his friends, instead focusing on the things taken from him in each of those major historic moments. It is not unrealistic that living through a pandemic, a global depression, and a world war since one's childhood would have that psychological effect of bearing down on the individual and creating a negative worldview and a feeling that the individual needs to be a problem-solver rather than a problem-maker. Clarence, as his guardian angel, and Mary, as his wife who ultimately saves the day, help George to shift his perspective and understand the good and benevolence he has brought into the world, effectively using his despair to reframe his nostalgia and look for the people helping each other through those nationally traumatic events.

In these ways, *It's a Wonderful Life* portrays an individual's fictional experiences of universal American history. What this does for the audience is first to allow them access points to relate to George based on their personal experiences with national hardships and subsequently to inspire optimism within them. Capra achieves this optimism by using a supernatural device, Clarence and the alternate world sequence, to encourage more positive self-reflection and an ultimate realization that rallying around loved ones is the best way to get through harsh realities.

Unlike previous Capra films tackling social problems in other eras, such as *Mr. Smith Goes to Washington* (1939), *It's a Wonderful Life* does not concern itself with a structural issue. In *Mr. Smith*, Jefferson Smith is a small-town man fighting against a corrupt political machine directly in Congress. Smith's adversaries are Senators with deep pockets and ties to the media, and Capra makes the point in this film that there are real issues in the US government and wider society that need addressing. *It's a Wonderful Life*, however, has a more nebulous villain in Mr. Potter, played by Lionel Barrymore, himself famous for many roles but particularly for his radio performances as Ebenezer Scrooge throughout the 1930s and early 40s.[100] Potter is a Scrooge-like character embodying that Dickensian character's iconic selfishness, malevolence, and greed with an added monopolistic flair to update him for the modern American audience. Instead of a specific systemic issue

---

100 Ed Dwyer, "Greatest Holiday Movies Ever!", *The Saturday Evening Post*, December 2012, 56, ProQuest.

with a clear path forward as in *Mr. Smith*, *It's a Wonderful Life* has no repercussions for Potter, no exposure of him as having committed his own crimes, no recompense for his moral failings or plan to overthrow his financial stranglehold on Bedford Falls. Instead, the film encourages the audience to remember that life is more than finances and that one's loved ones hold more value than one's bank account.

While this message is all well and good, it stands in stark contrast to Capra's Liberty Films partner William Wyler's *The Best Years of Our Lives*. Both films ultimately end on the same positive note of focusing on one's loved ones for support and benevolence and goodness, but the almost false optimism of *It's a Wonderful Life* – encouraging the audience by way of divine intervention to forget the structural issues for a moment and to breathe a sigh of relief that the war is over and their loved ones are gathered round in support – is not the same message as *Best Years*. *Best Years* has a much more realistic tone that sits with the historical moment's emotional weight. It does breathe a sigh of relief that the war is over, but it also carries on to acknowledge that many social issues are waiting for returning soldiers and that society had changed drastically in those four years that they were away. While *It's a Wonderful Life* depicts the historic events between 1919 and 1946 in an almost sterile way, watching characters age and focusing on the individuals in the town but not feeling a true sense of societal changes over that 27-year period, *Best Years* confronts specific societal changes directly.

The Best Years of Our Lives has been written about extensively, particularly famously by André Bazin commenting on Wyler's and cinematographer Gregg Toland's successes in creating such a sense of cinematic realism with the camera.[101] As this film has been analyzed by many film critics and historians, this chapter will highlight elements of the film that spoke to the moment in which it was made and which ground the Christmas films in this chapter in the wider context of Hollywood's outputs from the same period. *The Best Years of Our Lives*, having won seven Academy Awards including Best Picture, not only was a film reflecting the period's culture and social issues, but also was clearly highly regarded by the filmic community itself.

The Best Years of Our Lives is a film about the troubles of veterans returning home from World War II to their small midwestern town of Boone City. The movie follows three veterans of different ages, branches of the military, ranks, and social classes returning to different situations. The first of whom, Technical Sergeant Al Stephenson of the US Army (Frederic March), is an upper-class banker with a

---

101 See André Bazin, *Bazin at Work: Major Essays & Reviews from the Forties & Fifties*, trans. Alain Piette and Bert Cardullo (London: Routledge, 1997), 1–19.

wife and two children whose experiences in the war leave him with what would likely be diagnosed now as PTSD. Al turns to alcohol to mask his painful memories and fears that he is too damaged from the war to connect or interact positively with his family.

In one such emblematic interaction, Al's son tries to talk to his father about discussions in his high school science class concerning the mechanics of the atomic bombs. The conversation grows immediately uncomfortable for the two involved and the audience as Al is visibly thinking about the horrors of war and the juxtaposition of his son's exposure to it from a classroom begins to underline that these two individuals – and therefore many in the audience – had vastly different experiences for the last four years. Additionally, Al's son suggests that if humans do not learn to live in peace, then the world will end in the next war, trailing off into silence as the two allow that condemnation of the use of the atomic bomb to hover in the room and over the audience in the cinema, a heavy acknowledgement of the weight of being an American in 1946.

The second veteran, Petty Officer 2nd Class Homer Parrish of the US Navy (Harold Russell) is a young man returning to a fiancée whom he is afraid to embrace emotionally because of a disability he acquired in the war. Homer lost his hands and in their place has two hooks that the Navy trained him to use. The film's focus is not on his having lost his hands, nor does it question whether his service was worth that loss. Harold Russell, the actor playing Homer, was himself a veteran and an amputee, acting for the first time in this role and taking care to prioritize his own experience and speak for those disabled in the war effort.[102] Homer's primary concern is about the practicalities of his physical reintegration into society, his discomfort with others' discomfort around his disability, and his feelings of being a burden on his fiancée. Ultimately, she shows him that she is there to take care of him and to be by his side as he learns how to be himself not despite his disability but with it.

The third veteran, USAAF Bombardier Captain Fred Derry (Dana Andrews) is a lower-class man seemingly in his late 20s or early 30s, who has never trained for a trade and left his job at the drugstore soda counter to go to war. Fred's lack of job prospects upon his return and his severe PTSD, which he tries in vain to deny, lead to a situation in which his military bride, who had been living off his stipend and working in a nightclub, depletes his finances on lavish nights out and files for divorce. Fred simultaneously becomes romantically involved with Al's daughter Peggy (Teresa Wright), causing friction between the veterans.

---

102 Alison Macor, *Making The Best Years of Our Lives: The Hollywood Classic That Inspired a Nation* (Austin: University of Texas Press, 2022), 2.

In each of their situations, despite being from different economic classes, different ages, and different military branches, the ultimate resolution to the collective problem of fear of misunderstanding from those at home is to trust the women in their lives when they promise to be emotionally available for the veterans. The optimism in the film is paired with realism that the better days following the almost sarcastic title "The Best Years of Our Lives" will only come with hard work and emotional labor in a loving partnership. *It's a Wonderful Life* uses a supernatural element to change George's perspective in one night and finish on a note of blanket optimism, while *The Best Years of Our Lives* emphasizes the continued struggle to pursue a more perfect society that can and will provide emotional support to its servicemen.

Interestingly, and similarly to *It's a Wonderful Life*, the film does not suggest anything structurally will change; rather, to the contrary, it bitingly critiques the effectiveness of the Serviceman's Readjustment Act of 1944 – more commonly called the GI Bill – when Al, as a banker, is chastised for giving aid to his fellow veterans without proper financial security for the bank. As it is explained, the GI Bill is a promise from the government that banks will provide for the nation's servicemen, but the terms and limitations of the banks' willingness to comply were up to the banks to decide for themselves. This criticism of the GI Bill is a central issue for Al who looks critically at the world he has returned to, trying to move on with business as usual as though the war had never happened and his fellow veterans are not actively traumatized by it.

Criticisms of the GI Bill are not out of place. The Act did help many veterans get an education and housing, but by no means did it help every veteran. As recently as 2023, legal experts have made claims for reparations for Black veterans who were systemically denied access to education and housing benefits promised by the Bill.[103] Disabled veterans were likewise widely denied educational benefits or places in universities that refused to accommodate disabilities acquired during the war.[104] Discrimination such as this was common for minority veterans and was perpetuated in the ways *Best Years* identifies: the government making a promise that the free market was expected to keep on their behalf with few securities against banks' own financial risks. By making this allegation as early as 1946, questioning the efficacy of the GI Bill for low-income White veterans with no job training, assets to their names, or specialism because they spent "the best years of their lives" specializing in the new skills of war, *Best Years* is tapping into a profound

---

103 Micah Poulson, "Heroes Abroad, Forgotten at Home: The Case for Reparation for Black WWII Veterans", *Georgetown Journal on Poverty Law & Policy* 31, no. 1 (September 2023): 158.
104 Fred Pelka, *What We Have Done: An Oral History of the Disability Rights Movement* (Amherst: University of Massachusetts Press, 2012), 94.

social criticism. It is not enough to say "welcome home" to veterans; rather, it is necessary to provide a clear path forward to ensure their ability to live as prosperously, healthily, and happily as possible.

In these ways, *It's a Wonderful Life* and *The Best Years of Our Lives* both address social problems resulting from historical American experiences. Although they employ different philosophies on the subject, they both speak to their moment and the need for cultural outputs to offer not escapism but a comforting acknowledgement that things are difficult and also will get better. The four Christmas films released in the following year do just that by addressing a range of social issues.

Social and Psychological Problems Within Christmas Films

Having established that Hollywood in this post-war period was prominently engaged in reflections on the social problems and psychological issues confronting many Americans, this chapter will next explore the four Christmas films released in 1947: *The Bishop's Wife, Miracle on 34th Street, It Happened on 5th Avenue*, and *Christmas Eve*. Specifically analyzing these films for their depictions of the housing crisis, job insecurity and scarcity, and treatment of the elderly and infirm, this section will highlight social realities that are infrequently explored in the post-war period. According to two Gallup Polls, one dated December 21–26, 1945, and the other dated January 2–7, 1947, the three most frequent responses to the question "what is the most important problem that you and your family face today?" were, in the same order both times, the high cost of living, housing, and shortages of household equipment, food, automobiles, and clothing with the addition in 1945 of "finding a job".[105] These answers point to the reality of the post-war period that is commonly overlooked in favor of the imminent economic improvements in the 1950s and the so-called "Age of Affluence", discussed further in Chapter 4.

Using Christmas films as the genre in which to think about these social problems is particularly appropriate due to the aforementioned connections between the nostalgia, moralism, and outright calls for better social conditions that had become synonymous with the American Christmas tradition via the Dickensian Christmas model. Mid-1940s culture was already concerned with presenting the period's social problems to some degree – and rewarding those depictions as with the profits and Academy Awards for *Best Years*. Looking specifically at 1947's Christ-

---

105 George Gallup, *The Gallup Poll: Public Opinion, 1935–1971*, vol. 2 (New York: Random House, 1972), 554 & 622.

mas films for a deeper insight into such depictions aligns with traditional Christmas stories up to this point while emphasizing further the drastic decline in social problem and psychological films that is about to happen later in 1947 and for at least the next seven years.

Housing

In the immediate post-war period, the housing crisis, rooted in the Great Depression, affected many returning veterans. While this was a relatively short-lived phenomenon – it would be only four years before the economy recovered and the GI Bill of 1944 and Housing Act of 1949 allayed much of the housing crisis – it was a very real problem in American life that was faced by millions of Americans. In a 1984 report by the Community Service Society of New York tracking the history of homelessness in the United States, analysts Kim Hopper and Jill Hamberg emphasized that "in the immediate post-war period, substandard housing conditions were considered to be the most pressing housing problems."[106]

The predominant issue was that the housing crisis resulting from the Great Depression was not remedied prior to most of the men of this generation being mobilized for war.[107] With this large portion of the population not physically present in the US, housing issues were not as much a prevailing concern during the war itself. However, upon their return, the unaddressed problems became much more pressing. In response to the worsening housing crisis, Congress passed the Housing Act of 1949 to instigate "slum clearance" and "to aid materially in furnishing employment and in stimulating use of building materials."[108] The Act extended provisions from the Housing Act of 1939 for maintaining low-rent guarantees in public housing and set new regulations on construction costs and federal financial assistance to ensure the start of construction on up to 50,000 new homes within a 12-month period. This 1949 legislation reflects the dire situation many Americans found themselves in in the immediate post-war period; many of them, as emphasized in *The Best Years of Our Lives*, were returning veterans with little capital to their names or collateral to secure a mortgage.

Here too, *It's a Wonderful Life* offers an indirect and optimistic reflection of contemporary housing issues. George Bailey's multiple passionate speeches defend

---

106 Kim Hopper and Jill Hamberg, *The Making of America's Homeless: From Skid Row to New Poor, 1945–1984* (New York: Community Service Society of New York, 1984), 15.

107 Kenneth L. Kusmer, *Down & Out, On the Road: The Homeless in American History* (Oxford: Oxford University Press, 2002), 224.

108 "Provisions of the Housing Act of 1949", *Monthly Labor Review* 69, no. 2 (August 1949): 155.

the necessity of the Building & Loan's low rents and building contracts while fore-shadowing the sentiments of the Housing Act three years later. George remarks,

> What'd you say just a minute ago? They had to wait and save their money before they even ought to think of a decent home. Wait! Wait for what? Until their children grow up and leave them? Until they're so old and broken-down that they – Do you know how long it takes a working man to save five thousand dollars? Just remember this, Mr. Potter, that this rabble you're talking about, they do most of the working and paying and living and dying in this community. Well, is it too much to have them work and pay and live and die in a couple of decent rooms and a bath?

The Housing Act of 1949 stated its intended goal of providing "a decent home and a suitable living environment for every American family."[109] This emphasis, in both the legislation and *It's a Wonderful Life*, on the necessity of a decent living situation for every American family is a recurring theme in the subsequent filmic representations of homelessness and housing insecurity in the post-war period.

In Roy Del Ruth's *It Happened on 5ᵗʰ Avenue*, the entire plot revolves around the housing crisis on multiple levels. Firstly, the plot concerns an elderly homeless man, Aloysius T. McKeever (Victor Moore) squatting in the home of real estate tycoon and multi-millionaire Michael J. O'Connor (Charles Ruggles). Gradually, Mc-Keever acquires more squatters including ex-GI Jim Bullock (Don DeFore), two of his veteran friends and their families, O'Connor's daughter Trudy (Gale Storm) and estranged wife Mary (Ann Harding), and O'Connor himself, the latter three pretending to be homeless themselves as Trudy falls in love with the penni-less and homeless Jim. Ultimately, Jim and his GI friends develop a business plan that O'Connor agrees to fund to turn a former Army barracks into affordable housing for veterans.

Starting with the film's treatment of veterans and their housing concerns, Jim is evicted from his apartment early in the film on the orders of O'Connor's real estate firm. During the eviction, Jim handcuffs himself to his bed frame with cuffs he says he acquired during his WWII service. He argues with police officers about the legality of evicting a veteran who fought for the United States and cites "Section 40. Article 27 of the Housing Code – no discharged veteran can be evicted." The officer informs Jim that no such code exists to which Jim replies, "Well, there should be." Jim's indignation at the federal government allowing veterans to be evicted in the post-war period and his further claims about legislation that should exist to prevent such an eviction are a direct call for action beyond this film. When

---

[109] P. J. Madgwick, "The Politics of Urban Renewal", *Journal of American Studies* 5, no. 3 (December 1971): 265.

McKeever finds Jim, he is sleeping on a bench in Central Park bundled up in just a trench coat against the howling winds.

Shortly after, Jim encounters the wives and children of two GIs he served with on the street, living out of their car. The wives inform Jim that their husbands are viewing an apartment in the building behind them. Eager to see his old pals, Jim runs upstairs and blows their cover in front of the landlord when he asks how the wives and children are doing. The landlord abruptly refuses to rent the apartment to the veterans, claiming the apartment does not allow for dogs or children, and the ex-GIs lament that they are struggling to find housing. Jim offers them room and board for themselves and their families until they can find a place of their own. McKeever hesitantly relents and allows the families to stay, stating he cannot in good conscience turn a baby back to the streets. This dichotomy between a land-lord refusing to rent to a family with children and the homeless man with a heart of gold is a key theme throughout the film: the system in place is failing, and it takes the good nature of individuals to help correct the crisis.

McKeever's own presence in the film is a second level of attention given to the housing crisis. In this post-war period, there was a demographic shift in the US un-housed population. For those who were too old or unfit for military service at the start of the war and who were already economically disadvantaged or homeless then, their situation continued into the late 1940s when a large portion of the homeless population for the first time became older men incapable of working as opposed to young men or families.[110] McKeever, as a transient homeless man, is depicted more sympathetically than his counterparts living statically on skid-row, although, as Hopper and Hamberg write later, "the lore and lifeways of [...] 'hobohemia' proved no match for the realities of mass hardship" that is seen in the film among the amassing crowd of homeless individuals in the house.[111]

As the group of squatters grows in the millionaire's mansion, Jim and his fel-low veterans form their plan to purchase the old military barracks outside the city and turn it into low-rent housing for veterans and their families. This initiative, if carried out, could supply necessary housing to up to 200 families experiencing sim-ilar hardships, evictions, and refusals of leases as those Jim and his friends have suffered. The GIs contact their network of veterans and pool funds to bid on the lot, but after a bidding war with a mysterious third party, the veterans lose the barracks and their hopes of helping others in the housing crisis.

As it is a Christmas film and carrying on in the traditions of *A Christmas Carol* and *It's a Wonderful Life*, it is ultimately revealed that O'Connor is the mysterious

---

110 Kusmer, *Down & Out, On the Road*, 224.
111 Hopper and Hamberg, *The Making of America's Homeless*, 18.

bidder who purchased the lot. While living with the veterans and vagabonds, O'Connor completes his own redemption arc from miserly millionaire to kind-hearted individual, citing the Christmas period as the cause for this transformation. Being exposed to the hardships of the poor and downtrodden shows O'Connor the error of his ways in evicting veterans, buying property to turn into an air strip to further his globalizing business efforts, and looking down on those who are less fortunate in a system stacked against them. In a selfless act, motivated by a hearty Christmas Eve song around the tree and the sentiments of the season of giving, O'Connor gifts the Army barracks property to Jim and the GIs for free. This act of giving the lot to the veterans successfully redeems O'Connor, showing that the good nature of individuals, especially during the Christmas season, is crucial to fixing not only the housing crisis, but also the perceived disparity of morality between wealthy individuals and the working class.

Ultimately, *It Happened on 5th Avenue* is a film directly calling for awareness of and action on the very real housing crisis faced by not only the economically disadvantaged left ravaged by the Great Depression, but also the veterans returning from war who were promised support in exchange for their service. The film takes a stark look at how the housing crisis affects women, children, the elderly, and veterans and relies on a Christmas trope to ensure a happy ending in the face of massive structural issues. By calling for direct legislation and shaming for-profit real estate tycoons refusing to provide affordable housing to veterans, *It Happened on 5th Avenue* takes a highly critical look at the social problems around housing affecting many Americans in that 1947 audience.

Job Insecurity

As quoted at the start of this chapter, Koster's *The Bishop's Wife* addresses the concerns of the underfunded community in which the bishop and his congregation live. Mrs. Hamilton, the wealthy widow, turns her attention to the plight of her neighbors after the angel Dudley reminds her of her late love – not her late husband, but the man she loved when she was a young woman. Mrs. Hamilton loved a pianist but chose to marry another because, in her words, the musician "had nothing, and I was afraid of poverty." This fear of poverty was not only realistic but also relatable to many 1947 viewers. With the looming not-so-distant memory of the Depression, the horrors of wide-spread poverty were recent and, economically, many in the post-war period without many job prospects saw themselves as living in a threatening and precarious situation.

The economic crisis of the time is echoed in *It Happened on 5th Avenue* as well, as the veterans struggle to find work on top of navigating the housing crisis. Beyond the veterans who are portrayed similarly to Fred in *The Best Years of Our Lives*, i. e. as having missed out on a particular stage of career development while deployed in the military, the film comments on the prospects of both Trudy and McKeever. Trudy applies for a job as a piano player in a music shop and is quickly hired. This could be a commentary on the increased presence of women in the workforce or on Trudy's ability as a wealthy teenager to have learned skills unrelated to the war effort. Regardless, it stands in contrast to the men who cannot find jobs easily and must be industrious in finding their own employment. As early as 1944, the Women's Bureau at the Department of Labor was concerned with the questions of what women's roles would be in the post-war period since many had accepted positions in place of men.[112] While the national unemployment rate was not staggeringly high in this post-war period, it nonetheless represented a large increase from a low of 0.8 % in October 1944 to a high of 4.9 % in early 1946.[113] Including Trudy's immediate employment upon applying for a job, whether intentional or not, speaks to this period's confrontations between returning servicemen and women in the workforce.

McKeever, on the other hand, is portrayed as disinterested in working at all. As far as post-war cultural depictions of this older generation of homeless individuals went, McKeever is portrayed slightly more sympathetically than most, but certainly still within the stereotype of a grifter living off social assistance. The prevailing cultural view of an individual living on skid-row was as someone "uneducated, unemployable, and lazy", often associated with alcoholism and criminality.[114] McKeever, as a transient homeless man and not a skid-row tenant, is portrayed more evocatively as a sweet old man who has tricked the system by carrying himself as an educated man. With regard to working, McKeever says, "I believe that people who require money should work for it. As for myself, I gave up working years ago. I never could make enough to satisfy my lavish tastes, so I let other people work for it and I enjoy it." This attitude is played quite endearingly by McKeever but ultimately supports the harsher stereotype of the homeless population, perpetuating the stigma that they were living off social benefits paid for by the taxed labor of American workers.

In Edwin L. Marin's somewhat bizarre film *Christmas Eve*, the three adopted sons of an elderly millionairess, Matilda Reed (Ann Harding), are called upon to

---

112 See: Mary Anderson, "The Postwar Role of American Women", *The American Economic Review* 34, no. 1 (1944): 237–44.

113 Bureau of Labor Statistics, "Unemployment Rate and Timing of Changes to Current Population Survey Measurement, 1940–2017", 2018, accessed March 21, 2024, https://www.bls.gov/opub/mlr/2018/images/data/haugen-figure1.stm.

114 Kusmer, *Down & Out, On the Road*, 229.

return home from their drastically different lives to settle an inheritance dispute. Matilda's nephew, Phillip Hastings (Reginald Denny) has alleged to the courts that Matilda has become senile and contends that he should be named sole executor of her accounts. The film then breaks into three smaller narratives in which the sons are seen living their own lives. The first son is bankrupt, refusing to hold down a job in favor of his playboy lifestyle and pursuing marriage to a wealthy heiress to fund that lifestyle. The second son is reminiscent of Humphrey Bogart's Rick Blaine of *Casablanca* (1942), fighting a covert ring of Nazis out of a bar in Venezuela. The third son is an alcoholic all-American John Wayne-type rodeo star who arrives in New York and immediately gets involved in an illegal adoption ring he helps bust. The three mini-films come back round to the sons arriving on Christmas Eve with their respective love-interests, sorting out the inheritance debacle, and gifting Matilda three baby girls rescued from the human trafficking orphanage, all rounded out with a rather cold speech from Matilda about her wavering pride in her sons.

While this film is an amalgam of various things, the vignettes into the sons' lives offer views into different American stereotypes. Primarily of interest here are the playboy son, Michael (George Brent), who refuses to work, and the nephew, Phillip, whom the film exposes as a liar and a cheat, essentially embezzling money from his aunt and trying to take over her fortune entirely. Michael is rebuked as a disappointment early in the film for attempting to marry an heiress for the financial security she could bring him. However, by the end of the film, Matilda praises all three of her sons for their ambition and chastises Phillip for not being more like them and instead feeling the need to cheat her out of her fortune instead of making his own. Notably, none of her sons have made their own fortunes either, but the film does suggest support for a work ethic worthy of the American Dream by valorizing their effort in simply leaving home at all.

The Elderly

In each of these three films, *The Bishop's Wife*, *It Happened on 5th Avenue*, and *Christmas Eve*, the central elderly characters have largely been millionaires of some sort, save for the sole homeless vagabond with a heart of gold. Two of these wealthy elders experience moralizing arcs reminding them of hard-earned lessons that could seemingly only be learned by a harsh life in poverty, while the third is largely used as a plot device to allow the portmanteau of the three sons' short stories structure. Still, the portrayal of Matilda as a weak-minded and feeble woman lasts for most of the film as a believable reality for a woman of her age squirreled away from society in her mansion. Mrs. Hamilton and O'Connor, from *The Bishop's Wife* and *It Happened on 5ᵗʰ Avenue* respectively, were similarly separated from society, albeit financially able to distance themselves from the general population and remain largely unaware of the issues affecting their communities. Elderly characters shown as Scrooge-like, free-loaders, or in need of assistance are joined by the penniless elder of the fourth 1947 Christmas film: Kris Kringle (Edmund Gwynn) of *Miracle on 34ᵗʰ Street.*

Miracle on 34ᵗʰ Street follows the story of Kringle, who believes himself to be the real Santa Claus. While working at Macy's department store, Kringle shares his supposed identity with the store psychiatrist and is ridiculed for the mere notion that Santa Claus might be real, let alone working as the in-store sales prop by the same name. The psychologist Mr. Sawyer (Porter Hall) then recommends Kringle be incarcerated in a mental institution and the film becomes a courtroom procedural with a trial set to decide whether Santa exists and whether he is Kringle. The question of Kringle's sanity is at the heart of the plot and given extra veracity due to his age.

This plot speaks to a period in which perceptions of the elderly in society were changing. Prior to the 1940s, elderly individuals lived with family members, paid for their own care, or lived in poorhouses. However, the Social Security Act of 1935 prohibited poorhouses from receiving federal funding or assistance, and the elderly residents within them were forced to seek private equivalents akin to the modern nursing homes.[115] In the post-war period, a higher number of economically disadvantaged elderly individuals were living off Social Security benefits during a period when for-profit nursing homes started to become mainstream.[116] This development pushed the elderly from public communal spaces to the fringes of society, locked away in nursing homes or hospitals with varying levels of care administered in these for-profit, long-term homes.

The treatment of the elderly in this period became so much of a public health concern that the federal government recognized it as a potential long-term crisis. In November 1945, President Truman delivered an address to Congress in which he recommended a comprehensive health program to address economic concerns regarding the infirm. In this speech, Truman said,

> Millions of our citizens do not now have a full measure of opportunity to achieve and enjoy good health. Millions do not now have protection or security against the economic effects of

---

115 "Evolution and Landscape of Nursing Home Care in the United States", in *The National Imperative to Improve Nursing Home Quality: Honoring Our Commitment to Residents, Families, and Staff* (National Academies Press, 2022).
116 Kevin C. Fleming, Jonathan M. Evans, and Darryl S. Chutka, "A Cultural and Economic History of Old Age in America", *Mayo Clinic Proceedings* 78, no. 7 (July 2003): 918.

sickness. The time has arrived for action to help them attain that opportunity and that protection.[117]

In early 1948, at the direction of Truman's administration, the Federal Security Agency set up a Working Committee on Aging with the intention of addressing the concerns of an aging population. According to the October 1950 notes on the proceedings of the National Conference on Aging, "This action followed the recommendations of the National Health Assembly which had pointed out the need for consideration of the complex problems of aging that are related to, but actually distinct from, the problems of chronic illness."[118] The notes continue to acknowledge that "Aging affects not only the individual, but also his family, his community, and society as a whole."[119] The committee's establishment shows that how society should help the elderly was a primary concern in the post-war period with Truman himself reportedly "requesting a prompt assessment of the implications of the increasing proportion of the aged in the population" in a letter to the Federal Security Administrator.[120]

As this issue became more salient in the post-war period, and as privatization of elder care facilities became more popular, the 1947 Christmas films reflect this societal struggle to care for the aging population. The common answer among these films was to suggest that the elder character be sent to a mental institution as opposed to a care facility specifically designed for the elderly. When Mr. Sawyer recommends that Kringle be sent to Bellevue Hospital, out of sight and far from Macy's, the implication is that Kringle, at an advanced age and with questioned mental capacities, will be held away from the public eye. This phenomenon was a growing reality among the elderly population in this period. Likewise, when Phillip brings in a psychiatrist to evaluate Matilda in *Christmas Eve*, the implication is that she would be taken away to a facility out of the way while he assumes control of her estate. This conflation of the elderly being taken away from public sight and out of the way of people who see themselves as more capable is reflective of another cultural trend developing in the post-war period: the rise of psychoanalytic psychiatry.

---

117 Harry S. Truman, "Special Message to the Congress Recommending a Comprehensive Health Program", The Harry S. Truman Library and Museum, 19 November 1945, accessed April 14, 2024, https://www.trumanlibrary.gov/library/public-papers/192/special-message-congress-recommending-comprehensive-health-program.
118 Clark Tibbitts, "National Conference on Aging", *Public Health Reports (1896–1970)* 65, no. 42 (October 1950): 1370.
119 Tibbitts, 1373.
120 Tibbitts, 1370.

Psychoanalytical Psychiatry

The post-war period was a flourishing time for experts in their field. As Cold War cultural historian Elaine Tyler May succinctly states in *Homeward Bound*, "Physicists developed the bomb, strategists created the cold war, and scientific managers built the military-industrial complex … Americans were looking to professionals to tell them how to manage their lives."[121] Dramatic developments across many fields mixed with the astounding, unprecedented pressures of the immediate post-war period – including processing the national traumas and social problems shown in these films – led people to trust those who were certified experts in their fields to guide them safely through the turbulence. One such field, portrayed in several of these films, was psychiatry.

As this chapter is exploring social problem and psychological films of 1947, looking at the place of psychiatry in society at the time offers insight into the portrayals of it on screen. Psychoanalytic psychiatry was on the rise in the post-war period. Due to the prevalence of the use of psychiatry in the US military during World War II to "conserve manpower", discourses around it flooded the nation in the ensuing years. As Kaia Scott notes, "Cinema, among other media, was an essential tool used to disseminate psychiatric ideas and practices among millions of personnel in the US military."[122] This psychological cinema for personnel was largely military-made, but the practice of portraying psychological themes and psychiatry on screen carried over in Hollywood releases, especially in films from 1944 to 1947, before the sharp decline observed by Jones.

In effect, the purpose of showing films portraying psychiatry to the military, according to Scott, was both to destigmatize the widespread use of psychiatry within the military and to administer therapeutic treatment techniques to many service-members at once.[123] Destigmatizing psychiatry and mental health awareness was also necessary at home upon the post-war return of those service-members. As Thomas Doherty writes of this period of "psychiatricals": "With the enemy overseas vanquished, America and its cinema turned inward to ponder the domestic problems deferred for the duration."[124] "Psychiatricals" referred to the spate of Hollywood films released in the mid- to late-1940s that concerned psychological issues and included psychoanalytical responses to them. These films included Mitch-

---

121 May, *Homeward Bound*, 29 – 30.
122 Kaia Scott, "Managing the Trauma of Labor: Military Psychiatric Cinema in World War II", in *Cinema's Military Industrial Complex*, ed. Haidee Wasson and Lee Grieveson, 1st ed. (University of California Press, 2018), 116.
123 Scott, 116.
124 Doherty, *Hollywood's Censor*, 231.

ell Leisen's *Lady in the Dark* (1944), Billy Wilder's *The Lost Weekend* (1945), Alfred Hitchcock's *Spellbound* (1945), Stuart Heisler's *Smash-Up, The Story of a Woman* (1947), Anatole Litvak's *The Snake Pit* (1948), and Rudolph Maté's *The Dark Past* (1948). The psychiatricals of the 1940s met American audiences who "were so well drilled in the techniques of Freudian psychoanalysis" that process of destigmatisation by exposure worked alongside a growing popularity of popular psychoanalytical texts throughout the decade. According to Doherty, the "true repressed memory" of these psychiatricals was "the terror of the war", suggesting that the abrupt rise in Hollywood taking psychoanalysis seriously on screen was, in effect, a type of collective therapy after the national traumas felt by so many in the contemporary audience.[125]

According to Nathan Hale in his history of psychoanalysis in America, this post-war psychoanalytical psychiatry was led by a "generations of young psychiatrists convinced that the major causes of nervous and possibly mental illness were psychological and interpersonal."[126] This led to an emphasis in the profession on psychotherapies, or talking therapies, to understand underlying neuroses and, in this way, an emphasis on the individual as both the victim of their past and the champion of their own future.

This emphasis on the individual is at the heart of several best-selling psychoanalytical texts from the period. Books such as Dr. Benjamin Spock's 1946 *The Common Sense Book of Baby and Child Care* and minister Norman Vincent Peale's 1952 *The Power of Positive Thinking* were iconic markers of the profession at the time. These new age approaches to raising children and maintaining sanity during the Cold War were essential tools in a world so drastically different from the one just a few years earlier before the atomic bombs were dropped.[127] This individualist approach to mental health and behaviorism coincided with the American right's ideological movement – as explored in Chapter 1 – that emphasized the individual's role in promoting conservative social values. While these two areas are distinct in themselves, the overemphasis in this period on language centering the individual and the general shift towards a more individualist-focused mentality in multiple social and cultural spheres – as opposed to an emphasis on building connection in communities – is of significant note.

Another text particularly popular in this period was Ferdinand Lundberg and Marynia F. Farnham's 1947 *Modern Woman: The Lost Sex*. In *Modern Woman*, Lundberg and Farnham identify certain perceived neuroses of society, using Freu-

---

125 Doherty, 231.
126 Nathan G. Hale, *The Rise and Crisis of Psychoanalysis in the United States: Freud and the Americans, 1917–1985*, Freud in America, vol. 2 (New York: Oxford University Press, 1995), 245.
127 May, *Homeward Bound*, 31.

dian psychoanalytical theories to diagnose social problems, particularly along the gender binary. As a given starting place, they write, "With the loss of the self-contained traditional home, women's inner balance was disastrously upset" and they continue the argument by asserting that "Feminism, despite the external validity of its political program and most (not all) of its social program, was at its core, a deep illness."[128] *Modern Woman* made claims that were summarized by one contemporary reviewer as "the ills of the world are due to women's efforts to become men" by means of leaving the home for careers.[129] The text was prominent in American culture at the time and received its most thorough critical response 16 years later in Betty Friedan's 1963 *The Feminine Mystique.*

These examples highlight the ways in which psychoanalytical psychiatric texts were not merely developing the field academically, but rather were reaching public consciousness through national best-sellers. These books attempted to persuade a generation to think differently in an age of new challenges, and they were trusted by many members of the general public as scientifically reputable due to their authors' professional qualifications. This widespread public trust, or at least interest, in psychiatry was translated to the screen and became a critical part of the cultural landscape of the 1940s and 1950s.

Mr. Sawyer of *Miracle on 34th Street* is a psychologist by trade. When he dares to diagnose the young janitor, Alfred (Barry Greenberg), with a psychological condition, Kringle confronts him enraged. The actual conflict of the film, the instigating moment in which the plot takes a turn to the Bellevue psychiatric hospital and the trial deciding the "true" identity of Kringle, happens because Kringle accuses Mr. Sawyer of playing psychiatrist – a medical professional who can diagnose illnesses – when he is actually only a psychologist. Kringle asserts that he does have "great respect for psychiatry and great contempt for amateurs who go around practicing it." This inclusion at the heart of the film suggests the post-war importance of psychiatry. The film assumes that the average person would understand the difference between the two professions and accept it as the instigating factor of the film's conflict.

Further, Mr. Sawyer's diagnosis of Alfred is that he has a guilt complex stemming from his relationship with his father. This diagnosis is entirely based on the fact that Alfred volunteers to dress up as Santa Claus each Christmas and distribute gifts to children at the YMCA. As will be explored further in Chapter 4, this pathologizing of the act of giving children gifts at Christmas for free is an egre-

---

128 Ferdinand Lundberg and Marynia F. Farnham, *Modern Woman: The Lost Sex* (New York: Harper & Brothers Publishers, 1947), v.
129 Don Calhoun, "Woman as Log", *ETC: A Review of General Semantics* 5, no. 1 (1947): 58–61.

gious overstep on the part of Mr. Sawyer, and Kringle's response to it is a powerful declaration in favor of generosity, gentleness, and selflessness. For the villainous character, Mr. Sawyer, to claim that one of the most common gift-giving practices during Christmas – an older male gifting to young children – is a manifestation of a mental condition born of possible neglect suggests that American psychiatry's increasing focus on the individual is a potential problem. By looking solely at Alfred's role as a community Santa actor, Mr. Sawyer has separated him from the contextual significance of that role in American Christmas traditions, shedding light on the challenges of hyper-focused individualism.

This increasing individualism – at the expense of communal context – in the post-war period and the way it encouraged an inward focus on what the individual can control is, consequently, a by-product of the psychoanalytic turn of American psychiatry in this period. May suggests that mainstream psychiatric advice took the stance that political activism was too unhelpful and unrealistic an option for affecting real change.[130] The problems facing the US were too large to tackle with grassroots organizing and, in order to protect the individual's inner peace, the more sensible approach to dealing with issues of anxiety about the wider world was to turn inwards into the boundaries of the individual's immediately controllable life, i.e. the family unit and the home space.

Recognizing this developing idea of extreme individualization at the expense of the collective at a time when national domestic and foreign policy were at a crossroads with competing philosophies dealing with interventionism, containment, isolationism, and American exceptionalism brings depth to the condemnation of hyper-focused individualism in *Miracle on 34th Street*. The film does not necessarily reach that depth on its own, but it does when situated in and considered as a part of its appropriate historical context. As a microcosmic engagement with the popular psychiatry of the day that is informing the general population who read the decade's best-sellers, the film engages with this larger societal discussion of the value of turning inwards for a simulacrum of peace at the expense of the context of the outer world. *Miracle on 34th Street* effectively declares that there is a danger in isolating the individual from the collective by condemning Mr. Sawyer's assessments of Alfred and Kringle as deranged for their own personal generosity at Christmas.

---

130 May, *Homeward Bound*, 31.

Conclusion

This chapter has shown, through the vignettes of various social problems present in 1947 Christmas movies, a willingness on the part of these four films to engage critically with the pertinent structural social issues and psychiatric ideas of the time. Reflecting the experiences of the audience back to them through a medium embracing realism as a primary trend shows the audience that they are not alone in having troubles, concerns, and problems arising from failings of social structures. Further, this emphasis on realism and using narrative devices and tropes that have become emblematic of the American Christmas tradition by means of the Dickensian tradition reflects the 1947 atmosphere very well.

Simultaneously, with the success of *The Best Years of Our Lives* at the Academy Awards in March 1947, the Christmas films released throughout the year build on aspects of the social problems depicted in it and the spirit of its cinematic realism. Highlighting the plights of the housing crisis and the challenges facing returning veterans only a year after their return or engaging with the ideas of psychoanalytic thought in critical and thoughtful ways make these particular movies serious additions to other films belonging to the social problem and psychological film categories. This chapter shows that *It's a Wonderful Life* and the four Christmas films released in 1947 were not isolated from other Hollywood releases in those categories and were in fact in line with the year's Best Picture winner.

Such categories were about to experience a sharp decline and, as a result, the Christmas film genre would change as well. Films reflecting the harsh realities of the post-war experience for many Americans were commonplace and sometimes even critically acclaimed and award-winning. By the fall of 1947, however, only seven months after *The Best Years of Our Lives* received seven Academy Awards for its outstanding ability to capture lived experiences in a visually interesting, moving, and realistic way, Hollywood was placed on trial. The film industry was accused of potential communist subversion, and *The Best Years of Our Lives* was one of the alleged perpetrators.

In the same series of FBI reports in which *It's a Wonderful Life* was condemned as potentially subversive communist propaganda (Chapter 1), *The Best Years of Our Lives* was the immediate prior entry. The analyses of these two films are on the same page of the FBI report, and in both cases the films' portrayal of the upper class and particularly of bankers was decried. The primary concern with *Best Years*, according to the report, was that Al's boss, the head of the bank, was shown as "a mean, avaricious individual" specifically because when Al tells him he accepted a loan from a GI, "the banker's face changed and he registered disapproval of the former's action."[131] In the August 7, 1947 version of the report, *Best Years* is criticized for encouraging "an irresponsible economy in the name of moral responsibility", suggesting that the banker was correct to protect his bank's assets rather than fall victim to an emotional instinct in helping veterans as promised by the GI Bill.[132]

There are several references to Wyler's film in the various versions of the report as it was written, re-written, and expanded over the course of the FBI's monitoring of Hollywood and the perceived communist threat. For instance, the version of the report collated in May 1947 states that in April 1947, Dr. John R. Lechner, the Executive Director of the "anti-communist organization" of the MPA-PAI, made a list of ten films he "asserted contained propaganda." At the top of this list was *The Best Years of Our Lives*.[133] A subsequent July 1949 version reiterated FBI findings on the alleged communist presence in Hollywood by expanding on the concerns with *The Best Years of Our Lives*. In a section subtitled "Mobilization for Democracy" under part III, "Communist Infiltration of Intellectual Groups", the report quotes former California Attorney General Robert W. Kenny as calling J. Parnell Thomas, Chairman of HUAC, a "hatchet man for democracy." Kenny continued, "A movie like 'The Best Years of Our Lives' could not be produced in the future if the Thomas Committee continued to function."[134]

This chapter explored how the films of this post-war period reflected the real-life experiences of many in their audiences back to them, using the social problems of the time to invent positive, moralistic Christmas films with happy endings. The modern social problems audiences were likely experiencing or aware of replaced the Victorian Dickensian elements of tradition and helped form an even more specifically American Christmas tradition. Further, while the Christmas film genre is predisposed to addressing social problems due to that Dickensian tradition, these were not abnormal Hollywood releases, but rather were embracing the same filmmaking ideology that led Wyler to create the widely celebrated and successful *The Best Years of Our Lives* only a year before. However, this reflection of reality was now deemed potential communist subversion and labeled as un-American.

---

131 FBI, "COMPIC", file 100–138754, serial 251x1, 158.
132 As cited in John A. Noakes, "Official Frames in Social Movement Theory: The FBI, HUAC, and the Communist Threat in Hollywood", *The Sociological Quarterly* 41, no. 4 (2000): 663.
133 Federal Bureau of Investigation, "Communist Infiltration – Motion Picture Industry (COMPIC) (Excerpts)", file 100–138754, serial 157x1, Federal Bureau of Investigation, 121.
134 Federal Bureau of Investigation, "Communist Infiltration – Motion Picture Industry (COMPIC) (Excerpts)", file 100–138754, serial 1003 part 1, Federal Bureau of Investigation, 70.

The heart of the issue here is that a film depicting the struggles of veterans returning home from the war in a powerfully vulnerable three hours of character and societal studies on screen, not dissimilar to the Christmas films from the same period, was deemed un-American and used to further this fear-mongering campaign. Even in the trade presses, *The Best Years of Our Lives*, the film that Doherty describes as having "tapped into the post-war nervous-out-of-the-service mood and confirmed Hollywood's arrival as a mature art," was named un-American.[135]

The implications of the period's growing public fixation on anti-communism in the motion picture industry threatened the films that could be seen as addressing social problems and psychological issues. Beyond the direct assault on *The Best Years of Our Lives* by HUAC, the genre of social problem and psychological films confronting real-world conditions was a direct focus of the trials. As A.G. Kenny is stated as saying in the 1949 version of the FBI report, a film depicting such a nuanced critical view on how to improve society in line with American values and with respect to its veterans would not have been a secure investment for a filmmaker or studio in this period of HUAC's presence in Hollywood. Dorothy Jones's 1954 report supports this perspective with quantitative analysis asserting that very few such films were actually made in the period 1947–54 with HUAC and its lasting threat hanging over Hollywood. Christmas films as a genre – which are uniquely inclined towards depicting social problems and psychological issues as the context for the imminent optimism and happy ending emblematic of the holiday season – would prove particularly vulnerable to this political pressure.

The next chapter will explore more fully Jones's findings regarding this decline in social problem and psychological films as they pertain to the Christmas film genre. It will also lay out further historical context within Hollywood between 1948 and 1954 that made Hollywood more vulnerable – financially and politically – to the federal pressures that resulted in a fundamental change in Christmas films. In this period from 1949's *Holiday Affair* through 1954's *Susan Slept Here* and *White Christmas*, different elements of the genre were omitted as Christmas films expanded away from the Dickensian-inspired plots and Santa Claus mythologies popular in 1947 and into holiday romances, comedies, and musicals.

---

135 Thomas Doherty, *Show Trial: Hollywood, HUAC, and the Birth of the Blacklist* (New York: Columbia University Press, 2018), 298. It should be noted that much of the criticism of *Best Years* directly was within the trade presses and FBI report, as, according to Doherty, Samuel Goldwyn "had been crystal-clear in his denunciation of HUAC" and was "poised to come out swinging in defense of *The Best Years of Our Lives*, a film that even Thomas had come to realize was unassailable". Doherty, 291.

Chapter 3
The New All-American Christmas:
Rebranding Christmas, 1949 – 1954

Christmas in Hollywood is no different from Christmas all over the world. It's a day of peace.
- The Oscar, Susan Slept Here (1954)

Mark Christopher's (Dick Powell) golden screenwriting Oscar statuette stands atop his mantelpiece in Frank Tashlin's *Susan Slept Here* (1954). On Christmas morning, the Oscar tells the audience – via Art Gilmore's voiceover – that Christmas in Hollywood is the same as everywhere else: "it's a day of peace". This assertion from an icon of Hollywood that Christmas is a simple, homogenous, peaceful holiday stands in stark contrast to the films of seven years prior as discussed in Chapter 2, in which the social problems and psychological challenges of the day were presented as aligned with the American Christmas tradition. The five films from 1946 and 1947 – *It's a Wonderful Life*, *Miracle on 34th Street*, *The Bishop's Wife*, *Christmas Eve*, and *It Happened on 5th Avenue* – follow in the Dickensian tradition of confronting structural issues in society that affect individuals from differing socioeconomic backgrounds differently. All of these films culminate in a happy, feel-good ending precisely because it *is* Christmas in that tradition in which a moral lesson has been learned à la Scrooge, a belief in something fantastical beyond the tangible has been adopted, or a combination of the two. Yet these Dickensian aspects of Christmas all but disappear in the Christmas films released between 1949 and 1954: *Holiday Affair* (1949), *The Lemon Drop Kid* (1951), *Susan Slept Here* (1954), and *White Christmas* (1954).

Replacing Dickens was a new formula that would influence a subset of Christmas romance films well into the twenty-first century. These new-style films present simplistic, often formulaic plots with the sole goal of not only a happy, feel-good ending, but very specifically one placed within the confines of a heteronormative marriage. What disagreements there are in the films are interpersonal and not the result of larger systemic issues with societal structures as in the previous films. Christmas is reduced to simply romantic comedies, or in the case of *The Lemon Drop Kid*, a farcical comedy starring Bob Hope.

This simplification of narratives did not jeopardize the films' ability to reflect their contemporary mainstream American culture or political opinions. The focus of these new films, however, had changed from the earlier films' emphasis on identifying social problems to stories expressing far stricter social conservatism. As laid out in the Introduction, the use of "social conservatism" in this book refers to the growing emphasis on turning inwards towards the home, traditional domes-

∂ Open Access. © 2026 the author(s), published by De Gruyter. (cc) BY-NC-ND This work is licensed under the Creative Commons Attribution-NonCommercial-NoDerivatives 4.0 International License.
https://doi.org/10.1515/9783111631424-005

tic ideals, and a general conservation of these structures of society. These films, for instance, provide much more overt commentary on gender dynamics and the societal role of a happy family and marriage than their 1946 and 1947 counterparts. While those earlier films had elements of these themes within them, the new Christmas films released in the 1950s were in essence light-hearted comedies foregrounding the desire to show Christmas itself and the films set around it as peaceful, happy, non-consequential expressions of socially conservative American ideals and values.[136]

This chapter argues that in the wake of the turbulence within Hollywood and the wider nation in the post-war period, many within the film community succumbed to Cold War pressures and produced films that were in line with HUAC's preference for films less critical of US institutions and more favorable to what it regarded as "American" cultural ideals. Starting with Cold War contexts and the pressures on the industry, the chapter will then analyze four Christmas films released between 1949 and 1954 – a period in which HUAC was still a major influence, the FBI was continuing its observations, the blacklist was in full effect, the Supreme Court was altering Hollywood business practices, and McCarthyism was a significant force throughout the country. These four films generally align with Elaine Tyler May's concept of "domestic containment", a cultural adaptation of the foreign policy of "containing" the communist threat abroad as discussed further below.[137] After exploring the cultural ramifications of these pressures and how these films reflected a growing social conservatism in the wider culture of the US and within Hollywood, this chapter finishes by examining how Christmas romances changed between 1947 and 1954 in line with changing social and cultural perceptions in areas such as dating behaviors, marriage, and views of the military.

No one factor has sole responsibility for the drastic cultural changes evident on screens in this period; rather, the cultural ramifications are interwoven with the intense federal pressures on Hollywood, the perceived economic insecurity

---

136 Similar trends towards social conservatism and these expressions of Christmas as simplistic, happy narratives can be seen in the growing number of televised Christmas specials throughout the 1950s. While TV specials deserve a study in their own right, two examples of these increasingly popular and numerous episodes include season 2, episode 14 "The Christmas Show" of *The Amos 'n Andy Show* in 1952 and season 6, episode 12 "Company for Christmas" of *The George Burns and Gracie Allen Show* in 1955.

137 May, *Homeward Bound*, 16. For more analyses on domestic and cultural containment, see: Alan Nadel, *Containment Culture: American Narratives, Postmodernism, and the Atomic Age* (Durham, NC: Duke University Press, 1995); Laura McEnaney, *Civil Defense Begins at Home: Militarization Meets Everyday Life in the Fifties* (Princeton: Princeton University Press, 2000).

within the industry during these specific seven years, and the wider political landscape influencing the culture of the time. As a result, the Christmas films released from 1949 to 1954, representing the goodwill, feel-good nature of the holiday, followed the trajectory identified by Dorothy Jones of films moving away from highlighting social problems towards producing light-hearted, simplistic, and essentially conservative romantic comedies.

Cold War Contexts for an Escapist Christmas

Dispelling Dickens from the American Christmas tradition was not merely happenstance. At least three factors potentially contributed to this phenomenon. Firstly, the bustling US economy under Eisenhower's high taxes on the wealthy ushered in the Age of Affluence – perceptions of which are analyzed more fully in Chapter 4. Chapter 2 explored the phenomenon of films reflecting the general audience's lived reality, and as the economy changed, that social function of mainstream cinema changed with it. As the general ticket-buying audience became less financially precarious, more affluent, and could afford more luxuries than in previous generations, films began to reflect that changing economic reality. Films that reflected social problems were no longer as representative of the target audience for many Hollywood studios. By extension, escapism into aspirational cinema became more central to the target audience.[138] This escapist cinema also aspired to alleviate the mounting atomic fears of the 1950s, explored more fully below.[139]

Secondly, while the general economic situation of the US and its citizens largely strengthened, the financial situation of Hollywood itself weakened. The convergence of several issues – including the rise of television, the labor movement within Hollywood, several Supreme Court decisions, and the reluctance from banks to lend funds to studios – altered the motion picture industry's business drastically.

Finally, the effects of HUAC were more fully evident in the film community as observed and recorded by contemporary film analyst Dorothy Jones. Jones's research was published in John Cogley's 1956 *Report on Blacklisting* as an appendix which will be explored further below.

---

138 Jones, "Communism and the Movies: A Study of Film Content", 220.
139 May, *Homeward Bound*, 25.

Atomic Bombs and Precarity

As the social problems of the immediate post-war period began to dissipate for many Americans in the late 1940s, atomic fears gradually replaced those mainstream economic anxieties. A confluence of events deepening Cold War concerns over communism abroad and the future of nuclear weaponry ushered in an era of widespread terror, anxiety, and paranoia that persisted throughout the 1950s and into the 1960s as the world tried to come to terms with the power of the bombs.

From the moment the US dropped the first bombs on Japan in August 1945, the world was changed. Firstly, the effect on the human psyche of the power of the bombs cannot be overstated. In his history on American culture and thought in the wake of the bombs, Paul S. Boyer writes that the "entire basis" of existence was "fundamentally altered" when the US used the first atomic weapons.[140] Boyer continues, "from the earliest moments, the American people recognized that things would never be the same again."[141] In his emotional history of nuclear fears in the Cold War, Spencer R. Weart argues that nuclear anxieties had become "a condensed way of thinking about more than the forces of science and technology in general ... it also stood for the cruelest secrets of the heart: the drive to control others, or betray them; forbidden aggressive prying; and the urge to destroy."[142] This intense emotional reaction to the bombs had a lasting impact on the general public, creating, according to Boyer, "powerful currents of anxiety and apprehension [that] surged through the culture" throughout the early Cold War especially.[143]

Within the US politically, the dropping of the bombs introduced what historian Gary Wills suggests was a constitutional crisis. Wills writes that "the Bomb altered our subsequent history down to its deepest constitutional roots" as the US entered into what Eisenhower popularized as the National Security State – discussed more fully in Chapter 5.[144] This National Security State created a military perpetually ready for action and, with it, developed "an apparatus of secrecy and executive control" that, Wills argues, challenged the very foundations of the US govern-

---

140 Paul S. Boyer, *By the Bomb's Early Light: American Thought and Culture at the Dawn of the Atomic Age* (Chapel Hill: The University of North Carolina Press, 1994), 3.
141 Boyer, 3.
142 Spencer R. Weart, *The Rise of Nuclear Fear* (Cambridge, MA: Harvard University Press, 2012), 68.
143 Boyer, *By the Bomb's Early Light*, 12.
144 Gary Wills, *Bomb Power: The Modern Presidency and the National Security State* (New York: Penguin Books, 2010), 1.

ment.[145] The dropping of the bomb also induced the fear of retaliation. Weart claims that "everyone recognized that when the United States made atomic bombs it had opened up the possibility of being bombed in turn"; it was only a matter of time until other nations developed their own atomic technologies.[146] As acknowledged at the time by American military strategist Bernard Brodie: "to be sure, the monopoly" that the US held over atomic secrets, "is bound to be temporary."[147]

In 1949, four years after the US dropped its bombs, news of the Soviet Union's first atomic bomb tests spread internationally. Subsequently, multiple nations developed atomic technologies throughout the 1950s as the US began its race against the Soviet Union to develop the first hydrogen bombs.[148] Simultaneously, communist ideology spread further abroad. Significantly and by way of example, after Mao Zedong's Chinese Communist Party won the civil war in 1949, the People's Republic of China became a central adversary for American anti-communist sentiments, prompting conflicts including the imminent Korean War as Chinese- and USSR-backed North Korean troops invaded South Korea.[149] President Truman's administration and aggressive anti-communist foreign policies were largely blamed for the "loss" of China and the incitement of the gradually unpopular Korean War, a factor in the eventual 1952 election that saw the end of the two decades of Democratic control of the presidency.[150] The atomic age was even more of a pronounced threat for the average American while the perceived communist threat

145 Wills, 1.

146 Weart, *The Rise of Nuclear Fear*, 61.

147 Bernard Brodie, 'The Atom Bomb as Policy Maker', *Foreign Affairs* 27, no. 1 (1948): 18, https://doi.org/10.2307/20030159.

148 For more on the impacts of the nuclear race, see: *Allan M. Winkler, Life under a Cloud: American Anxiety about the Atom (Oxford: Oxford University Press, 1993); Boyer, By the Bomb's Early Light; Matthew Grant and Benjamin Ziemann, Understanding the Imaginary War: Culture, Thought, and Nuclear Conflict, 1945 – 90 (Manchester: Manchester University Press, 2016); Weart, The Rise of Nuclear Fear.*

149 For more on the history of Communism in China, see: Chen Jian, *Mao's China and the Cold War* (Chapel Hill: The University of North Carolina Press, 2001); Tetsuya Kataoka, *Resistance and Revolution in China: The Communists and the Second United Front*, 1st ed., vol. 11 (Berkeley: University of California Press, 2023); Yung-fa Chen, *Making Revolution: The Communist Movement in Eastern and Central China, 1937 – 1945*, 1st ed., vol. 26 (Berkeley: University of California Press, 2023); Ralph A. Thaxton, *Salt of the Earth: The Political Origins of Peasant Protest and Communist Revolution in China*, 1st ed. (Berkeley: University of California Press, 2024).

150 Steven Casey, "Confirming the Cold War Consensus: Eisenhower and the 1952 Election", in *US Presidential Elections and Foreign Policy: Candidates, Campaigns, and Global Politics from FDR to Bill Clinton*, ed. Andrew Johnstone and Andrew Priest (Lexington: University Press of Kentucky, 2017), 83.

persisted and an era of suspicion ravaged the country.[151] As the macro context for the changes in the cultural outputs of Hollywood throughout this early Cold War period, the shift towards conservative politics and the atmosphere of fear and suspicion added to the pressures on the motion picture industry to lean further into social conservatism.

Distrust and Antitrust in Hollywood

Hollywood in the late 1940s and early 1950s was experiencing immense turbulence. The combination of three decisions handed down by the Superior and Appellate Courts of the State of California, the Department of Justice, and the Supreme Court of the United States between 1944 and 1948 had a significant impact on the industry's business practices and therefore its finances and working relationships with creatives. Simultaneously, that same working culture within the industry was split into two warring factions along political lines as explored in Chapter 1. As cinema scholar Janet Staiger observes about post-war shifts in the mode of production, "rather than an individual company containing the source of the labor and materials, the entire industry became a pool for these." Further, Staiger attributes the move away from mass production and towards fewer, more specialized projects to "income losses, divorcement of exhibition from production and distribution, and new distribution strategies" leading to this new "package-unit system" typifying Hollywood by the mid-1950s.[152]

In addition to the Cold War contexts of anti-communist investigations in the industry and a general looming threat of nuclear war, Hollywood's financial and labor situations added pressure to create films that would receive positive attention and overall approval not only from HUAC but from media publications as well. The judicial actions and their subsequent financial consequences were not coordinated with the actions of HUAC or any other federal pressures on Hollywood in this period. Rather, they created a vulnerability within the motion picture industry that made compliance with growing social conservatism a more attractive approach to filmmaking than the financially and politically risky approach of, for instance, social problem and psychological films that challenged US institutions. While these legal challenges and labor disputes may not have been directly related

---

151 May, *Homeward Bound*, 25.
152 Janet Staiger, "The Package-Unit System: Unit Management after 1955", in *The Classical Hollywood Cinema: Film Style & Mode of Production to 1960*, by David Bordwell, Janet Staiger, and Kristin Thompson (New York: Columbia University Press, 1985), 330–331.

to the specific ideological issues studied here, their ramifications aided Hollywood's conservative shift in the 1950s.

Legal Challenges

Several legal challenges to the business practices of the studio system in the late 1940s and early 1950s had a significant impact on the period's filmic outputs. By altering both the means of production and the avenues for exhibition, the combined effects of these judicial actions meant Hollywood as a business was less secure about its future. Three such decisions between 1944 and 1948 exemplify the growing financial stresses on Hollywood that would add to the precarity of the motion picture industry throughout the period studied in this project.

In 1944, after nearly a decade of contractual disputes brought against studios by stars such as James Cagney and Bette Davis, Olivia de Havilland won her own legal challenge against Warner Brothers (*De Havilland vs. Warner Bros.*). De Havilland believed that her time at Warner Bros. was not as productive to her career as her work on films made with other studios on loan from her seven-year Warner Bros. contract. Loans from the studio landed her two Oscar nominations for her roles in *Gone With the Wind* (1939) and *Hold Back the Dawn* (1941) while, she argued, the roles offered at her home studio were "indifferent" and did not allow her to showcase her talent or capitalize on her growing fanbase.[153] De Havilland rejected these roles, forcing a suspension of her contract for a cumulative nine months by Warner Bros., who then attempted to use this suspension as justification to extend her contract beyond the usual seven-year period. The lawsuit brought by de Havilland was decided in her favor in the Superior Court and upheld by the Appellate Court when Warner Bros. appealed the decision. This decision reaffirmed the California Civil Code Section 1980/Labor Code Section 2855 allowing studios to contract major players for seven years, but simultaneously afforded creatives more freedom, effectively "providing a legal path for freelancing in the film industry" after the fulfilment of contractual obligations.[154] Ultimately, de Havilland's case was indicative of the trend Staiger observed in the post-war period in which the studio system was gradually shifting towards a more independent model. Instead of longer-term contracts and studios' attempts to maintain control over their players, "one-time packages reduced fixed costs and allowed more studio flexibility."[155]

---

153 Emily Carman and Philip Drake, "Doing the Deal: Talent Contracts in Hollywood", in *Hollywood and the Law*, ed. Paul McDonald et al. (London: Bloomsbury Publishing, 2019), 319.
154 Carman and Drake, 322.
155 Staiger, "The Package-Unit System", 332.

In 1947, the Department of Justice sued Eastman Kodak Company and two other Technicolor companies for monopolistic practices in *United States v. Technicolor, Inc., Technicolor Motion Picture Corporation, and Eastman Kodak Company.* The allegations of anti-competitive practices surrounded the "stranglehold" Technicolor had on Hollywood with "its proprietary three-strip color additive process, which required the use of Technicolor's own cameras and cameramen."[156] Over the next three years, the named defendants were forced to sign consent decrees requiring them to license a significant number of their patents to all applicants. This decision, while minor, impacted the physical production of films and their exhibition as both studios and cinemas were eventually able to replace film cameras and projectors with those from cheaper competitors. Technicolor, in response, reduced their prices of color prints by 6.6%, effectively saving its customers "about $1,800,000 annually" from 1953.[157] Interestingly, both Christmas films released in 1954 – *Susan Slept Here* and *White Christmas* – were produced in color with *White Christmas* being widely marketed as the first film ever made in VistaVision, Paramount's own widescreen process using Technicolor.[158]

The delayed financial gratification of this 1947 decision, however, was met with a financial blow from a Supreme Court decision the following year. In 1948, the Supreme Court finally delivered a 7–1 decision after multi-decade challenges alleging violations of the 1890 Sherman Antitrust Act in Hollywood business practices.[159] According to contemporary legal and business expert Michael Conant in his in-depth 1960 dissection of antitrust law in Hollywood, *United States v. Paramount Pictures* upheld the District Court's ruling of illegality in "the horizontal and vertical agreements fixing admission prices, the uniform systems of runs and clearances adopted by the distributors, formula deals and master agreements, block booking, pooling agreements, and certain other discriminatory license terms."[160] The five majors studios – Paramount, Warner Bros., MGM, RKO, and Fox – were ordered to divorce and divest from their cinema holdings and comply with new practices for an exhibition system largely separated from the industry's production and distribution sides. The full effects of this divorcement and divest-

---

156 Wheeler W. Dixon, *Death of the Moguls: The End of Classical Hollywood*, Techniques of the Moving Image (New Brunswick: Rutgers University Press, 2012), 21.

157 Michael Conant, *Antitrust in the Motion Picture Industry: Economic and Legal Analysis* (Los Angeles: University of California Press, 1960), 197.

158 *White Christmas* Pressbook, Paramount Pictures, 1954, microform, Reuben Library, British Film Institute.

159 Jennifer Porst, "The Preservation of Competition: Hollywood and Antitrust Law", in *Hollywood and the Law*, ed. Paul McDonald et al. (London: Bloomsbury Publishing, 2019), 180.

160 Conant, *Antitrust in the Motion Picture Industry: Economic and Legal Analysis*, 106.

ment were gradual over the 1950s due to several studios filing appeals and extensions, with MGM being the last to establish an exhibition subsidiary and transfer its holdings in 1954.[161] In effect, the decision proved "to dismantle the vertical integration of production, distribution, and exhibition" that the Studio System "used to dominate the film industry for decades."[162]

None of these decisions in themselves changed Hollywood, nor did they together in a vacuum. These were just a few of the challenges Hollywood was facing – within itself, let alone as a significant industry in the American cultural sector – and the consequences of these decisions would play out over the next seven years as the legal ramifications took effect. However, they were a significant factor in destabilizing the industry's security in itself, and particularly the control that the studio heads sought to maintain in these post-war years. As Conant writes in his reflection on this period: "The *Paramount* decrees were but one of many causes of the revolutionary changes in the motion picture industry in the post-war period."[163] Hollywood legal historian Jennifer Porst likewise writes that the legal decisions, as well as the "disruption of television and the social and cultural changes in American society post-World War II forced Hollywood into a period of significant change."[164]

These antitrust suits were one part of a confluence of events that led to substantial changes in Hollywood's business end in the 1950s. Acknowledging the legal history of these judicial actions and considering their ramifications provides necessary context for why securing funds and evading federal suspicions of communist sympathy were crucial in this period. Filmmakers eager for work in the 1950s were required not only to avoid any suspicions of communist sympathies, but also to navigate the financial struggles of an unstable industry reeling from federally mandated changes to its business practices. In that situation, compliance with socially conservative expectations of filmic content – e. g. simplifying narratives and producing more romantic comedies such as *Holiday Affair* or *Susan Slept Here* – was a safe approach to retaining one's place in the industry. The financial uncertainty within the industry compounded with the labor struggles earlier in the 1940s and the federal pressures regarding American loyalty in terms of both industry employment and content of films encouraged compliance from filmmakers to create such pro-American media.

---

161 Conant, 107.
162 Porst, "The Preservation of Competition", 182.
163 Conant, *Antitrust in the Motion Picture Industry*, 107.
164 Porst, "The Preservation of Competition", 182.

Guilty by Suspicion

Distrust ran in both directions for laborers and employers in Hollywood in the late 1940s and early 1950s. Labor disputes continued – both with the organized strength of Hollywood unions and after de Havilland's legal win in 1944 – to have reverberating impacts on the business practices and modes of production within the motion picture industry. Meanwhile, HUAC returned to Hollywood with its second round of investigations commencing in 1951 bringing a renewed wave of conservative expectations to Hollywood. The second round of investigations and the continued labor issues added to Hollywood filmmakers' increasing vulnerabilities, raising the stakes for those risking non-compliance.

Labor disputes from 1945 and 1946 were still echoing in Hollywood by the end of the decade. The sometimes-violent strike action is largely agreed among scholars to be a contributing catalyst for the vehemence of the Second Red Scare in Hollywood with historian Donald Critchlow even alleging that, without these strikes, "the subsequent Hollywood Red Scare might not have occurred."[165] While this is quite an extreme position, it illustrates the lasting significance of the Conference of Studio Unions (CSU) disputes discussed in Chapter 1. Reynold Humphries also supports this assessment that the union infighting weakened the filmmaking community and strengthened the studio heads while also encouraging them to retaliate with allegations during HUAC testimonies.[166]

Historian Wheeler Winston Dixon, though in broad agreement, returns some agency to the actual workers within Hollywood. Arguing that the labor disputes of the 1940s were a major instigating factor for some studio heads to allege communist infiltration of Hollywood in their HUAC testimonies, Dixon suggests that in the fallout from the hearings, many filmmakers were aware that the studio heads would stop at nothing to maintain control. Dixon writes that the "anti-communist, right-wing purge of the late 1940s and early 1950s" ultimately made "employees realize it was time to become free agents rather than deal with capricious, dictatorial, and ultimately cowardly overlords who would capitulate to political pressure."[167] Either way, the labor disputes in the 1940s had a lasting impact for the industry with distrust between employer and employee sown deeply.

This distrust mounted in the creation of the blacklist that would remain in effect until 1960 after a painstakingly gradual chipping away of its power throughout the decade. In the early 1950s, however, the blacklist was still a major threat to the

---

165 Donald T. Critchlow, *When Hollywood Was Right: How Movie Stars, Studio Moguls, and Big Business Remade American Politics* (New York: Cambridge University Press, 2013), 81.
166 Humphries, *Hollywood's Blacklists*, 65–67.
167 Dixon, *Death of the Moguls*, 19–20.

film community – a threat reinforced when HUAC re-entered the scene. Having been on hiatus while the legal proceedings of the Hollywood Ten persisted in the courts, the HUAC investigations resumed in Hollywood in 1951.[168]

In his comprehensive history of HUAC in Hollywood, Victor Navasky argues that this second round is when "the blacklist became institutionalized." Navasky writes of the significance of this second round of hearings: "No Hollywood Communist or ex- who had ever been accused, or called to testify, or refused to sign a studio statement would get work in the business – at least under his own name – unless he went through the ritual of naming names."[169] As a result of the names named during the 1950s investigations in Hollywood, HUAC published an annual report "that conveniently listed names and namers in the appendix, which could be clipped and pasted" by organizations such as the MPAPAI, the American Legion, or the Catholic War Veterans.[170] The ensuing results were deeper division within Hollywood and greater distrust between filmmakers, their colleagues, and the studio heads themselves.

Both the legal challenges altering the business practices of Hollywood in the post-war period and the direct effects of the distrust sown within the industry as colleagues were pitted against one another in Congressional testimonies destabilized the motion picture industry in the mid-century. These issues, of course, were not the only factors adding to that destabilization as television rose in prominence, cinema ticket sales declined, and the Baby Boom's early effects began to take hold – as discussed in more depth in Chapter 5. However, they were part of the maelstrom affecting Hollywood during this period of intense anti-communist scrutiny with very real effects on the careers of many individuals in the industry. With the insecurity of the industry in mind, this chapter will next consider the contemporary data illustrating the "revolutionary changes" Hollywood experienced in the post-war period as collated by film analyst Dorothy Jones and as evidenced on screen in the four Christmas films released between 1949 and 1954.

Dorothy Jones and the Rise of the Conservative Romantic Comedy

Chapter 1 discussed the ideological approach chosen by the FBI, HUAC, the MPAPAI, as well as other organizations within and outside of Hollywood to root out communists. By following Ayn Rand's *Screen Guide for Americans* as an exemplary text on

---

168 Navasky, *Naming Names*, 84.
169 Navasky, 84.
170 Navasky, 85.

how to analyze film content for communist leanings, these organizations chose an ideological approach from a right-wing group that did not have the professional training or expertise to analyze propaganda. This choice was in opposition to someone such as Jones whose career began with writing practical texts on identifying propaganda. While fully acknowledging that Jones had her own biases and was writing in a left-leaning publication, it is still valid to suggest that her perspective on the industry and its outputs had actual evidence behind its claims. This chapter will now analyze Jones's extensive quantitative research into both communist propaganda and motion picture content to assess how cultural outputs shifted in this seven-year period in alignment with the pressures on the industry.

Dorothy Jones and the Report on Blacklisting

Dorothy Jones is an underutilized resource in mid-century Hollywood history. Her life's work was dedicated to developing paradigms for analyzing propaganda and film content from a seemingly liberal perspective. Jones's first publications established the metrics for analyzing communist propaganda in Chicago in the 1930s, and in the 1940s, she turned to the film industry while working for the Office of War Information in the Motion Picture Analysis Division in Los Angeles. By the 1950s, these two focuses combined when Jones was enlisted to conduct a study into the actual basis of HUAC's fear-mongering surrounding allegations of un-American subversion in Hollywood to determine whether there actually *was* communist propaganda and infiltration in the motion picture industry. In 1956, Jones completed and published her multi-year research project analyzing the validity of HUAC's claims.

Jones's full study "Communism and the Movies: A Study of Film Content" was published as an appendix to the first volume of John Cogley's book *Report on Blacklisting*.[171] Cogley's *Report on Blacklisting* was initiated by the left-leaning Fund for the Republic in September 1954 when, as chairman of the Fund Paul G. Hoffman wrote, "many Americans had become disturbed by the revelation of blacklisting practices in the radio, television, and motion picture industries."[172] This timing also coincided with the undermining of McCarthyism as a mainstream movement after Senator Joseph McCarthy was exposed as an unserious man with

---

171 The first volume of the *Report on Blacklisting* concerns movies, and specifically in some chapters, Hollywood business practices, while the second analyses both radio and television.
172 John Cogley, *Report on Blacklisting* (Fund for the Republic, 1956), vii.

"no decency" in the Army-McCarthy Hearings between April and June of 1954, before being censured by the Senate in December of that year.[173]

The Fund for the Republic was a liberal organization seeking to bridge the ideological differences between those in favor of and those opposed to the practice of blacklisting in private businesses. As Hoffman writes in the report's foreword, this ideological bridge would be built by "supplying the data on which such knowledge and understanding may be established" as an "educational undertaking in the field of civil liberties in the United States."[174] Cogley's report comprises multiple extensive studies into entertainment industries and their blacklisting practices with analyses of their causes and repercussions. As a result of the first volume's publication and its direct refutation of HUAC's claims about the film industry, Cogley was interrogated by HUAC in 1956, though nothing significant came of the interrogation in a post-McCarthyism world.[175]

Within her appendix to the report, Jones found no real communistic threat or presence of subversive communist propaganda in her analysis of 283 films from the period of 1947 through 1954. This sample included the 159 films of the Hollywood Ten and 124 other films from the 29 ex-communists who testified at the second round of HUAC hearings in 1951 and 1952.[176] She did, however, conclude that something in Hollywood changed substantially, with several significant shifts in the content and types of films being produced over these seven years.

In particular, Jones notes a dramatic decline in the production of films concerning social problems and psychological issues. In the second half of 1947, 28.0 % of films screened by the Production Code Administration were classified as "Social Problem and Psychological" films; by 1953, however, this percentage dropped to a low of 9.2 %.[177] This statistic is a crucial result in Jones's findings. Jones suggests that while HUAC found no communism to root out, it did have a perceivable impact on Hollywood's productions. The threats of the industry's blacklist and HUAC's federal legitimization of it seemingly had a measurable effect on those

---

173 Michael Gauger, "Flickering Images: Live Television Coverage and Viewership of the Army—McCarthy Hearings", *The Historian* 67, no. 4 (2005): 678.

174 Cogley, *Report on Blacklisting*, x. While the report itself claims a balanced ideological perspective, it is clear that there is a liberal slant from both Jones's personal politics and the associations between The Fund for the Republic, the report's contributors, and other alleged and accused socialist organizations and individuals – such as *The Daily Worker* and Chairman of the Fund Paul G. Hoffman.

175 Fried, *Nightmare in Red*, 160.

176 Jones, "Communism and the Movies", 201.

177 Table 15 "Predominant Classifications of Feature-Length Motion Pictures Approved by The Production Code Administration of the MPAA" in Jones, 282.

filmmakers who would challenge US institutions and the so-called "American ideals" as laid out in Rand's *Screen Guide* and reinforced by the FBI's use of it.

This stark decrease in focus on social and psychological problems in Hollywood cinema can be understood through all the pressures discussed above. The FBI and HUAC investigations feeding the distrust and suspicions of the blacklist, the turmoil of uncertainty with the industry's business practices, and the wider social and cultural shifts putting various economic and political pressures on the industry aligned with the substantial changes in filmic outputs observed by Jones. Fear surrounded the potential accusations of communist ties and subversion that could have led to subpoenas to appear before Congress or, worse for both the immediate and long-term livelihoods of filmmakers, actors, writers, and crew members, blacklisting from their professions.

When taken contextually with the rest of the report and the even more interesting findings explored below, this statistic can be read to shed light more broadly on Hollywood in the early Cold War. HUAC's interference with the motion picture industry had a perceivable effect on what films were being produced with lasting ramifications throughout the 1950s. In her analysis of the data she collected, Jones writes, "Thus the years 1950–1952 can be described as a period when the industry radically reduced the number of social theme movies and devoted itself to escapist fare of various kinds. And it was the period when the bulk of Hollywood produced anti-Communist films came to the screen."[178] Writing between 1954 and 1956 as she conducted this research for the Fund for the Republic, Jones identified shifting trends in Hollywood using her expertise as a film and propaganda analyst. Her role has since been undervalued and her contributions to the understanding of Hollywood's mid-century politics overlooked.

The Results

In an adjoining chapter (using Jones's research) "Communism in Hollywood", Cogley offers an overview of the history of the Communist Party in Hollywood, as well as his professional opinion of their effectiveness and that of HUAC. Detailing the relationship between known communists during the war years 1941–45 and their opposition, Cogley remarks that the majority of the attacks levied towards the communists were anti-labor and racist more often than not and that anti-Communists in Hollywood "belonged with the right-wing extremists."[179] Writing retrospectively in 1946, Cogley also notes that the HUAC investigations into Hollywood were ill-conceived and invokes George E. Sokolsky, a key radio broadcaster and

---

178 Jones, 220.
179 Cogley, *Report on Blacklisting*, 40.

syndicated columnist advocating for the rampant anti-communist movement during McCarthyism.[180] Cogley writes that the motion picture industry was "never formally absolved" but that, by 1955, the question of communist subversion in films had become so "muted" that Sokolsky "in a lapse of memory, could assert in his nationally syndicated column that Congressional investigators had never believed that they would find Communist content in the films" at all.[181] Sokolsky's admission suggests that, at least in retrospect, he believed the hunt for Reds in Hollywood had been purely fear-mongering.

Cogley goes on to explain how any attempts to get subversive communist ideologies into films would have been thwarted by the hundreds of minds that collaborate on an individual film, echoing the same arguments expressed by studio heads Jack Warner and Louis B. Mayer in their testimonies as "friendly" witnesses before HUAC.[182] Using Jones's quantitative analysis of filmic content and expertise in propaganda, Cogley went so far as to say that even films created by known Communist Party members were "not susceptible to overt preachment" and that "more than one of their pictures ends as a complete vindication of capitalist and religious values."[183] Finishing this analysis of Jones's work, Cogley writes: "Perhaps there will never be an accurate assessment of the extent to which the Communist Party influenced cultural life in Hollywood. On the positive side, the Communists can be credited with much of the industry's long-delayed awareness of racial and minority problems."[184] Cogley reinforces Jones's conclusions put forward in her report: that communist subversion in Hollywood films was not only not present, but also not possible, and if there was any real impact by communists in Hollywood, it was principally to highlight issues relating to the problems faced by marginalized communities.

In her report "Communism and the Movies: A Study of Film Content" in the appendices of *Report on Blacklisting*, Jones analyses the films of the Hollywood Ten and other critically acclaimed and award-winning films from 1947 through 1954. As noted above, the part of her report most frequently quoted is a very significant conclusion using the data she gathered to explain the drastic decrease in social problem and psychological films in the HUAC years. However, the report also gathers a number of other intriguing data points that give a fuller perspective to how Hollywood reacted to HUAC's incursion into the motion picture industry.

---

180 Andrew Justin Falk, *Upstaging the Cold War: American Dissent and Cultural Diplomacy, 1940–1960* (Amherst: University of Massachusetts Press, 2010), 143.
181 Cogley, *Report on Blacklisting*, 42.
182 Humphries, *Hollywood's Blacklists*, 92.
183 Cogley, *Report on Blacklisting*, 42.
184 Cogley, 44.

More precisely, the repeated statistic used in most citations of Jones's report is that there is a decline in socially critical cinema from 28.0% in the second half of 1947 to 11.7% in 1950 and 9.2% in both 1953 and 1954.[185] There are two methodological issues arising from these statistics. Firstly, the first percentage given only concerns films from the second half of 1947, so the number of actual films (and hence the percentage) could be higher or lower when the full year is taken into account; however, that analysis is not available from Jones. Moreover, when social problem and psychological films are split into two categories, psychological films decrease from 7.1% in 1947 to 0.5% in 1951 and reportedly none in 1954. For social problem films alone, those numbers become 20.9% in 1947 down to 8.1% in 1953 and 9.2% in 1954.[186]

Secondly, these percentages are a part of a whole. As social and psychological films decreased, other genres of films increased over that time. Filling that gap, Jones's research shows a number of shifts in the content of Hollywood films in this seven-year period. She notes that there is an uptick in "farces" from 1.7% in the second half of 1947 to as high as 8% in 1952 before dropping back to 3% by 1954.[187] Romantic films also experience a significant rise from a low of 8.8% in 1949 to a high of 17.6% in 1952 and 15.7% in 1953. Musicals vacillate between 3.7% and 5.9% throughout the period with the highest percentage recorded for 1954. Military films – which Jones distinguishes from war films – also have a stark change from the post-war period into the early 1950s. With zero military films in 1947 and 0.2% in 1948, that number sharply increases to its height in the period at 7.6% in 1951, declining to 6.8% in 1953 and 6.3% in 1954.[188]

All of these shifts in Hollywood's generic outputs from 1947 to 1954 support Jones's analysis that social cinema was in decline, and the significance for this chapter lies in what replaced it. Comedies, romances, and military films all increased in this period of political pressures that dissuaded filmmakers from creating films

---

185 In a 1950 article laying out her methods of quantitative analysis, Jones includes a list with descriptors that qualify a film for the category of "problems of society". This list includes issues of inheritance, family issues including orphanage, corrupt politics, discrimination, and more. While this is an earlier list, it is a helpful inclusion for understanding the qualifications of her analyses. Dorothy Jones, "Quantitative Analysis of Motion Picture Content", *The Public Opinion Quarterly* 14, no. 3 (1950): 554–558.

186 Table 16, Detailed Breakdown on Classification of Feature-Length Motion Pictures Approved by The Production Code Administration of the MPAA in Jones, "Communism and the Movies", 283–284.

187 Table 14, Types of Feature-Length Motion Pictures Approved by The Production Code Administration of the MPAA in Jones, 281.

188 Table 16, Detailed Breakdown on Classification of Feature-Length Motion Pictures Approved by The Production Code Administration of the MPAA in Jones, 283–284.

that addressed and assessed the social problems of the time. This distancing from rigorous social and political commentaries – such as, for example, the call for legislation prohibiting the evictions of veterans in *It Happened on 5th Avenue* (1947) discussed in Chapter 2 – and shift towards lighter films is crucial for understanding the cultural ramifications of the aforementioned pressures on the industry in this post-war, early Cold War period.

With regard to the Christmas films in this study, Jones does specifically mention *It's a Wonderful Life* (1946), *Miracle on 34th Street* (1947), *The Bishop's Wife* (1947), *The Lemon Drop Kid* (1951), and *Susan Slept Here* (1954) in the report, namely in the sections concerning top box office successes and award-winning films from 1947 through 1954. *White Christmas* presumably was released too late to be included in Jones's assessment as it was released in October 1954 – while *Susan Slept Here*, having been released in July, is listed under the section heading 1953–54.[189] Each of these Christmas films is included for both their positive responses from critics and financial successes with audiences. As Jones writes on the period:

> The switch to escapist fare is reflected in the type of films which won top acclaim from the critics in these years. And not least significant in describing the 1950–1952 change in content is the fact that Hollywood itself, voting for the best film of the year through the Academy of Motion Picture Arts and Sciences, named 'pure entertainment' films as the best in each of these years.[190]

The Christmas films released between 1949 and 1954 are a part of this increasing focus on escapist fare, most evident to Jones between 1950 and 1952. The films also reflect the changing trends towards more comedies, romances, and military films in line with Jones's findings. Ultimately, Jones's study – retrospectively analyzing the presence of communists in Hollywood, the US government's searches for them in the film industry, the industry's reaction of implementing the blacklist in 1947, and the ramifications of all these ideological decisions as read through the data on categorizations of top-grossing and award-winning films – shows that the political body encroached on and effected change in the cultural sphere. These effects as identified by Jones can be further analyzed and supported by turning to the Christmas films from this period as a case study examining the cultural impacts of not only HUAC's presence in Hollywood but also the myriad other pressures on the industry in this post-war, early Cold War moment.

---

189 Jones, 299.
190 Jones, 220.

The New All-American Christmas

Christmas films from 1949 through 1954 established the paradigm for romantic comedy Christmas movies that is still largely in use today. The films redefined the genre of Christmas films away from Dickensian models concerned with social issues – such as *It's a Wonderful Life, The Bishop's Wife, Christmas Eve*, and *It Happened on 5ᵗʰ Avenue*, explored in Chapter 2 – or traditional mythologies around Christmas – such as the Santa Claus model in *Miracle on 34ᵗʰ Street*, explored in Chapter 4 – and towards more simplistic, feel-good, escapist plots. This shift towards a focus on playful adult romantic relationships speaks to the prevailing cultural state of the United States in the early Cold War period with an increased emphasis on inter-personal connections, a theory put forward by Elaine Tyler May in her book *Homeward Bound.* These films did not, however, depart completely from presenting real-world issues or acknowledgements of concerns that their audiences may have been experiencing throughout the turbulent 1950s. Instead, they present a more sanitized version of those concerns than in the Christmas films from the late-1940s and offer a largely joyous and jovial atmosphere from start to finish. As a holiday into which the most idealized vision of American values and messaging is imbued, Christmas became a hyper-exaggerated caricature of its already mythologized self through its portrayal in the increasingly socially conservative films released between 1949 and 1954.

Adapting a Genre

While the threat of HUAC loomed over Hollywood, filmmakers began to adapt their work to fit the more surveilled and suspicious atmosphere. As the new structure for American Christmas films developed, filmmakers tried different approaches including shifting the focus of the films to a singular romantic plot or attempting a gangster comedy set at Christmas. The attempts were met with middling success until *White Christmas* became the highest grossing film of 1954.[191] In shifting the focus of these films to a simplified romantic narrative, the romances and their conflicts take center stage as opposed to any larger plot or conflict that does not immediately serve the focus on the primary couple(s).

    Holiday Affair (1949) depicts the romantic relationship between Connie (Janet Leigh) and Carl (Wendell Corey) as it is made more complicated by newcomer Steve (Robert Mitchum) for whom Connie begins to develop romantic feelings.

---

191 "1954 Box Office Champs", *Variety* (Los Angeles, January 5, 1955), ProQuest.

From a relationship perspective, the film is not entirely different from the relationship depicted between Doris (Maureen O'Hara) and Fred (John Payne) in *Miracle on 34th Street*. Both women are living in the past and resist the desire to engage in a new relationship, aiming more to be attentive single mothers to their children while working in department stores to support their households. Both women are then seduced into romances with a new and exciting partner.

Tonally, however, these relationships are entirely different. In the 1947 film, the romantic relationship between Doris and Fred is a subplot with loose connections to the primary plot and ultimately comes back into play in the final scenes to depict a happy family ending. By 1949, Connie's romantic entanglements are the entire plot of the film with her child as a subplot used only to reinforce her romantic interests. Connie is made to choose between security with Carl and love with Steve, whom she does ultimately choose in the film's final moments as she runs off with her son to follow Steve to California. This shift may be explained as a difference between two films that set out for different purposes, but it reflects a significant shift in the genre that shaped Christmas film releases over the next decade and beyond.

For the first time in the films in this study, Christmas is used to enhance the plot rather than to facilitate it. *It's a Wonderful Life* (1946), *It Happened on 5th Avenue* (1947), *Miracle on 34th Street* (1947), *Christmas Eve* (1947), and *The Bishop's Wife* (1947) are all Christmas movies that center the Christmas season as an integral part of the films' climaxes. From *Holiday Affair* through *White Christmas* – and even more so in the films of 1961 – Christmas films are a dual genre, meaning that the primary layer of the film, for example, is a romantic comedy that uses Christmas tropes to form a hybrid genre of Christmas Romances. Chapter 2 discussed the social and psychological problems embedded within the Christmas films of 1946 and 1947, a natural pairing because of the American Christmas traditions built on Dickensian models and the Santa Claus mythology. From 1949 onwards, the Christmas film genre expands into straightforward romantic comedies, doing away with Dickens and Santa in Hollywood feature film releases until the 1980s.

By expanding the genre, the hallmark tropes of it begin to change. Whereas before, the Dickensian and Santa elements of the Christmas stories were essential to the efficacy of the "Christmas spirit", now the films began to develop new signifiers that would carry through the rest of the century and beyond in a subcategory of romantic Christmas films that specifically focus on the romance. By contrast, in *The Bishop's Wife*, Dudley (Cary Grant) is an angel whose purpose is to remind the titular bishop, Henry (David Niven), of "what really matters". Ultimately, "what really matters" is equally his love for his wife Julia (Loretta Young) *and* redirecting money meant for the cathedral to the town's less fortunate. The film rounds out both of these plots. Henry promises to devote more of his attention to his wife and child and also closes the film with a sermon on the true meaning of Christmas: "loving kindness, warm hearts, and an out-stretched hand of tolerance. All the shining gifts that make peace on earth." Addressing the concerns of the townspeople and using Christmas as a reminder of those social problems are equally as important as the love story playing out in the film. By 1949, *Holiday Affair*'s sole focus is Connie's relationship conflict with Carl and Steve.

This development in the Christmas film genre can be read retrospectively as a way to adapt the holiday film around the political and economic pressures bearing down on Hollywood in this crucial moment. As the pressures on Hollywood mounted to move away from Dickensian tropes of social problems or away from moral stories based on beliefs in the seemingly "socialist" fantasies of Santa Claus, the genre pivoted to align with the overall changes in Hollywood Jones observed. This pivot manifested in the Christmas film genre as an embrace of light-hearted, simplistic romantic comedies, farcical comedies, and musicals while carrying with it certain elements of the American Christmas tradition. For instance, with *Holiday Affair*'s release in 1949, Christmas on screen was reaffirmed as a commercialist venture – as explored in Chapter 4 – and also reintroduced as a romantic holiday.[192]

Holiday Affair had a lackluster response from critics. Bosley Crowther from *The New York Times* called it "an amiable little romance in which a boy meets a girl at Christmas-time, and the sentiments are quite as artificial and conveniently sprinkled as the snow is provided." Crowther goes on to state that it is "a strictly holiday item", "light-weight in story and treatment, it is one of those tinsel-trimmed affairs which will likely depend for popularity upon the glamour potential of its stars." Lambasting the sentimentality of the film further, he writes, "Shepherded by Don Hartman, who produced and directed this film, these lambs – for, of course, that's what they all are – are led through a cozy little tale of giving and receiving at Christmas under the cumulative influence of love." Crowther found the film "much too saccharine for either credibility or de-

---

192 It should be noted that there were even earlier romantic Christmas films from Hollywood that predated the films in this study. These films such as *Love Finds Andy Hardy* (1938), *Meet Me in St. Louis* (1944), and *Christmas in Connecticut* (1945) laid the foundations for the romances of the 1950s. However, all of these films showcase large ensemble casts and convoluted plots. These films reflected their own period's dating trends and carried larger plots with societal concerns beyond the immediate couples, marking a stark difference from the Christmas romances released in the 1950s.

light."[193] This critical response suggests the troubles filmmakers in this tumultuous era of Hollywood experienced when attempting to bring romance to the fore in a Christmas film. Crowther previously had taken issue with the saccharine ending of *It's a Wonderful Life* but wrote in his review that that sentimentality was offset in the film by the performances and the majority of the plot save for the ending scenes.[194] By stripping away those other layers of a more complex plot and offering only "a cozy little tale", filmmakers were up for a challenge in adapting the multi-layered Christmas genre into simplistic but still enjoyable romances and comedies.

In addition to the necessity of simplifying the films away from Dickensian social problems and Santa Claus mythologies in order to avoid possible allegations of communist subversion, the pressbook for *Holiday Affair* gives insight into how these films were marketed in this new paradigm for Christmas films. In the publicity materials for *Holiday Affair*, each of the lead actors was given a short biography for cinemas and newspapers to use if they wished. Mitchum, Leigh, and Corey are presented as average Americans: Mitchum takes his two young sons fishing while Leigh is "a capable cook" but maintains her "delectably-distributed 115 pounds … no matter how much she eats". The materials also describe *Holiday Affair* as Leigh's tenth film "since Hollywood summoned her from a life of quiet domesticity." Despite the inherent misogyny directed towards Leigh, the biographies fitted the cast into safe, unchallenging parameters as all-American types, but none more so than Corey. Corey is described in publicity material as new to Hollywood, but it is also quickly established that he is a full-blooded American with familial roots he can trace back to the American Revolution.[195] These assertions of the Americanness of the cast, particularly the relatively unknown Corey, can be read as statements addressing HUAC and the inherent distrust of members of Hollywood that the Committee had planted in the public consciousness. In developing this new extension of the genre and maneuvering around the political pressures on Hollywood, these star biographies stand out from the other pressbook materials for the films in this study as ardent declarations of loyalty to the US.

The next Christmas film to be released was not until two years later with another all-American player in the titular role exhibiting another inventive new approach to the genre. *The Lemon Drop Kid* (1951) is a wide departure from any of the Christmas films that came before it. Starring Bob Hope as the Lemon Drop Kid, the

---

193 Bosley Crowther, "'Holiday Affair,' Tinsel-Trimmed Trifle with Mitchum and Janet Leigh, at State", *The New York Times Film Reviews*, November 24, 1949.

194 Bosley Crowther, "It's a Wonderful Life", *The New York Times Film Reviews*, December 23, 1946.

195 *Holiday Affair* Pressbook, RKO Radio Pictures, 1949, microform, Reuben Library, British Film Institute.

film is an adaptation of a Damon Runyon short story about a conman in financial trouble with a gangster. Hope was given ample freedom to make the character an extension of himself with comedic gags, quippy wisecracks, and overly long slapstick routines throughout the film. As "the single most popular comic" of the 1940s and United Service Organization (USO) darling, Hope was a safe choice to adapt the Runyon work into a feature-length comedy, though the film did not quite reach the levels of critical success hoped for with Hope involved.[196]

The Lemon Drop Kid opens on Hope's lead character – only ever referred to as The Lemon Drop Kid – scamming gamblers at a horse track in Florida and accidentally going $10,000 into debt with the gangster Moose Moran (Fred Clark). The Lemon Drop Kid strikes a deal with Moran that he can get him the money by Christmas Day, leading to the Kid's shenanigans in New York City attempting to raise the funds by scamming people at Christmas. The Kid first begs his girlfriend Brainey Baxter (Marilyn Maxwell) and rival scam artist Oxford Charlie (Lloyd Nolan) for the funds, calling the latter a "communist" when he refuses. When these requests fall through, he sets up a fake charity home for elderly women in Moran's abandoned casino during a gambling prohibition and runs a number of scams including sending his fellow conmen and thugs to dress as Santa Claus and collect donations, mimicking the Salvation Army technique. Ultimately, the ruse of the charity is found out and Charlie steals the money. The Kid recovers the funds to open the home for the elderly properly, devises a trap in the casino on Christmas Eve, has Charlie and Moran arrested for operating an illegal gambling hall, and proposes marriage to Brainey.

Variety reported in 1952 that *The Lemon Drop Kid* was the 28th highest grossing film of 1951 (of 131 films listed) with a recorded gross of $2.3 million.[197] Critically, the film was poorly received. One review in *Harrison's Reports* calls the film a "let down" for the "nefarious methods employed by Hope" to pay his debts. The review goes on to say some scenes may "prove somewhat objectionable to many movie-goers" including the shady enlistment of Santa Claus "hoodlums" to exploit people at Christmas. It condemns his actions, claiming, "his enlisting the unwitting aid of a group of gentle old ladies to carry through the scheme may not sit so well with those who have a dignified respect for the aged." The review finishes: "the low moral values make it unsuitable for children."[198]

---

196 Ron Miller and James Bawden, "Bob Hope", in *Conversations with Classic Film Stars* (Lexington: University Press of Kentucky, 2016), 359.

197 "Pictures: Top Grossers of 1951", *Variety* (Los Angeles, 2 January 1952), 70, ProQuest.

198 "'The Lemon Drop Kid' with Bob Hope, Marilyn Maxwell and Lloyd Nolan", *Harrison's Reports*, March 10, 1951.

The film's critical reception foreshadows that of another Christmas film based on a Damon Runyon story a decade later: Frank Capra's *Pocketful of Miracles* (1961). As will be explored further in Chapter 5, a growing dissatisfaction with the throwback gangster plot suggests that such morals, values, and even plots were out of touch with audiences in both 1951 and 1961. These types of stories glorifying criminal activity were falling out of fashion. In 1951, this may be due to the proximity of the film to "glorifying depravity", an item on Rand's *Screen Guide for Americans.* Although the film and its creators were not investigated by HUAC, the movie's reception provided evidence of a changing culture within and outside of Hollywood as this film, with one of the hottest comedians of the day, the all-American Bob Hope, was scolded for its immorality and exploitation of people at Christmas. Ultimately, its middling box office success and poor critical response, as well as those of *Holiday Affair,* suggest that opinions were forming about these films specifically regarding their presentations of Christmas, offering judgements on what can make or break a Christmas film.

Interestingly, these two films do make an attempt at commenting on the wider world and moments in which they were released. In *Holiday Affair,* Carl and Steve have an uncomfortable conversation while they wait for Connie. Carl remarks that it looks like there will be a white Christmas, but that the snows are not the same as when they were kids. The two agree the weather has changed and Carl states, "probably got something to do with the atomic bomb." The scene between two competing love interests is meant to play uncomfortably for laughs, but the choice of dialogue is significantly the only reference in the film to something that was seen as controversial at the time.[199] World War II is mentioned many times tangentially as Connie's late husband died a soldier, but the blasé reference to the atomic bomb makes it seem as though it is something normal, albeit uncomfortable, in conversation. Compared to the handling of discussions about the atomic bomb in *The Best Years of Our Lives* – as analyzed in Chapter 2 – this scene reads as an attempt to normalize conversation about the atomic bomb just three years later. Mention of the bomb is the punchline to a joke and embodies the overall shift in Hollywood of currying political favor by subduing complex conversation around atrocities committed by the US.

Similarly, the comedy of *The Lemon Drop Kid* wades into several additional contemporary issues. In one scene, as referenced above, the all-American Bob Hope uses "communist" as a comeback to Oxford Charlie as a punchline. Accusa-

---

199 According to a Gallup Poll from October 18, 1947, 55% of Americans were still in favor of the dropping of the atomic bombs, while 38% thought it was a "bad idea" and 7% had no opinion. Gallup, *The Gallup Poll,* vol. 2, 682.

tions of communist subversion were a very real threat to those in Hollywood and in the audience as McCarthyism was still an active threat in the public consciousness in 1951. To make light of the allegation of calling someone a communist in a Hollywood film and to use it as one of Hope's quippy comebacks is a pointed, if stunted, shift for the Christmas films of the era. Communism is used as the punchline to a joke but, ultimately, Charlie is arrested at the end of the film, suggesting that the acceptable use of an allegation of communist sympathies is towards a character who will have a comeuppance.

The film also boasts a variety of contemporary discriminations including misogyny, homophobia, racism, and ageism for the sake of its comedy. Interestingly, the only concern about marginalized communities targeted in the film which Crowther draws attention to in his review is with ageism. By leaning into jokes about marginalized communities, *The Lemon Drop Kid* seems to be currying favor with the conservative factions of Hollywood in the post-war period. As Cogley highlights, right-wing aggression towards communists in Hollywood was frequently "anti-labor and racist-minded" due to the aggressors' ignorance of what communism actually is.[200] The film comfortably situates itself in that right-wing category of films by promoting unchecked racist, homophobic, and misogynist ideas so blatantly.

Notably, the conservative-leaning film *The Lemon Drop Kid* was released after a slew of significant racially focused films in 1949 and 1950. These films centered Black narratives with stories about the racial hardships African Americans faced in the mid-century, effectively making up a majority of the social problem films released in those years. As noted above, Jones observed a significant decrease in social problem films from 20.9% of all films in the latter half of 1947 to 16.5% in 1949 and an even more dramatic 8.9% in 1950.[201] Films such as *Home of the Brave, Lost Boundaries, Pinky,* and *Intruder in the Dust,* all from 1949, and Sidney Poitier's debut *No Way Out* in 1950 were branded as "message movies" that tackled various, emotionally intense topics relating to race relations in this period.[202] These message movies about racism can be seen to have largely filled the quantities of social problem films that were previously centered on white characters in social and financial plights.

---

200 Cogley, *Report on Blacklisting*, 40.
201 Table 16, Detailed Breakdown on Classification of Feature-Length Motion Pictures Approved by The Production Code Administration of the MPAA in Jones, "Communism and the Movies", 283–284.
202 Aram Goudsouzian, *Sidney Poitier Man, Actor, Icon* (Chapel Hill: The University of North Carolina Press, 2004), 65–66.

This abrupt increase in message movies concerning Black experiences may be due to multiple factors. Sidney Poitier biographer Aram Goudsouzian suggests that this increase may have been due to progress in normalizing Black presences in positive roles in the public sphere, for instance with Black veterans, musicians, and athletes, such as Jackie Robinson. More widely, Hollywood historian Thomas Doherty adds the gradual shifting of narratives of racial equality into the mainstream with the integration of the US armed forces in 1948 and an increasing sentiment among progressives that Jim Crow was "an un-American activity", emboldening Hollywood "to liberalize its own admissions policies."[203] Outside of the industry, Goudsouzian also highlights the start of suburban white flight echoing historian Thomas Cripps who earlier had argued that shifting urban economics had encouraged filmmakers to produce movies that would speak to the realities of changing audience demographics in cities.[204] The message movies of 1949 and 1950 – and the imminent rise of these types of films pioneered by Poitier and other stars such as Ossie Davis and Ruby Dee – stood apart from the general decline in social problem films in these years as documented by Jones, by developing a new approach to the category, concerning race as opposed to earlier topics such as economics, crime, and corruption.[205] Likewise, Cogley highlights that the one thing communists in Hollywood did do to some extent was direct attention to racism on screen: "The Communists may have done more than their share to banish from the screen the stereotyped Negro, the dim-witted Italian and red-nosed stage Irishman. But uniquely Marxist values were rarely if ever inserted."[206]

Although message movies on race were becoming more prominent, racism itself still appeared in films such as *The Lemon Drop Kid.* Further, through its gratuitous conservative perceptions on the subject, *The Lemon Drop Kid* can be read as upholding and even celebrating racist ideologies through its comedy. Yet, despite aligning itself with socially conservative ideas on race, sex, and gender, *The Lemon Drop Kid* did not generate much enthusiasm either at the box office or from critics. The divergence of social politics in these films – the message movies concerning racism and *The Lemon Drop Kid* – shows the changes emerging in the cultural content of films in this period. As white storylines about financial challenges and communal hardships within the social problem category abruptly dis-

---

203 Doherty, *Hollywood's Censor*, 235.

204 Thomas Cripps, *Making Movies Black: The Hollywood Message Movie from World War II to the Civil Rights Era* (Oxford: Oxford University Press, 1993), 255–256.

205 For more on this era of Hollywood's emerging Black celebrities, see Emilie Raymond, *Stars for Freedom: Hollywood, Black Celebrities, and the Civil Rights Movement*, A Capell Family Book (Seattle: University of Washington Press, 2015).

206 Cogley, *Report on Blacklisting*, 43.

appeared from screens, they were replaced with the social problems embedded in Black narratives about racism. Significantly, what replaced many of the storylines about white characters – as that demographic started to become more affluent and social problem films about economic inequities declined – were the simplistic films identified by Jones and exemplified here by *The Lemon Drop Kid* and *Holiday Affair.*

Both of these films from 1949 and 1951 were released to mediocre financial and critical success, failing to effectively navigate the cultural challenges in the industry as HUAC's presence in Hollywood was still very much felt, the impacts of the blacklist were fresh, and the industry reeled in the economic and political tumult of its changing business practices in a changing world. *Holiday Affair* and *The Lemon Drop Kid* attempted to incorporate social commentaries into the films for comedic value but fell short of critical success. In later Christmas films from the 1950s, filmmakers found more success with bridging the genre's expansion into romantic comedies while still retaining crucial elements of the holiday. However, when the films endeavored to levy social criticisms in more serious ways, the attempts were met consistently with backlash from the critics. As the attempts to lighten social commentaries continued, the effects of HUAC on Hollywood identified by Jones in her 1956 report are even more evident as the pressure to minimize those commentaries comes both internally from Hollywood as well as externally from critics.

Developing the Formula for Domestic Containment

In the following two Christmas films from the 1950s, *Susan Slept Here* (1954) and *White Christmas* (1954), the Dickensian model was fully left behind and the romantic comedy formula that is still in use today began to form. *Susan Slept Here* is a romantic comedy first and foremost while *White Christmas* is the first Christmas film of this study to embrace the feature-length musical.[207] These two films enjoyed more commercial success than the first two attempts at adjusting the genre in 1949 and 1951, even finding that success in some cases with social commentaries embedded within them.

Within these two films from 1954 the tropes of romantic Christmas films really began to develop. Formulaic Christmas romances generally follow a set pattern that can first be read in *Holiday Affair* but became more successfully executed in *Susan Slept Here* and *White Christmas*. In general, the dominant story structure

---

207 While *White Christmas* is a remake of the earlier Bing Crosby film *Holiday Inn* (1942), *Holiday Inn* is not a Christmas movie specifically but rather incorporates federal holidays from every month for its plot and musical numbers.

centers on a hard-working and/or headstrong woman, commonly living and working in a city. This woman has a chance encounter with a stranger, normally a man, for whom she initially has disdain and eventually comes around to like, before a challenge interrupts the budding romance. This challenge is ultimately resolved just before or around Christmas Day, when the two profess their love for one another. This structure frequently relies on three distinct tropes. Firstly, the woman has a demanding life which she supposedly enjoys but secretly wishes were simpler and that she were partnered in a traditional relationship. Secondly, a child – or the promise of children – is a linchpin for the main couple. Thirdly, a miscommunication or lack of communication provides the conflict for the two lovers to overcome by Christmas Day, showing the ultimate strength of the pair. These tropes are born out of this era of increasing social conservatism and growing emphasis on the family unit as a place of security and fulfilment.

A version of these three central tropes is initially evident in *Holiday Affair*. Connie's uncommunicated reluctance to marry Carl, her son's distance from Carl and growing closeness with Steve, and the ultimate decision in the Christmas period to leave her life behind in pursuit of Steve with her child in tow all set the groundwork for these tropes to be further solidified in future Christmas romance films.

The three tropes speak to the growing popularity in this period of what Elaine Tyler May describes as domestic containment. Domestic containment, for May, is the conceptual framework of a cultural response to the US foreign policy of containment abroad popularized and enforced by the Truman administration and policies such as the Truman Doctrine. The policy of foreign containment was the idea that the US could restrain the communist threat and prevent it from spreading beyond the USSR and its allies in the interest of US domestic and international security. In practice, domestic containment was the idea of creating one's own security in the comfort and control of the domestic sphere where the suspicions of the outside world – including communism – stayed external to the strength and safety offered by the nuclear family unit. As May writes, "the familial ideology that took shape in these years helps explain the apolitical tenor of the middle-class post-war life." May continues to explain that the popular rise of psychiatry – explored in Chapter 2 – gave way to an era that "offered private and personal solutions to social problems."[208] This gradual shift towards individualism mixed with the pressures on Hollywood filmmakers to avoid addressing social problems afflicting collective communities developed these tropes as a reaction to the changing political and social culture in the US. Simplifying narratives away from ad-

---

208 May, *Homeward Bound*, 17.

dressing social problems and towards a focus on the individual's private affairs developed the tropes that center on the strength and security that ultimately come with the promise of a nuclear family unit at the film's end.

Having established that a substantial shift in Christmas films is evident after the tumultuous effects of the myriad political and economic pressures on Hollywood, this chapter will next examine that shift's cultural ramifications. Moving further towards social conservatism and domestic containment, the next two films depict unconventional romances that ultimately end in the same heteronormative marriage with the promise of creating a nuclear family unit. Using the three core tropes identified above to look more in depth at *Susan Slept Here* and *White Christmas*, this section will show how the subgenre of romantic Christmas films developed its socially conservative foundations. It will also explore a case study on how depictions of teen marriage changed in Christmas films between the late 1940s and mid-1950s as well as offer an in-depth look at the sentiments towards the US military expressed in *White Christmas*. Finally, it will return to Jones's research and argue that not only did these films demonstrate the increase in romances, comedies, and musicals, but they also gravitated towards the right in line with contemporary socially conservative expectations of Hollywood.

Susan Slept Here

Susan Slept Here was a critically successful film that also earned $2.25 million at the box office, according to *Variety*'s year-end totals, placing it as the 50th highest earner out of 114 movies recorded.[209] *Harrison's Reports* framed the film as "a good romantic comedy" that "provokes laughter almost all the way through." The review also states, "it is a sort of bedroom farce, but because the sex angle is inoffensive and quite innocent, the picture may be deemed to be suitable for the family trade."[210] *Susan Slept Here* offers an approach to the three new tropes of Christmas romance films that fully embodies the first and the last: Susan (Debbie Reynolds) secretly wants to be a wife and it is a climactic misunderstanding that ultimately brings the couple closer together. As for the child who is integral to the relationship, controversially that too is Susan, as the film revolves around her coming-of-age story as she develops from an emotionally wise but erratic teenager into a refined wife.

---

209 "1954 Box Office Champs", 59.

210 "'Susan Slept Here' with Dick Powell and Debbie Reynolds", *Harrison's Reports*, July 3, 1954.

In essence, the film is about a 17-year-old girl, Susan, who, in a scheme to avoid arrest, marries the 35-year-old Mark (Dick Powell) who is, for all intents and purposes, a stranger to her. Ultimately, Susan decides she wants to stay married to Mark when he attempts to annul the marriage, and she endeavors to become a perfect wife by studying hard, reading *Ladies' Home Journal,* and practicing her husband's interests. The fact that *Harrison's* calls this a family film is an interesting perspective as most of the film revolves around the concept of consummation of the marriage in order to remain married, with several jokes about the much older Mark receiving Susan as a "Christmas gift" and a "humorous" miscommunication that Susan has gotten pregnant with a man other than Mark.

Seeing this film as one suitable for the whole family brings to light some of the cultural context around the film's release. Firstly, by the mid-1950s, a growing resistance to – and even outright defiance of – the Production Code had begun to influence moral expectations and perceptions of the medium.[211] As a film with multiple seduction scenes – played specifically for comedy – by a minor with whom the audience is expected to sympathize despite her introduction as a criminal, the film surely would have at least raised suspicions under the 1930 version of the Code.[212] The loosening of the Code may also be due, as Thomas Doherty argues, "post-war revolutions in manners and morals" as well as the expansion of both television and First Amendment protections for cinema.[213] While this film would almost definitely have been produced differently in an earlier time – if at all – the mere existence of it in 1954 speaks to both the overall changing cultural tone of the early Cold War and changes within the motion picture industry itself specifically.

Secondly and as part of those overall changes in American mid-century society, *Susan Slept Here* engages successfully with the relatable social context of the mid-1950s, in particular with the emerging concept of the "teenager" and how teenagers carved out a space for themselves in American society. As Doherty writes elsewhere, "the teen years became a unique transitional phase between childhood and adulthood, in some senses an autonomous and in most cases a privileged period in an individual's life."[214] This new liminal status in 1950s society brought with it new cultural experiences that allowed the younger members of the Silent Generation to distinguish themselves from their parents' generation

---

211 Doherty, *Hollywood's Censor,* 294.

212 Terry Ramsaye, "What the Production Code Really Says", *Motion Picture Herald,* August 11, 1934.

213 Doherty, *Hollywood's Censor,* 312.

214 Thomas Doherty, *Teenagers and Teenpics: Juvenilization Of American Movies* (Philadelphia: Temple University Press, 2002), 34.

or the younger Baby Boomer children.[215] One such way in which they distinguished themselves was by developing their own paths in dating and marriage.

Many American teens aspired to marry younger than their parents' generation had, and a key component to this increase in young marriages was the security the arrangement could offer the young girl in the partnership as she graduated high school and emerged into adulthood. Although the farcical relationship in the film is an exaggeration for dramatic effect – Mark must marry Susan as a charitable act to keep her from spending Christmas in a juvenile detention facility – the underlying instigator for their marriage is to provide an illusion that she is financially secure and supported socially. A case study on these issues of security, teens, dating culture, and young marriage will help explain what changed from the 1940s to the 1950s and how *Susan Slept Here* tapped into wider cultural developments more successfully than other films in this study.

Case Study: Teenagers and Security in Young Marriages

Unlike many of the other themes explored in this study, the portrayal of a marriage proposal and the family unit as a promise of security, both financially and in terms of trust, remain consistent throughout the entire 15-year period. However, the nature of these filmic relationships changed from the 1940s through the 1950s. While the lived reality of many Americans was not consistent with this filmic portrayal, as divorce rates peaked following World War II and declined again throughout the 1950s, the films do echo and represent cultural ideals and fantasies around the security both marriage and families could offer in the early Cold War.[216] The offer of marriage is presented as a gift that brings characters together both in sentimental bonds and mental reassurance during an age of increasing suspicion and distrust for anyone outside of the family circle. According to May, marriage and "a home filled with children would create a feeling of warmth and security against the cold forces of disruption and alienation."[217] The pressures of the early Cold War were vast and strong, creating an incentive for settling down and building a family in early adulthood.

Beyond these pressures, marriage was on the rise for young couples in the 1950s for a number of reasons that are also reflected on film. For instance, Julie Solow Stein acknowledges that in the post-war period, young marriages were on

215 Doherty, 35.

216 Laura Oren, "No-Fault Divorce Reform in the 1950s: The Lost History of the 'Greatest Project' of the National Association of Women Lawyers", *Law and History Review* 36, no. 4 (November 2018): 851.

217 May, *Homeward Bound*, 26.

the rise specifically with regard to white, middle- and upper-class women – similar to those depicted in many of the films in this study – due to the development of a distinctive teenage culture. Stein writes that the drive for young marriages was due in part to teenage rebellion, as in the mid-twentieth century, changes to the culture including "universal high school education and the emergence of teenage culture" encouraged young people to assert their maturity by marrying young.[218] Susan in *Susan Slept Here* is a prime example of a young 17-year-old girl who marries an older man and spends the remainder of the film trying to convince him of her maturity and ability to be a good wife.

In addressing this teenage behavior, Stein states, "For those who found the wait too difficult, marriage was one way of laying claim to adulthood without waiting for societal approval."[219] *Susan Slept Here* escalates that already shortened timeline and portrays the complications a young bride faces in terms of societal approval. Susan's task of convincing not only her husband, but also the audience of her ability to be a wife are underscored throughout the film by her childish demeanor until the final moments of the film in which she stands her ground and informs her husband that she has read the advice and checklists of every reputable magazine teaching her how – by 1954 standards – to be a proper, fulfilling, and loving wife to her partner.

Teenage rebellion as a motivating factor for young marriages also suggests that the desire to distance oneself from one's immediate family by starting a new one of one's own was increasingly common for young people in the 1950s. In a period when the new age construct of "teenager" was emerging, early marriage became a sign of growth, maturity, and adulthood. In situations in which children were expected to stay at home longer and be dependent financially and emotionally on their parents until they finished high school in their later teens, the drive to be independent was higher and coincided with the earlier-mentioned domestic pressures and fears of communist subversion and suspicion of those outside of the immediate family. For young people entering this tumultuous world, establishing strong familial ties to a partner was a desirable goal. Not all of these relationships worked out well, and some were annulled by the young newlyweds' irate parents, as Stein recounts, but the goal on the part of many young people to achieve a new and stable family unit cannot be overlooked.[220]

In terms of Christmas films, not every marriage proposal portrayed on film involved a young couple; however, a high portion did. Additionally, not every pro-

---

218 Julie Solow Stein, "Early to Wed: Teenage Marriage in Postwar America", *Journal of the History of Childhood and Youth* 6, no. 2 (Spring 2013): 360.
219 Stein, 360.
220 Stein, 361.

posal offered the same financial security. This case study will explore the specific changes in dating and marriage between the 1940s and 1950s and then analyze their filmic portrayals in *It Happened on 5th Avenue* (1947) and *Susan Slept Here* (1954). Specifically, this case study examines the marriage proposals themselves within these films as acts of generosity, gift-giving, or charity, as well as the relative securities they promise in giving this gift of familial protections. *It Happened on 5th Avenue* features a unique proposal in which the young woman originally is against marriage entirely but changes her mind when she falls in love with and actively pursues her partner in a cross-class relationship in which she is wealthy, and he is not. Similarly, *Susan Slept Here* portrays the young 17-year-old Susan in her efforts to convince her much older husband she deserves their relationship. Fitting these relationships into the wider cultural changes in dating and marriage among teens will contextualize these films and show how such cultural developments impacted motion pictures in the mid-1950s.

Case Study: Teenagers and Security in Young Marriages

As noted above, the post-war period saw a major cultural shift with the emergence of the "teenager". Stein explores the increase in young marriages through census data and suggests that this increase in early marriage among wealthier young girls in particular was due to the arrival of the new and distinct sphere of teenage culture. The sharp increase in teenage enrolment in high school through the post-war period indicated, for Stein, a need for teenagers to assert their newfound identity as young adults rather than as older children. One way to assert this independence was to marry young, effectively, in their eyes, stepping into a markedly adult phase of their lives. Other historians studying this period, such as Beth Bailey and John Modell, offer differing conclusions about this increase in teenage marriages and the emerging culture they inhabited. To understand the seemingly abrupt increase in teens seeking marriage in the post-war period, a brief understanding of how the dating culture shifted is necessary.

Beth Bailey, in her 1989 book *From Front Porch to Back Seat* and subsequent works, suggests that the changes in teenage dating styles in the late 1940s and 1950s were due to the advent of "going steady". In previous decades, young dating trends were predominantly looser in that one girl would have several male callers who would literally call on her at home and be invited in for a chaperoned date. Likewise, at youth dances, one girl would dance with several boys who expressed interest and vice versa. This trend was consistent throughout the 1920s and 1930s but began to change with the onset of World War II. Bailey comments on the dating mentality before the war, stating that to be desirable, "men needed outward, material signs: an automobile, the right clothing, and money" while women needed to "cultivate the impression that they were greatly in demand".[221] Due to the expected long courtship period and the high number of dates one was expected to go on, Bailey suggests, engagements were longer and marriage was put off in favor of dating.

When World War II started, there was far less time to cultivate these personas with which to establish a reputation of popularity among one's peers. This loss of time for traditional dating started the emergence of the dating trend known as "going steady". Going steady meant a faster monogamous, exclusive relationship formed between two partners with a focus on each other much more than in previous decades. Rather than delaying marriage until a soldier returned from service overseas, many American teens turned to promises of loyalty to their single partner and in some cases even earlier marriages. By the 1950s, going steady was the predominant dating trend for American teens. This dating trend baffled these teens' parents since their own dating traditions in their youth were the multiplicity of partners and competition between each other for reputations of popularity. Dating trends going from a multitude of partners to nearly immediate monogamy marked a significant difference between the older and younger generations.[222]

The clash between the generations was also indicative of larger changes in the world. Cultural, social, and political changes in the 1940s and 1950s provided immense challenges for young people who did not feel that the older generation's experiences matched the changing world. As May writes, "the wisdom of the earlier generations would be of little help to post-war Americans who were looking toward a radically new vision of family life and trying self-consciously to avoid the paths of their parents."[223] These young people turned to the advice of perceived experts in social science and psychology who were encouraging the domestic containment policy of finding safety and security within the boundaries of the family unit. Regardless, the clash between the generations regarding their dating trends played out in popular media of the day.

Going steady in the 1950s was seen by some adults as a genuine issue for young people. Many magazines – including such publications as *Woman's Day* and *Ladies' Home Journal* – warned about the new dating trend and the ways in which it might affect the sociability of American youth. A 1958 article in *Woman's Day* features a frightful warning that "the boy you're dating" could be "a

---

221 Beth Bailey, "From Front Porch to Back Seat: A History of the Date", *OAH Magazine of History* 18, no. 4 (July 1, 2004): 24.
222 Bailey, 24.
223 May, *Homeward Bound*, 31.

teen-age menace in a quiet town like yours" reinforcing this divide between the younger and older generations, the latter of which was concerned with the former getting too close to only one teen partner.[224]

Concern that the younger generation was getting too serious too quickly with someone they did not know was conflated with a security threat in these publications. In one issue of *Ladies' Home Journal* from July 1949, the section "Profile of Youth" featured an article entitled "Going Steady ... a National Problem". The article warns that "going steady is a custom exclusively teen-aged" and explains for parents and adults unfamiliar with the youth tradition how it actually works: "For some teen-agers, this 'exclusive friendship' is the normal expression and result of mutual affection ... for others it is simply a means of social security ... and for the candid few, going steady is important because 'you can go further with a girl if you're going steady with her.'"[225] This article continues, "quite frequently a couple will decide to go steady but, fearing parental disapproval, will date someone else 'just every little while to throw [their] parents off the track.'"[226]

As a publication predominantly read by women and mothers, this article interprets the phenomenon of "going steady" as a foreign idea and introduces a psychological approach to undermine the new dating trend. It continues to claim that "teen-agers are not fully mature" and that "unless there is economic security or a willingness on the part of the parents to subsidize marriage, boys and girls just out of high school are likely to encounter hardship that kills romance."[227] From the parental perspective, the trend of going steady was a harmful introduction into teen lives, supporting Stein's and Bailey's arguments of a generational divide on the perceptions of young marriage. The article also highlights the faults of Hollywood in popularizing this trend, stating, "Teen-agers who marry are inclined to expect the perfect romance, as pictured in movies and fiction, and to be impatient when it doesn't work out that way."[228]

In an earlier 1942 article, "Quantitative Analysis of Motion Picture Content," Dorothy Jones had also questioned the role of Hollywood in constructing romances for young people. Jones writes in her conclusion:

> Our material that the film holds ideal marriage above every other value yet rarely carries the hero and heroine beyond the marriage ceremony. If marriage is idealized in the movies, but

---

224 Susan Bennett Holmes, "Teen-Age Menace", *Woman's Day* (New York, May 1958), 68, ProQuest.
225 "Going Steady... A National Problem", *Ladies' Home Journal*, July 1949, Women's Magazine Archive, 128, ProQuest.
226 "Going Steady", 131.
227 "Going Steady", 131.
228 "Going Steady", 131.

rarely realistically shown, what effect, if any, does this have upon the success of marriage in our culture? Do Susy Smith and Johnny Jones, who attend the movies at least once a week, really expect that when they marry they will achieve the kind of bliss that is promised the screen heroes and heroines in the final fade-out?[229]

Jones's questions about the portrayal of reality align with the real anxieties parents – and magazine columnists – had later in the decade and echo concerns about the impact of certain portrayals on screen. If the screened romances stop at the big kiss or promise of marriage, as most do, then the idealization of marriage is less about the marriage itself and more about the aspirational idea of being engaged. These filmic promises of security are not necessarily portraying the reality of married life, but rather an exceptionally idealized goal of acquiring a proposal and the subsequent securities promised that come with it.

To reach her conclusions from the teenage perspective, Bailey analyses teen magazines, advice books, and other contemporary teenage-related cultural outputs. She focusses on the teen experience over the decades through the media with which they would have interacted and draws conclusions on the economic changes throughout the twentieth century as indicative of the opportunities teens would have. For instance, as the title of her book suggests, Bailey emphasizes the affluence of the 1950s and the increased number of teenage-centric locations available to suburban white teenagers with access to cars as a reason for this cultural change. Dates were no longer in the home and chaperoned or at youth dances that were also chaperoned by adults, but rather dates could be at amusement parks, soda shops, or even in the intimate privacy of one's own car much more than ever before. Stein, Bailey, and Modell agree that the increased intimacy and privacy teens had access to accelerated their desires for expediting not only dating, but also sexual exploration. Dating in the 1950s now included "necking, petting, and going steady" with the hopes of speeding up the possibility of an engagement and the time until marriage.[230]

In his 1991 book *Into One's Own*, Modell agrees with much of what has been said above by Bailey and Stein. Through census data and youth surveys, Modell argues that the increased sexuality of the younger generation led to the uptick in youthful marriages in the 1950s; however, he does not see the same significance for marriage that Stein argues in her study. Modell claims, "In a curious fashion, the very ease – and earliness – of marriage now marked it out as less the moment of entry to the status of adult than as a continuation of the prior stages along that

---

229 Jones, "Quantitative Analysis of Motion Picture Content", 423–424.
230 Stein, "Early to Wed", 361.

road."[231] For Modell, this change in the increase of youthful marriage only served to diminish the cultural importance of marriage more generally and moved the marker of true adulthood to parenthood.

In this period, it was common for the youngest married couples to continue to live at home with their parents until they were economically stable enough to live on their own. For Modell, this economic instability suggests that teenage marriage was merely another step of adulthood appropriated by young, inexperienced teens. Stein agrees with most of this assertion that the power of marriage was widely diminished; however, she also more accurately acknowledges, through the use of census data, teen magazines, and other teenage cultural outputs, that from the teenage perspective in the 1950s, the significance of marriage was not diminished. Teens in the post-war period throughout the 1950s saw marriage as the important next step in asserting their independence and newfound identity as young adults distinct from their school experience and home life with their often less-than understanding parents.

Bailey's overarching argument concerning teens going steady aligns with Stein's analysis of young marriage and takes it further into understanding the teenage mindset. In agreement with May, Bailey contends that the main reason for American youth's newest and most popular trend of seeking a single partner in the post-war and early Cold War was the promise of security.[232] Amidst the pressures and threats in the 1940s and 1950s of atomic bombs, nuclear annihilation, communist subversion both at home and abroad, and more, Bailey suggests that the safety of having a single, dependable partner was the most appealing option. She writes, "As going steady was a simulated marriage, relationships could and did develop within its even short-term security, monogamy, and, sometimes, love."[233] This simulated marriage reverberated into the trends Stein maps through census data of actual marriages among American youth that were not necessarily, as Modell argues, true assertions of independence, but rather charades of simulated adulthood through the appropriation of an adult tradition. In looking at teenage marriage as a simulation of adulthood with this contextual understanding of the mid-century shift in dating trends, the two films most centrally concerning teenage relationships and their developments into marriage proposals – *It Happened on 5ᵗʰ Avenue* and *Susan Slept Here* – can more accurately be seen as reflecting the fantasies American teenagers had about their young romances.

---

231 John Modell, *Into One's Own: From Youth to Adulthood in the United States, 1920–1975* (Berkeley: University of California Press, 1991), 256.
232 Bailey, "From Front Porch to Back Seat", 23.
233 Bailey, 25.

Filmic Proposals, 1947 and 1954

Trudy O'Connor (Gale Storm) in *It Happened on 5th Avenue* (1947) is an 18-year-old strong-willed girl who runs away from boarding school in the hopes of becoming independent. She returns to her father's mansion on 5th Avenue to procure some clothes – including a mink coat – for a job interview and meets Jim Bullock (Don DeFore) and Aloysius McKeever (Victor Moore), vagabonds who are squatting in the mansion. After a briefly contentious exchange in which Jim threatens to call the police on her and mocks her for wanting the mink coat for an interview in a music shop, Trudy quickly becomes enamored with him and decides to join the pair in their charade as interlopers in the mansion. The next day, Trudy and Jim run into ex-GI friends of Jim's and invite them as well as their wives and children to stay in the mansion. Within a day of meeting Jim, Trudy asks one of the veterans' wives, Margie (Dorothea Kent) how long she has been married and how her husband proposed.

This rapid shift in character is almost indiscernible. Trudy's first appearance is when she is shown entering her father's home, and she is only briefly mentioned in the scene before this when her headmistress at boarding school informs Mr. O'Connor (Charles Ruggles) that she has run away again. The shift seems to suggest that her immediate and rapidly deepening infatuation with Jim takes her from a runaway teen to a young woman ready to settle down. During her conversation with the veteran's wife, Margie accuses Trudy of being "a little crazy about Jim" to which Trudy responds, "oh he's nice, but he doesn't know I'm alive." The conversation continues:

> Trudy: He calls me "Cookie". What does Whitey call you?
>
> Margie: "Sugar." 'Cuz I was hard to get.
>
> Trudy: Tell me. What made him propose?
>
> Margie: Well, it happened at the movies. Gregory Peck and this blonde were getting married, so I said to Whitey, I said "Gee. I sure wish that was us." And Whitey said, "uh-huh." And then I said, "Ain't marriage wonderful?" And Whitey said, "uh-huh." And then I said, "Well why don't we get married?" And Whitey said, "uh-huh." And, well, after all how can you say no when a fella coaxes you like that?

This exchange confirms that Trudy is interested in a proposal from Jim and also reflects the World War II dating trends that Bailey examines. Margie states that she and Whitey have been married for seven years, roughly putting their marriage around 1940, which is also supported by the joke that sugar would have been difficult to procure in the late Depression era and early War rationing. In line with Bailey's analysis, Margie was "hard to get" and also the instigator for their proposal, showing this transition from a multiplicity of partners to a quick and sudden marriage as WWII dawned. While this recounting is a bit anachronistic, as Gregory Peck's first film, *Days of Glory*, was released in 1944, the idea that Hollywood has some sort of influence over the marriage trends of American youth, about which Jones wrote in 1942, is also asserted in this Hollywood film.

This quick conversation leads Trudy to immediately don an elegant ballgown and dramatically enter the room where Jim and the rest of the interlopers are congregated. She asks for a light for her cigarette with hand on hip and visibly trying to seem elegant and desirous. When Jim becomes entranced with her and lights her cigarette, he asks why she's dressed so nicely, to which Trudy responds, "I have a date." The scene plays as though Trudy is clearly forcing herself to embody the vision of a popular, in-demand girl on the dating scene; however, she does not have a date and both of them know this. The scene almost parodies the pre-war dating traditions of the multiplicity of partners in a scenario in which none of them are leaving the mansion and the only unmarried and viable match for Trudy in the house is Jim. In the following scene, Trudy picks up a billiards cue to play with Jim and then clumsily picks up one of her father's shotguns. Jim falls for her ploy and scolds her for her mishandling of the gun, offering to show her the army technique for holding and aiming a gun, wrapping his arms around her while leaning in closely. Trudy presses herself against him and leans her head up for a kiss, which Jim, entranced again, gives her.

Trudy's rapid transformation from a headstrong girl to a woman preparing to be a wife and expressing interest in her partner's interests continues to intensify throughout the film. Within mere days, her father arrives at her place of work, and she informs him that she is in love. He tells her that she is too young and that this is ridiculous, but Trudy responds saying, "My goodness, a girl of 18 is practically middle-aged nowadays. Women get married at 11 in India." This stark line points to the divisiveness between the older and younger generation's views of marriage. O'Connor does not come around to the idea of Trudy marrying Jim until the very end of the film and actively tries to separate them and sabotage their love affair throughout. He goes as far as to arrange a job opportunity for Jim abroad and convince him that he is too poor and too independent to be settling down with Trudy. Ultimately, after O'Connor's reunion with his own wife, Trudy's mother Mary (Ann Harding), and the young lovers' quarrel over the job abroad and potentially lost future between them, O'Connor is convinced the two truly love one another and are ready for marriage. The film ends with the two announcing their plans to marry and proclaiming they will have plenty of space for guests; however, it is unclear whether Trudy tells Jim by the end of the film that she is the millionaire's daughter.

It Happened on 5ᵗʰ Avenue reflects transitioning views on dating from 1940 to 1947. Trudy's awkward behavior when trying to engage with the antiquated ritualistic performance of presenting oneself as popular on the dating scene, desired, and in-demand shows how absurd the younger generation felt when trying to adopt those dating traditions. Trudy is more successful in her advances towards Jim when she attempts to show interest in his interests, something which Bailey highlights as common advice in teenage magazines on how to secure a husband.[234]

In a 1958 advice column from *Seventeen* entitled "How to Let a Boy Know You're Alive", one 15-year-old wrote in saying she has trouble flirting with boys her own age and is much more attractive to older boys. In response, columnist Abigail Wood advised allowing boys to take charge of the conversation and "dwelling on the interests and thoughts [she] share[s] with a boy." The columnist continues, suggesting,

> Think, too, of the many subjects he knows more about than you do: this year's new sports cars, the chances of the school's football team reaching the top of the league, his summer job. Use your intelligence to guide the conversation into areas in which he can take the lead and you can learn from him.[235]

According to this columnist, by expressing interest in the boy's hobbies and playing down her own interests, intellect, and "seriousness", a girl could make herself more attractive to boys her own age. This strategy of making oneself appear more interesting to a partner by adopting his hobbies is also highlighted in the 1954 film *Susan Slept Here.*

Mark in *Susan Slept Here* marries Susan as an act of charity towards the 17-year-old to protect her from becoming a ward of the juvenile court. Susan has been picked up by the cops for throwing a beer bottle and brought to Mark, a struggling Hollywood screenwriter, to be used as research for his next plot about teenage delinquents. In order to protect her from jailtime, Mark must prove she has "a viable means of support". When his friend Virgil (Alvy Moore) jokingly suggests he "could fool the court by marrying the girl and supporting her on what you haven't got", Mark formulates the plan to marry her. The illusion of security in the relationship that unfolds when Mark takes Virgil's advice and marries Susan in Las Vegas is the crux of the filmic marriage. The instigation for the 1954 teenage marriage is specifically to create the illusion that she is secure financially and socially supported so as not to have her turned back over to the courts as a teenage delinquent.

---

234 Beth L Bailey, *From Front Porch to Back Seat: Courtship in Twentieth-Century America* (Baltimore: Johns Hopkins University Press, 1989), 14.
235 Abigail Wood, "How To Let a Boy Know You're Alive", *Seventeen* (New York, August 1958), 191, ProQuest.

This situation works out to save Susan from the courts; however, neither in the partnership is wholly happy. Susan is offended that Mark is not truly in love with her and wants a "real" marriage in which she is rightfully his wife and he rightfully her husband. Mark leaves Susan in his home and instructs his friends to watch out for the girl while he is away for several months writing his next screenplay in a cabin. In order to shift the illusion of the simulated marriage into a real one, Susan spends her time while he is away learning how to be a perfect wife. She reads advice columns, teenage magazines, and *Ladies' Home Journal*, explores his interests, and has an amusing scene in which she tries to understand his hobbies. Susan watches old home movies of Mark skiing, horseback riding, and golfing with his ex-fiancé and immaturely mocks the woman's mannerisms and figure in all of the films. Immediately following this, Susan returns home after practicing horseback riding, limping in pain from another failed attempt. She practices golfing in the living room despite derision from Virgil who comments "it takes more than sports to make a wife." Susan curtly responds, "anything that society girl can do, I can do." Angrily, Susan hits a golf ball into the aquarium, breaking the glass. Susan even takes up smoking to impress her husband, just as Trudy had to attract Jim in *It Happened on 5ᵗʰ Avenue*.

When Mark returns home after Susan has refused to sign annulment papers and Virgil spreads a rumor that Susan is pregnant, Mark is irate, and Susan is annoyed at not being taken seriously. She sets the table for dinner and leaves notes around the apartment denoting "his" and "hers" chairs, "Susan's husband" on one plate and "Mark's wife?" on another, with candles lit and a romantic record playing. Wearing an elegant evening dress and a more mature hairstyle, Susan greets Mark in the kitchen before realizing she had taken her heels off while waiting for him. She runs out to properly re-enter the kitchen with her make-up refreshed and heels on. The two have a strained conversation in which Mark realizes the pregnancy rumor was just that before the two are interrupted by Mark's friends bidding farewell and going on their own journeys. Virgil, in saying goodbye to Susan, tries to convince her to make Mark admit he cannot live without her. Susan dejectedly responds, "Oh, it's too late now. A woman has her pride" then realizes with glee "But I'm not a woman. Yet." In realizing she is 17 years old, Susan feels emboldened to speak to her husband blatantly and honestly in a way older married women likely wouldn't dare.

Susan indignantly confronts Mark on the balcony and informs him he cannot live without her. He admits that he cannot, prompting a conversation about how to move forward with Mark immediately saying they should do nothing because he is too old for her. Susan retorts that she has been reading books reiterating an implication throughout the film that a woman learns about sex by reading about it in feminine publications. Mark continues refuting on the basis of their age gap as she is only 17, and Susan retorts, "17? I'll be 18 in 4 months. I can climb on a horse alone, I shoot golf in the low 140s, I belong to the best book of the week club, I read the parts of the *New York Times* I can understand, I can smoke a cigarette half down, and I know how to mix drinks." Susan proceeds to list recipes for daiquiris, martinis, scotch over rocks then says, "Now, Mark, what more do you want in a wife? I'm a doll and you know it." Mark backs away responding, "I'm too big to play with dolls" and that he's old enough for "the armchair, television, small dog to bring [his] slippers", to which Susan rushes forward to grab his lapels while panting and saying, "arf, arf." She backs him around the apartment and to the bedroom door while he lists reasons of why he is too old and why their age difference is unfair. Mark claims Susan will be in her prime at 31 when he is 50, all reasons refuted by Susan as she pulls him into the bedroom.

This confrontation scene highlights both Susan's young age and willingness to use her youthfulness to entice her husband further as well as the desire she has for a true marriage like the ones she reads about in her magazines and books. Susan spent their months apart gaining an illusion of maturity in line with how the teenage advice magazines both in the film and reality suggested she do, by educating herself on his hobbies, mixology, and sex. The relationship between the two started specifically as a form of security to save her from herself and developed into her maturing into a proper wife so that she may offer the reciprocal social securities and benefits of marriage for her husband. The transition from a headstrong young woman into a woman fit for marriage echoes the representations of teenage marriage in *It Happened on 5th Avenue* with both Susan and Trudy following the advice of the day to engage with their partners' interests and hobbies and to prove they are mature enough to be a proper wife. However, the key difference between these two films is the focus on Susan as a teenager in the later film.

It Happened on 5th Avenue follows Trudy and Jim's relationship as one of several storylines in the film with the largest plotline concerning the structural inequalities within New York and the wealth disparity evident in the city. By 1954, the primary focus of the Christmas film genre is the romantic storyline. Other plotlines within the film – if any – are minimalistic and easily resolvable. Susan and Mark's relationship was the primary focus and central plot of *Susan Slept Here.* By excising plots that speak to larger social, political, or cultural narratives – such as the wealth disparity of New York – the new American Christmas films of the 1950s limited their potential for political criticism and stuck to simplified one-story romantic narratives. Further, Susan's age is also a central focus of that romantic narrative in *Susan Slept Here*, reflecting the cultural changes evident in the emerging teenage category. Trudy's age is briefly mentioned, but she is understood as a young woman, an adult with a job and responsibilities throughout the film. Susan uses her youthful age to her advantage in elevating her status from a young girl to a married woman.

While both films align in commenting on the change in dating trends that began in the 1940s, the later film is much more successful at foregrounding the romance and updating it to better represent cultural developments in the real world. *Susan Slept Here*, by simplifying the narrative, excising negative social commentaries, and tapping into the cultural response to the emergence of teenagers, proved a very commercially successful film in the context of the mid-1950s.

White Christmas

While *Susan Slept Here* was a financial and critical success, *White Christmas* was the highest grossing film of 1954. According to *Variety*, Paramount's *White Christmas* grossed $12 million at the box office, with the second highest earner, *The Caine Mutiny*, earning $8.7 million.[236] Critically, *White Christmas* was not as well-received as *Susan Slept Here*, with Crowther of *The New York Times* disapproving of the storyline and specifically the sentiments towards the US military expressed in the film. While *Susan Slept Here* dealt well with its social commentary and engaged a wide-spread community of teenagers in an allegedly family-appropriate film, *White Christmas* tried to appeal to an older generation by invoking nostalgia around the US's involvement in World War II.

Returning to the cultural impact of this early Cold War moment on the future of the Christmas film genre, *White Christmas* again offered an application of the three tropes of Christmas romance films. This time, however, with a slightly older cast. After the first two romantic films analyzed above – *Holiday Affair* and *Susan Slept Here* – show a young war-widow with a small child and an adolescent herself becoming a wife to an older man, *White Christmas* offers another way of proving the benefits of domestic containment for a different age group using the same unifying tropes: secret desires of the two leading ladies to be the wives of the leading men, the promise of children looming as the instigating factor for these relationships, and a misunderstanding based on a lack of communication that must be resolved at the climax of the film.

White Christmas follows four entertainers, Bob Wallace (Bing Crosby), Phil Davis (Danny Kaye), Judy Haynes (Vera-Ellen), and Betty Haynes (Rosemary Clooney), from the moment they meet through their romances as Bob and Betty and Phil and Judy pair off to find love. The romances are a major driving force and cen-

---

236 "1954 Box Office Champs", 59.

tral focus of the film, but there is a secondary plot that facilitates the romance. This storyline concerns Bob and Phil's ex-commanding officer, General Waverly (Dean Jagger) who owns a financially encumbered inn in Vermont. The quartet plan to put on a show at the inn to draw guests, effectively establishing the remote romantic setting in which they fall in love.

Early in the film, Phil attempts to set his performing partner Bob up romantically with a showgirl in their ensemble. Bob rejects this woman and is offended by Phil's assumed role as matchmaker offering "unserious" women with whom he should consider settling down. Phil explains that Bob works them both too hard and says, "I want you to get married. I want you to have nine children. And if you only spend five minutes a day with each kid, that's 45 minutes, and I'd at least have time to go out and get a massage or something." The emphasis on starting a family is stark from the beginning and continues to be a powerful theme driving the plot that sees Phil and Judy fake an engagement as a ploy to bring Bob and Betty together. Bob and Betty are enjoying a budding romance until a miscommunication drives them apart when Betty hears a rumor that Bob is looking to exploit General Waverly by publicizing the show. Without confronting Bob, Betty leaves abruptly to pursue a solo singing career in New York City. Ultimately, Betty realizes her mistake and surprises Bob at the grand opening performance of the show for General Waverly back in the remote setting of Vermont on Christmas Eve. The film closes on a romantic view of a snow-covered carriage and both happy couples embracing during a rendition of the titular song "White Christmas."

The foundations of the three Christmas romance tropes identified above – desire to be a wife, importance of children, and overcoming a miscommunication – are all evident in *White Christmas*. These conservative social values embedded in the film work even better with the concurrent theme of nostalgia for the military, making it a much more openly conservative film than any of the others. Still, the budding romance between Betty and Bob – and its subsequent troubles – are the film's focal point precisely because they are the least likely to embrace domestic life and leave show business behind, yet still come around to the ideas of domestic containment by the film's end.

Domestic containment is the ultimate goal which the film does achieve successfully not only for Betty and Bob but also for Phil and Judy, whose sham proposal becomes real by the closing rendition of "White Christmas". Unlike the other two romances – *Holiday Affair* and *Susan Slept Here* – this film does carry a second storyline that facilitates these romantic ones. That nostalgia for the military frames the film and deserves more attention for the perspective it brings to this mid-1950s period.

Nostalgia for the Old Days

White Christmas heavily employs nostalgia for an emotional effect in its audience. Not only does the title song itself automatically trigger a deep nostalgia for togetherness in difficult times, but the film also leans into cultural touchstones of the past to elicit this emotional response. By framing the film with sentiments for the WWII military and having numerous numbers that hark back to an earlier song and dance-style entertainment, *White Christmas* reacts to the contemporary 1954 moment by suggesting a more socially conservative past is nostalgically appealing.

Despite its proximity to the Korean War, *White Christmas* is framed by scenes of and reminiscence for WWII. The film opens on a battle-torn town in 1944 with American soldiers holding a Christmas Eve show to raise morale. As General Waverly arrives with his replacement, the latter remarks that the men should be lined up and awaiting inspection ahead of the following morning's plans to move out. Waverly remarks that he's correct, adding, "there's no Christmas in the army, Captain." He then suggests to the sergeant driving the captain back to headquarters to "take the shortcut," so as to keep the captain busy while the men finish their revelry in peace, undisturbed by their reality of being on an active battleground. General Waverly silently joins the men as they dream of a Christmas far away with their loved ones, punctuated by Bob's singing of the hugely popular and iconic title song "White Christmas." After tearful shots of uniformed men leaning on guns and longing for home, Bob laments that the General could not be present, offering a heartfelt speech praising his value as a strong, compassionate leader. The General himself interrupts this speech to mockingly condemn the revelry before thanking the men genuinely for their service and is played off the stage by a "slam bang finish" entitled, "The Old Man."

This opening scene is crucial for introducing two plot elements. The first of which is General Waverly's character and value not only as a military leader, but also as a righteous and upstanding man, exaggeratedly reminiscent of the current US president, former General Dwight D. Eisenhower. The men admire and look up to Waverly – even singing "we love him" in unison during the second song – because he values their service and individual lives more than seeing them as a collective unit of unnamed soldiers. This trait of seeing soldiers and veterans as unnamed numbers was depicted in both *It's a Wonderful Life* and *It Happened on 5th Avenue* as a selfish, negative trait of both villainous characters, Mr. Potter and Michael O'Connor. *White Christmas* touches on this briefly but pointedly in the interaction between General Waverly and the replacement captain and emphasizes it in each of his interactions with the men as he takes the time to shake hands with many of them while the song unfolds. This connection that General Waverly has with his men sets up the rest of the plot as a decade after the war,

Bob and his partner Phil drop everything in their own business to selflessly provide financial and emotional support for their former general.

The second plot element established in this opening scene is a framing of the film against a backcloth of the Second World War, which was largely viewed by the American public as a war fought for the greater good. *White Christmas* makes no reference to a military event after 1945. This framing is significant as *White Christmas* is the only one of the Christmas films in this study to interact with perceptions of the military directly and in a large-scale way. In doing so, it favors nostalgia for WWII while choosing not to acknowledge any events that could be seen as divisive with regard to the military, most obviously US participation in the Korean War of 1950–53. Support for the Korean War waned over time with more and more Americans losing faith in the initial justifications for entering the war. In a Gallup Poll on April 2, 1952, for instance, when asked "Do you think the United States made a mistake in going into a war with Korea, or not?" 51% of respondents said yes, 38% said no, and 14% had no opinion.[237] By not invoking the Korean War and focusing on the nostalgic feelings for WWII many Americans harbored, *White Christmas* evaded the dangers of raising the controversial topic of a war fought against communism that many Americans had come to oppose.

The usage of WWII as a plot device is not unique to *White Christmas* and, according to historian Christian Appy, "provides a blanket of moral certitude" for the audience, introducing a positive view of a military action with which the audience cannot disagree.[238] By opening the film in this way and centering the plot largely on helping the General with his inn as a way to facilitate the happy ending, *White Christmas* evades controversy and celebrates a façade of patriotism in promoting both the military and traditional domesticity.

In the film's climactic performance, there are three songs that invoke nostalgia for the war. In the first, entitled "Gee, I Wish I Was Back in the Army", the quartet sings about the advantages of serving in the US military. These advantages include, for the men, "three meals a day, for which you didn't pay" and the benefit of having "someone higher up where you could pass the buck". For the women, the song alleges there were "a million handsome guys/ with longing in their eyes/ and all you had to do was pick the age, the weight, the size." This song also uses the hook "there's a lot to be said for the Army" several times while extolling the virtues of military service to the audience and repeatedly claiming a wish to return to the military of a decade ago.

---

237 Gallup, *The Gallup Poll*, vol. 2, 1052.
238 Christian G. Appy, "'We'll Follow the Old Man': The Strains of Sentimental Militarism in Popular Films of the Fifties", in *Rethinking Cold War Culture*, ed. Peter J. Kuznick and James Burkhart Gilbert (Washington DC: Smithsonian Institution Press, 2001), 74.

In the other two songs, Bob and Phil reprise "The Old Man" and "White Christmas" with the whole of the New England regiment gathered round as a surprise for General Waverly that brings the old man to tears. "White Christmas" would have had a particular resonance for the 1954 audience as a distinctly WWII-era song filled with nostalgia, as the first public performance of "White Christmas" had been delivered by Bing Crosby at the Kraft Music Hall on December 24, 1941, mere weeks after the bombing of Pearl Harbor.[239] The song was then featured in the 1942 film *Holiday Inn*, but its true cultural resonance was in the weeks after the bombing of Pearl Harbor and its resurgence the following Christmas of 1942 by which point American soldiers were fighting abroad over the holiday season.

In the film, General Waverly was swayed by his granddaughter and housekeeper to wear his military uniform for presumably the first time since the war after their sly trick to send all his civilian clothes to the cleaners. The General stands before his unit once again in full uniform and mockingly condemns their revelry just as he had ten years prior:

> I am not satisfied with the conduct of this division. Some of you men are under the impression having been at Anzio entitles you not to wear neckties. Well, you're wrong. Neckties will be worn in this area. And look at the rest of your appearance. You're a disgrace to the outfit. You're soft. You're sloppy. You're unruly. You're undisciplined. And I never saw anything look so wonderful in my whole life. Thank you all.

This speech in particular, as Appy suggests, is the "high-water mark of post-war sentimental militarism."[240] While openly praising the military presence and uniforms of the men, General Waverly also praises their relaxed, "sloppy" peacetime appearances. This scene suggests that there will always be reverence reserved for military personnel while also proclaiming a preference for a peacetime standing military as opposed to an active wartime one. Further, with Waverly depicted as an Eisenhower figure, this visual representation of a standing military is an idealized and exaggerated representation of the aspirational goal of Eisenhower's administration: to be ready to defend national security with a standing military but to not have to call them into battle. Simultaneously, with the growing national security state and a shift towards a permanent wartime economy, this idealized presentation of retired WWII soldiers as a "wonderful" sight echoes contemporary

---

239 James Kaplan, "What Is a War Song?", in *Irving Berlin, New York Genius* (New Haven, CT: Yale University Press, 2019), 202.
240 Appy, "We'll Follow the Old Man", 80.

public concern over the covert military tactics of the Cold War.[241] The juxtaposition of retired soldiers from a war seen as fought for the greater good against the contemporary audience's potential feelings of unease about the US military's involvement in Korea reinforces this nostalgic preference for the WWII military.

Despite the US not being at peace in the years leading up to this film, *White Christmas* takes care to heavily insinuate that the military had not been in active duty since the end of WWII, with only one exception that alludes briefly to the differences between the militaries of 1944 and 1954. In a short scene that encourages Bob and Phil to add the particularly special and sentimental surprise to the show, General Waverly reveals to Bob that he re-applied for active duty. Asking Bob to read the letter due to his failing eyesight and need for reading glasses – a subtle nod to the direction the letter is going – the general is harshly rejected from re-enlistment, with the letter adding that it was a laughable idea for a veteran of his age to think there was a place for him in the military of 1954. This scene is the only direct indication that the military is still a functioning force; however, it also serves to remind the audience that the military in which Bob, Phil, and General Waverly originally served no longer exists. There is no longer a place for the type of military that helped to win WWII in a 1954 world.

Prompted by this conversation, Bob goes on the *Ed Sullivan Show* to sing a song entitled "What Can You Do with a General?" highlighting the plight of ex-generals who had a hard time finding employment in the post-war period. He sings that it is not hard to understand that the GIs were taken care of, but the generals were over-qualified and therefore often under-employed. This direct statement about the lack of US government aid for retired senior military personnel is powerful and reflects the tone of disappointment that was evident in the 1947 film *It Happened on 5th Avenue* concerning the treatment of veterans after WWII. The major difference between these two films, however, is that the earlier one depicted a veteran being forcibly removed from his home and made homeless while shouting protests about the current structural problems thousands of Americans were facing. *White Christmas* pulls on the heartstrings of nostalgia and says this one general is down on his luck now because of issues that occurred in a distant past. This song, General Waverly's rejection from re-enlistment, and the overall framing of the film within the reverential nostalgia for the US military of WWII all reflect the sentimental militarism Appy identifies.

---

241 Raymond Millen, "The Post–Korean War Drawdown under the Eisenhower Administration", in *Drawdown: The American Way of Postwar*, ed. Jason W. Warren (New York: New York University Press, 2016), 190.

Sentimental militarism refers to the ways in which Americans in the Cold War period held a romanticized and nostalgic view of the US military without directly rejecting or acknowledging its realities.[242] By denying, evading, or justifying the Korean War effort and harkening back to the pride and respect for the US military during WWII, the popular view of the military could be framed as favorable. In the ode to General Waverly, "The Old Man", the veterans sing of how they loved their general both in the war and ten years later at their reunion but reject the idea of continuing to serve. In the song, they sing that they would "follow the old man wherever he wants to go/ Long as he wants to go opposite to the foe" and they'll "stay with the old man wherever he wants to stay/ Long as he stays away from the battle's fray." When initially sung on the battle-torn stage, the song is interrupted by a quick bombing raid before resuming, grounding the lyrics in the reality of their present surroundings.

When the song is reprised in the safe country-inn in Vermont, it seems to take on a more meaningful message that American veterans still support their country and are still behind the sentiment of the military, but do not want to re-engage in active fighting. The veterans who sing the song in the final production are older, larger, quite literally not fitting in their old uniforms, and labeled as family men. These men are unfit for military service and when they sing the reprise of "The Old Man", this group of gentlemen who served the US in WWII are saying they want to go opposite to the foe and stay away from the battle's fray while retaining their sense of patriotism in what can be read as a plea to the nation to disengage military action.

White Christmas has a strong message about American sentiments towards the military during the 1950s. In a post-Korean War America, WWII veterans were no longer in touch with the contemporary Cold War military. In this filmic depiction, WWII veterans celebrated and fostered their more nostalgic views of patriotism rather than supporting the more complex and, at times, covert military ventures in the early Cold War. This depiction of the sentiments towards the military of former GIs in the mid-1950s is striking and was met with mixed reviews. In its year-end review, *Variety* contributor Gene Arneel wrote, the film "has come to be the most successful musical on the books, copping the crown held by *This is the Army*", another pro-US military musical by Irving Berlin from 1943 starring a young Ronald Reagan.[243] While it worked for Arneel, the overt sentimental militarism was the downfall of *White Christmas* for *The New York Times*'s Bosley

---

242 Appy, "We'll Follow the Old Man", 80.
243 Gene Arneel, "'54 DREAM PIC: 'WHITE XMAS'", *Variety* (Los Angeles, January 5, 1955), 5, ProQuest.

Crowther. Crowther wrote, "Sometimes nostalgia for the war years and the USO tours has taken the show awry" and disparaged the several musical numbers devoted to the military with "Three numbers are given over to the admiration of generals and Army life, which seems not alone an extravagance but a reckless audacity."[244] Despite Crowther's disappointment with the overemphasis on adulation of the military, the heavy-handed nostalgia for American heroism in WWII was certainly in line with contemporary conservative ideologies.

One additional nostalgic element of the film is in the minstrel number comprising of three songs: "I'd Rather See a Minstrel Show", "Mr. Bones", and "Mandy". In the earlier 1942 film *Holiday Inn* on which *White Christmas* is based, there is blackface in a minstrelsy number. The use of blackface was likely omitted from the later release as a reaction to the current culture and the slow progress being made regarding racism in Hollywood films. As mentioned earlier, the message movies of the late 1940s and early 1950s challenging racism in the US were a crucial step in this progress. This slow march towards civil rights was also supported by the US federal government.

In 1948, President Truman signed Executive Order 9981 ordering the desegregation of the US Armed Forces. As Elizabeth Lutes Hillman argues, "Because the armed forces were more visible internationally than any other American organization, the rhetoric and appearance of racial equity in the military was especially important to the United States' effort to claim the moral high ground in the war against communism."[245] The public perception of the US abroad was of critical importance and with that perception came an expectation of equality for the Black members of the Armed Forces who had fought in WWII and would soon in the Korean War as well. The desegregation of the military was a significant step towards civil rights for Black Americans. After several smaller strides towards domestic desegregation – including the desegregation of the nation's capital in 1953 via *District of Columbia v. John R. Thompson Co., Inc.* – the Supreme Court decided *Brown v. Board of Education* in 1954 declaring segregation in schools unconstitutional and ushering in an era in which, as historian Ben Keppel argues, Americans had to develop "new habits of citizenship" in order to navigate a new era together.[246] These strides in the culture were happening from the late 1940s onwards, however gradually, with one particular cultural distancing away from blackface in 1951, the same year *Brown* was originally filed.

---

244 Bosley Crowther, "White Christmas", *The New York Times Film Reviews*, October 15, 1954.
245 Elizabeth Lutes Hillman, *Defending America: Military Culture and the Cold War Court-Martial* (Princeton: Princeton University Press, 2005), 93.
246 Ben Keppel, *Brown v. Board and the Transformation of American Culture: Education and the South in the Age of Desegregation* (Baton Rouge: Louisiana State University Press, 2016), 6.

In Melvin Patrick Ely's *The Adventures of Amos 'N' Andy: A Social History of an American Phenomenon*, Ely records the history of the early twentieth-century radio show *Amos 'N' Andy*, a minstrel show created and voiced by two white men, Freeman Gosden and Charles Correll. The radio show was a hit across demographics, but in 1951 when the show moved to television, Gosden and Correll stepped down from the roles and cast black performers. This decision was made because an earlier attempt to bring *Amos 'N' Andy* to a Hollywood screen in 1930 flopped badly. In 1951, Correll reportedly said of that film, "The truth is that we don't look believable in blackface. We look like something out of a burlesque or minstrel show."[247] Gosden and Correll's radio show was a minstrel show by all accounts, but by the 1950s, the visual representation of blackface on screen was deemed unacceptable in the cultural climate.

With this context in mind, *White Christmas* did choose to omit blackface from the film; however, the minstrelsy number in the show exudes nostalgia for the minstrel tradition. The first number's title, "I'd Rather See a Minstrel Show", is already a nod towards the longing for that style of entertainment. The lyrics emphasize the desire for minstrelsy with lines such as "I'd rather see a minstrel show/ Than any other show I know" and "I'd pawn my overcoat and vest/ To see a minstrel show". Clooney later sings in "Mr. Bones", "That's a joke/ That was told/ In the minstrel days we miss" before Crosby and Kaye chime in with all three in unison "When Georgie Primrose would sing and dance to a song like this". The song following, "Mandy", is an elaborate song and dance number. These three songs performed in rapid succession have some of the highest production detail of all of the film's numbers.

This overt nostalgia for the minstrel tradition does comply with the period's wider moves towards desegregation and follows the lead of *Amos 'n' Andy* in excising visual blackface while still decrying the loss of the tradition's earlier social acceptability. In line with the derogatory and discriminatory jokes made in *The Lemon Drop Kid*, *White Christmas* holds values consistent with the more socially conservative attitudes held in Hollywood. This social conservatism mixed with the romantic plot and its adherence to the three tropes in Christmas romances that deliver domestic containment by the film's end support the argument that in this period, Christmas films were complying with the pressures to portray more socially conservative messaging with "American" values in line with the views of HUAC, the FBI, the MPAPAI, and Rand.

---

247 "Amos 'n' Andy Look for Exit as They Plan New TV Show", *Reading Eagle*, June 17, 1951, ProQuest.

Conclusion

As a result of the pressures on the motion picture industry in the late 1940s and early 1950s as well as the wider changing culture, Christmas films abandoned Dickensian plots and supernatural Santas in order to expand the genre into inoffensive, simplistic romances, farces, and musicals. By dispelling Dickens and replacing concern for collective issues with ones contained within the domestic sphere, Christmas films reflected changes both within Hollywood – by adhering to the content limitations implied by the Hollywood blacklist and other pressures on the industry – and the wider culture – by portraying marriage as the ultimate goal for safety and security in the tumultuous world off-screen. These depictions of romances in Christmas films from 1949 to 1954 echo the wider cultural, political, and social changes in the US in the late 1940s and early 1950s while simultaneously supporting the shift in Hollywood away from social problem films as observed by Jones and fulfilling the audience's appetite for feel-good escapism.

The first three chapters of this project have provided the political, cultural, and social context for analyzing Christmas films released in the immediate postwar period through 1954. The federal pressures on Hollywood, legal challenges within the industry, and labor strife created the conditions in which filmmakers were forced to make decisions about whether to comply with changing expectations within the motion picture industry or to risk suspicion or even blacklisting for speaking out against those expectations. Ultimately, those pressures and the responses of both the industry's executives and workers had an effect on the films' cultural outputs. These first three chapters have tracked those changes by analyzing the changes in a genre in direct conversation with historical contexts.

The next two chapters will diverge from this framework by each taking a different perspective on the 15-year period between 1946 and 1961 as a whole. Chapter 4 will analyze depictions of commercialism and consumerism as an element of the Christmas holiday. By placing filmic depictions of shopping in conversation with changing contemporary attitudes to the practice in a period of increasing economic affluence, the chapter will show the Christmas films in this study are not aberrations of Hollywood, but rather are reflections of the social and cultural attitudes around their production. Tracking a specific theme integral to the modern American Christmas tradition likewise emphasizes that while there are changes to the generic form, the holiday components at the center of it remain consistent.

Chapter 4
A Case Study for Christmas: Changing Attitudes towards Commercialism and Consumerism on Film, 1946–1961

> A lot of bad 'isms' floating around this world, but one of the worst is 'commercialism'.
> - Alfred, *Miracle on 34th Street* (1947)

George Seaton's *Miracle on 34th Street* (1947) did not hesitate to state clearly the position of the film's various Santa Claus characters when reacting to the gradually increasing commercialism and consumerism of the late 1940s. Alfred (Alvin Greenman), the young janitor in the film who volunteers as a Santa figure at the local YMCA, remarks that the growing trend of commercialism in post-war New York culture was arguably worse than other "isms", presumably likening the threats of it to those of communism, as discussed in Chapter 1. Similar straightforward presentations of ideas around commercialism – the ways in which stores market and capitalize on their brand – and, by proxy, consumerism – the process of purchasing – are evident in many of the films from the 1946 to 1961 period analyzed in this study. Such views develop from Alfred's standpoint to reflect the period's ever-evolving attitudes towards commercialism and consumption as the post-war American economy rebounded, rebuilt, and flourished, allowing more and more people to engage with the newfound purchasing power of an emerging age of the "affluent society".[248]

This 15-year period of growing economic prosperity throughout the late 1940s and early 1960s is captured in the films in a variety of ways. The focus on Christmas in each of the films provides a unique opportunity to examine where and how people shopped both on screen and relative to the off-screen world, as well as what items were most likely to be purchased and given at Christmas. Christmas has been associated with the tradition of gift-giving as early as the Biblical stories of Christ's birth and the Three Wise Men, on through the folklore around Saint Nicholas, and into the modern era with the classic American poem *The Night Before Christmas* (1823). This tradition of gift-giving and the conceptualization of Christmas as the "Season of Giving" allow for analysis of filmic reflections and representations of the changing attitudes towards both commercialism and consumerism in the wider world, as well as a closer look at the histories of particular commodities

---

[248] John Kenneth Galbraith, *The Affluent Society* (Boston: Houghton Mifflin, 1958).

that develop new – and evolve existing – social resonances throughout the 15-year period.

In bringing these ideas of the external trends, attitudes, and behaviors surrounding the practice of shopping into relationship with Hollywood's filmic representations of them, this chapter will examine three main subjects. First, the main places in which people shopped – specifically department stores – and the ways in which commercialism was displayed in these stores via the exploitation of a synthesized vision of the most prevalent Christmas iconography and its leading figure, Santa Claus. Second, the chapter will analyze how people shopped, bringing together advice from women's magazines and catalogues on the one hand and the practices of Hollywood's filmic shoppers on the other. Third, the items purchased as gifts within the films themselves will be closely scrutinized with a case study examining one recurring item across several films: the mink coat. This case study will explore the cultural and social attitudes towards mink coats and their associations with class status as they changed from the immediate post-war era through the 1950s and into the early 1960s.

Ultimately, this chapter argues that the cultural trends relating to the expanding economy in the post-war period not only introduced modernized ideas of consumerism and commercialism but also inspired interpretations of these "isms" in mainstream cinema. The Christmas films in this study do not stand alone in Hollywood's filmography of the era with their commentaries on these changing social ideas around consumption and rampant commercialization. However, they do offer a unique perspective in analyzing these trends with the recurring tropes of purchasing, selling, and transferring tangible items during the Christmas season and all of its associated traditions.

As Chapter 2 examined the Christmas film genre's reflections of current social problems in the wider world as a result of the holiday's connection with Dickensian tropes, this chapter looks at a specific theme recurrent in the Christmas tradition that becomes increasingly inseparable from the holiday. As will be argued, shopping and gift-giving were already an increasing part of the synthesized American holiday, especially when done through the central Christmas figure of Santa Claus. However, as observed in Chapter 3, after *Miracle on 34th Street* Santa is no longer a central figure in Hollywood Christmas releases until a brief mention in Disney's 1961 *Babes in Toyland* and then not again until the 1980s.[249] This chapter

---

249 A small number of low-budget films in the 1980s center on a magical Santa Claus plot: TriStar Pictures' box office flop *Santa Claus: The Movie* (1985), Disney's *One Magic Christmas* (1985), and Orion Pictures' *Prancer* (1989) to name a few. These films had minimal success at the box office with the next very successful and mainstream Santa-centric film being Disney's 1994 *The Santa Clause*.

shows that Christmas films adapted with the times culturally and socially over this 15-year period as non-extricable elements of the holiday – namely commercialism and commodities – were essential to their storylines. This analysis of the film's cultural elements shows consistency in the genre's inclusion of commercialism as well as change in how commercialism itself adapts over time to fit the needs of the contemporary economic climate.

Here Comes (the American) Santa Claus

"Christmas" in this book, as explained in the Introduction, refers to the idealizing American Christmas tradition born out of the consolidation of local and disparate community celebrations around winter, Saturnalia, and Christian holy days. Prior to the 1840s, historian Penne Restad argues, Christmas traditions "reflected a broadening sense of regional and cultural identity" across the US.[250] These local traditions, as Restad continues, began to consolidate and nationalize the holiday between the 1840s and 1870s for a number of reasons including the expansion of national media, developments of marketplace and industry, and the Civil War melding American cultures and promoting a more unified nationalized identity. These nineteenth-century political, social, and cultural influences raising Christmas up as a prominent secular American holiday began its gradual progression towards its ultimate identity as a civic holiday in the early 1910s when over 160 towns and cities held public, communal Christmas festivities.[251]

Throughout the nineteenth century, as these local celebrations began to coalesce in the public consciousness and as the streamlining of collective, public traditions developed, canonical imagery began to emerge as well. Iconography for the collective imagination of Christmas started to take shape with poetic and literary representations of the holiday. One of the earliest widely printed versions of Christmas traditions in America was in Washington Irving's 1809 *Knickerbocker's History of New York*. Irving's biographer Andrew Burstein suggests that Irving "considered the *idea* of America something with enduring sentimental potential" and from this began to develop a larger Christmas narrative from minor customs. For instance, Irving offered the addition that families of New Amsterdam hang stockings in the chimney for St. Nicholas to fill with gifts on "St. Nicholas

---

250 Restad, *Christmas in America*, 91.
251 Restad, 91.

Eve".[252] Through his writings, Irving was the first to widely publicize the idea of St. Nicholas as a fun-loving gift-giver for American families.

Another founding text in the construction of a standardized American Christmas was the classic American poem *A Visit from St. Nicholas* – more commonly known as *The Night Before Christmas*. Published in 1823, *A Visit from St. Nicholas* offered the iconic modern description of Saint Nicholas that would define his image for centuries:

> He was dressed all in fur, from his head to his foot,
> And his clothes were all tarnished with ashes and soot;
> A bundle of Toys he had flung on his back,
> And he looked like a pedlar just opening his pack.
> His eyes—how they twinkled! his dimples how merry!
> His cheeks were like roses, his nose like a cherry!
> His droll little mouth was drawn up like a bow
> And the beard of his chin was as white as the snow;
> The stump of a pipe he held tight in his teeth,
> And the smoke it encircled his head like a wreath;
> He had a broad face and a little round belly,
> That shook when he laughed, like a bowlful of jelly.
> He was chubby and plump, a right jolly old elf...[253]

This poem established for the first time that Santa Claus travelled by a reindeer-drawn sleigh, came on Christmas Eve, and looked like a sweet, portly, white-bearded old man, while, crucially, removing the burden of Santa's moral judgements of children.[254] This image and character of Saint Nicolas was popularized with the 1823 poem and became a mainstream version of him that has endured in the public consciousness, in part due to the comparably lasting illustrations that came to accompany this poem and other renderings of the character.

---

252 Andrew Burstein, *The Original Knickerbocker: The Life of Washington Irving* (New York: Basic Books, 2007), 86 https://hdl.handle.net/2027/heb07705.0001.001.

253 Although the poem is most commonly attributed to professor of divinity Clement C. Moore, the descendants of American Revolutionary War veteran Henry Livingston Jr. contend that he was the rightful author. The Livingston argument claims that the poem was composed in 1808 and recited to his children. Regardless of authorship, the popularization of the poem, and therefore the imagery within it, did not come about until 1823 when it was anonymously published in the Troy, New York, *Sentinel*. Cf. Bruce David Forbes, *Christmas: A Candid History* (Berkeley: University of California Press, 2007).

254 Forbes, *Christmas*, 87–88.

Thomas Nast's illustrations of Santa Claus for *Harper's Weekly*, beginning in 1863, resembled the figure described by Moore in the earlier poem. This nineteenth-century American portrayal of Santa Claus was an "amalgam of American, Dutch, and English traditions" that reflected the complex identity of the US, blending many immigrant communities and their traditions.[255] J. M. Golby and A. W. Purdue argue that these representations of Santa Claus by Nast and Moore and the myriad others developed upon Nast's physical depiction in the late 1800s lean heavily towards a modern Saturnalia rather than a Christian tradition. By omitting any reference to the nativity or Christian touchstones in the poem, they contend that modern Christmas might be "the Saturnalia of an increasingly urbanized, humanitarian, family-centered, and child-loving civilization."[256]

Other such depictions of Santa Claus developed from these first traditions and either leaned into secularism or highlighted the Christian elements of the holiday. However, as Richard Horsley argues in his "Christmas: The Religion of Consumer Capitalism", American Christmas and its traditions were "only very partially and superficially 'christianized' in the late nineteenth and early twentieth centuries."[257] These characterizations of American Christmas as decidedly secular in its portrayal led to, as Restad and Horsley argue, the formation of Christmas as a civic festival.

The idea of Christmas as a civic festival separate from religious connotations that could be associated with it – whether Pagan, Christian, or otherwise – raises a complex question about American identities. The default naming convention for the holiday and its figures are most apparently associated with its Christian context. Despite the nature of Christmas celebrations becoming a civic holiday connected to patriotic emblems and a sense of American community across religions and backgrounds, Christian connotations are inextricable from the name and ostensible ownership of the holiday. Christmas, however, especially in American traditions and through the last two centuries, is a complex amalgamation of various cultural traditions and religious customs distilled into a standardized public holiday under the guise of Christian nomenclature. For instance, as Mark Connelly writes, the name Kris Kringle is "one of Santa's pseudonyms, a mispronunciation of the German Lutheran term *Christkindlein*, meaning a messenger of Christ, a gift-

---

255 J. M. Golby and A. W. Purdue, *The Making of the Modern Christmas* (Athens, GA: University of Georgia Press, 1986), 75.
256 Golby and Purdue, 75.
257 Richard Horsley, "Christmas: The Religion of Consumer Capitalism", in *Christmas Unwrapped: Consumerism, Christ, and Culture*, ed. Richard Horsley and James Tracy (Pittsburgh, PA: Trinity Press International, 2001), 165–187.

bearer."²⁵⁸ The Santa Claus traditions and the secular nineteenth-century portrayals of him as the holiday's central figure work to separate the Christianized version from the synthesized American holiday; however, it is still important to be aware of the tendency to default towards the connotations of the holiday as ostensibly Christian.

Among these varied and numerous origins and alongside Santa Claus imagery, depictions of other Christmas traditions were developing as well throughout the nineteenth century. The popularity of Dickensian villages and vague iconography of old English villages mapped onto the identity of American Christmas by tapping into a sense of false nostalgia for many adults. As historian of Christmas Karal Ann Marling writes, the Dickensian iconography was the opposite end of the cultural touchtone spectrum from Santa by invoking "a universal good cheer, benevolence, and simplicity that stood in strong contrast to the commercial bustle of the modern, Santa Claus holiday."²⁵⁹ In the first half of the twentieth century, one such touchstone was Norman Rockwell through his illustrations on the cover of the *Saturday Evening Post*. Rockwell's covers depicted a range of iconography including extensions on the Santa Claus and Dickensian mythologies and also, more pointedly, realistic portrayals of the commercialism of the holiday, such as with his December 1947 *Tired Shop Girl on Christmas Eve*. With these covers, Rockwell helped to solidify public consciousness regarding Christmas for many Americans between the 1910s and 1950s.

The aesthetic of a standardized American Christmas developed out of these pieces of poetry and art that became the touchstones they are because of repetition and various media building on the myriad intersections of smaller communities' traditions that merged into a canonical national identity for the holiday. American Christmas is not just one thing, but rather a standard set of images, ideas, and icons that create a complex cultural phenomenon. This cultural phenomenon was then updated and adapted, amalgamating further for each subsequent generation and their modes of interacting with their own times and their own American identity. One particularly American influence on this mainstream vision of the man, the myths, and the legends of Christmas was the uses of them in commercial advertising, experiences, and entertainments within department stores and eventually in Hollywood.

---

258 Mark Connelly, "*Santa Claus*: The Movie", in *Christmas at the Movies: Images of Christmas in American, British and European Cinema*, ed. Mark Connelly (London: I.B. Tauris Publishers, 2000), 84.
259 Marling, *Merry Christmas!*, 138.

Commercialism in Stores and on Film

One of the most prominent locations in American Christmas nostalgia and iconography is the department store. In understanding how and why Christmas developed as it did in the American psyche and public traditions, the history of commercialism and consumerism is essential. Specifically, department stores played a major role in the construction and development of a standardized American Christmas. Emerging from early local immigrant populations' communal traditions through the poetry that prompted the imagery, the development of the modern American Christmas narrative then went to the stores that spread it nationwide and the film that eventually crystalized who Santa was at the center of it all from the mid-twentieth century on.

"Palaces of Consumption": Department Stores and Christmas

Many social, cultural, and business historians agree that the first department store was Le Bon Marché, established in Paris in 1852; however, beyond this fact there is much contention about which stores elsewhere could also be categorized as "department stores".[260] Here, the department store is defined as a commercial center within which specialist retailers using departmental units cater to many of the consumer's needs all under one roof. As historian Daniel Boorstin notes:

> The distinctive institution which came to be called the department store was a large retail shop, centrally located in a city, doing a big volume of business, and offering a wide range of merchandise, including clothing for women and children, small household wares, and usually dry goods and home furnishings. While the stock was departmentalized, many of the operations and the general management were centralized.[261]

Boorstin, although conceding that European department stores, such as Le Bon Marché, were the first to be established, argues that "if the department store was not an American invention, it flourished here as nowhere else."[262] This flourishing of the department store in America can be seen in the sudden emergence of

---

260 For more on mid-century views on department stores, see: John William Ferry, *A History of the Department Store* (New York, Macmillan Company, 1960); Harry E. Resseguie, "Alexander Turney Stewart and the Development of the Department Store, 1823–1876", *Business History Review (Pre-1986)* 39, no. 3 (Autumn 1965): 301–322.
261 Daniel J. Boorstin, *The Americans: The Democratic Experience* (New York; Random House, 1973), 101.
262 Boorstin, 101.

these grand complexes – "Palaces of Consumption" as Boorstin terms them – in cities around the country. Some of the largest retailers founded in the nineteenth century were A. T. Stewart's (established 1823), Lord & Taylor (1826), Arnold Constable (1852), and R. H. Macy's in New York City (1858), Jordan Marsh in Boston (1841), John Wanamaker in Philadelphia (1876), Field, Leiter & Co. – later Marshall Field & Co. – (1852) and the Fair in Chicago (1874), and smaller but well-known local stores including Lazarus in Columbus, Ohio (1851), and Hudson's in Detroit (1881).[263] These palaces of consumption quickly became highly important economic centers in growing cities, impacting the metropolises and the cultures in which they were built and ultimately becoming a defining feature of urban life.

As John Ferry wrote in 1960, "No city of any size in the world today is without its department stores. They are part of the make-up of urban areas just as are the churches, theatres, hotels, art galleries, and museums."[264] Harry Resseguie wrote in 1965 that the "principal obstacle" in defining what a department store is "has been its dynamism: its ability to change its characteristics while maintaining its outward form." This ability to change is a necessary reminder in discussing the abrupt and enveloping evolution of commercialism between the mid-nineteenth and mid-twentieth centuries.

On this evolution, Resseguie continues, "The early department store, for instance, prided itself on its ability to sell national brands of merchandise at substantial reductions from the manufacturer's suggested resale price."[265] This price-competitive aspect of department stores and the ability to meet many of their customers' needs in a single location helped establish and maintain their widespread popularity through uncertain economic times. Boorstin, in 1973, devoted a full chapter to department stores in the final instalment of his trilogy on the history of American society, *The Americans: The Democratic Experience*. In this chapter entitled "Consumers' Palaces", Boorstin argues that "the new department store grandeur gave dignity, importance, and publicity to the acts of shopping and buying – new communal acts in a new America."[266] As the twentieth century went on and particularly in the post-war sprawl from urban centers to new suburban towns, these department stores ventured into the suburbs with much of their clientele and served as the anchor stores in district shopping malls.[267]

---

263 Boorstin, 101.
264 Ferry, *A History of the Department Store*, 1–2.
265 Resseguie, "Alexander Turney Stewart", 302.
266 Boorstin, *The Americans*, 101.
267 Robert J. Gordon, *The Rise and Fall of American Growth: The U.S. Standard of Living since the Civil War* (Princeton: Princeton University Press, 2016), 349.

With department stores acquiring such importance and status in the late nineteenth and early twentieth centuries, it is not surprising that these commercial centers and their new communal activities were integral in the streamlining of American Christmas. Capitalizing on the Christmas holiday shopping season, department stores nationwide began creating elaborate window displays for December and integrating Christmas into their marketing strategies. As Marling notes, window displays curated for the Christmas shopping season began in the 1820s "when the first recorded holiday decorations – evergreens, flowers, and 'patriotic emblems' – appeared in the window of a New York City shop."[268] These patriotic emblems highlighted an early form of the intense relationship between Americanism and celebrating Christmas as a secular, patriotic tradition. Stores began to put Kris Kringle figures in their shop windows as early as 1840 in Philadelphia and the 1870s in Boston. Gradually, as the popularity of dressing shop windows for Christmas spread across the country throughout the late nineteenth century, Macy's began to emerge as one of the most iconic and best-known institutions for their elaborate and beautiful displays.[269]

Owing in part to the large bank windows on the corner of Sixth Avenue and 14th Street at the main entrance of the original R. H. Macy Dry Goods store in New York City, Macy's became synonymous with the grandeur and design of Christmas celebrations. By 1924, following the lead of Gimbel's in Philadelphia in 1920, the flagship Macy's store in Herald Square on 34th Street introduced their Thanksgiving Day parade "with Santa Claus presiding".[270] By introducing these parades with Santa at the helm, Macy's and the like were co-opting "the domain of the street festival and street fair, colonizing the mummers' world and working-class celebrations with their own spectacles that were eventually staged more for the consumption of television audiences than for the folks on the avenues."[271] Macy's participation in these Christmas festivities helped to synthesize regionally specific Christmas traditions into a mainstream, standardized view of American Christmas traditions that ultimately was transferred to the small and big screens.

Simultaneously, as Macy's developed their brand for Christmas, the department store industry capitalized on the benefits of children believing in Santa Claus. In 1897, *New York Sun* editor Francis Church received a letter from a

268 Marling, *Merry Christmas!*, 83.
269 Marling, 87–88.
270 Leigh Eric Schmidt, *Consumer Rites: The Buying & Selling of American Holidays* (Princeton: Princeton University Press, 1995), 145.
271 Schmidt, 145–146.

young girl named Virginia asking if Santa Claus was real. Church published his response as an open letter, writing:

> Yes, Virginia, there is a Santa Claus. He exists as certainly as love and generosity and devotion exist, and you know that they abound and give to our life its highest beauty and joy. Alas! How dreary would be the world if there were no Santa Claus! It would be as dreary as if there were no Virginias. There would be no childlike faith then, no poetry, no romance, to make tolerable this existence. We should have no enjoyment except in sense and sight.[272]

This response echoed and encouraged the societal belief in Santa and without any reference to Christian elements of Christmas. The faith in Santa was distinct from a religious faith but emphasized as a net positive to make the world more tolerable. The presence of Santa was a collective imperative for parents to sustain with their children and for the rest of American adults to cultivate as much as possible. One manifestation of this societal responsibility was the establishment of the Santa Claus Association in New York for "the express purpose of preserving children's belief in St. Nick."[273] Ultimately, however, just as the image of Santa was co-opted by department stores and, most egregiously, Hollywood for commercialist propagandizing and maximizing corporate profits, the Santa Claus Association eventually devolved from its purportedly sincere foundations into a monetized grift in itself further exploiting the Santa Claus image for financial gain.[274] Regardless, by the 1930s, a standardization of the Santa image became necessary as he was being used more and more in person and in advertising. In response to this need, schools began popping up in major cities to train men on how to look, act, and be the perfect Santa Clauses.[275]

Macy's remained a leader in the preservation of the myth and identity of Santa Claus, perfecting the use of Santa as a wholesome character, consistent across all stores. Simultaneously, however, this wholesome image of preserving the myth of Santa was not only for the sake of children or the protection of their innocence; Santa was also a marketing gimmick to get families into the store. As William Waits writes, "Santa was effective because, according to his myth, he did not use money and was not engaged in making profit." Waits describes Santa as a "decontaminator of manufactured items" and continues that,

---

272 As quoted in William B. Waits, *The Modern Christmas in America: A Cultural History of Gift Giving* (New York: New York University Press, 1993), 132.
273 Waits, 133.
274 For the full story of how the Santa Claus Association became a vehicle for financial exploitation, see: A. Palmer, *The Santa Claus Man: The Rise and Fall of a Jazz Age Con Man and the Invention of Christmas in New York* (Guilford, CT: Rowman & Littlefield, 2015).
275 Restad, *Christmas in America*, 158.

"he made no trip to the toy store to buy the toys, nor even a trip to purchase raw materials. Santa's motivation for his monumental undertaking was free of market considerations."[276] Because of Santa's purity from manufacturing, he was used in advertising nationwide for a range of products. As the posterchild for Coca-Cola and a figure in over 20 % of toy ad campaigns in *Ladies' Home Journal* and *The Saturday Evening Post*, by the 1930s, Santa had become the official spokesman of commercialism, especially when marketing toward children.[277]

This contradictory idea of Santa as both pure of and the spokesman for the commercialism that increasingly was tainting the American Christmas in the early twentieth century led to even more complex manipulations of the figure. Macy's used Santa and his clean image, decontaminated of manufactured items, to sell manufactured items. This ostensible innocence, the use of Santa's long and storied image as a jolly, sweet figure, a grandfatherly type whose image Americans honed for years as an ethereal saint denoting positivity and generosity, was the perfect image to exploit for corporate profits in the palaces of consumption themselves.

Macy's department store itself became a symbol of the shopping season incorporating much of the iconography associated with the idea of an American Christmas. The connection between the store and the holiday grew organically from the importance of department stores to their local culture and the increasing attempt to captivate an audience of all classes who could stare into shop window displays and live a fantasy in relation to the items in the tableaux.[278] With Macy's deeply entrenched connection to the holiday and its increasing commercialization of Christmas via their advertising resources, including the parade, window displays, and store Santa Clauses, Macy's became the perfect backdrop for Valentine Davies's 1947 novella and the subsequent George Seaton film, *Miracle on 34th Street*.

Miracle on 34th Street Steals Christmas

Department stores in the mid-twentieth century were well-established cultural centers integral to a city's identity. Their Christmas displays, merchandise, and gimmicks helped to streamline the commercial view of what a mainstream American Christmas looked like, especially for the cities in which they were located. Just as department stores helped to standardize the public consciousness of Christmas in the late nineteenth and early twentieth centuries, Hollywood cinema took this

---

276 Waits, *The Modern Christmas in America*, 25.
277 Restad, *Christmas in America*, 163.
278 Marling, *Merry Christmas!*, 84.

process to a new level. Santa had been depicted on screens a few times prior to the 1940s, but no film did more for the image of Santa Claus, and the updating or modernization of him, than *Miracle on 34th Street* (1947).[279]

Miracle on 34th Street is a masterpiece of evasion and manipulation of the audience, of Santa Claus and Christmas imagery, and of straightforward messaging. In the first example of this complex manipulation, the film was originally billed as a romantic comedy, downplaying in all of the promotional materials the film's central Christmas spirit and plot. As the concept of a Christmas film was not yet an established genre and because the film was releasing in June 1947, the marketing for the film emphasized the romance between Maureen O'Hara and John Payne's characters in all of the posters and publicity. Even in the five-minute trailer for *Miracle on 34th Street*, the Christmas elements of the film were entirely evaded.

The trailer describes the film as "Hilarious! Romantic! Delightful! Charming! Tender! Exciting!" In a meta spin, the trailer pans back to a producer watching the trailer for *Miracle on 34th Street*, enraged at this characterization of the film. He exclaims:

> That won't work – it's no good. What do you make a trailer for? To give the public an idea of what kind of a picture to expect. Hilarious! Romantic! Tender! Exciting! Make up your minds. It can't be all of those things. Tender, exciting, why they're practically opposites. You've got to decide what kind of a picture this is. Is it a romantic love story? Is it an exciting thriller? Is it a hilarious comedy? Make up your minds. Now go to work and fix it up.

The producer subsequently leaves the viewing room and encounters a number of celebrities on the studio lot and enquires if they have seen *Miracle*. None of these stars are in the film but are used in the promotional materials for it. Anne Baxter very nearly gives away the Christmassy elements of the plot and that there is even a Santa Claus in the film at all but stops herself in time, saying "no, I'm not going to spoil it for you." The trailer is brilliantly self-referential and as evasive as the film in refusing to deliver a straightforward message.

This evasion of purpose and manipulation of the audience even prior to their seeing the film was an excellent marketing strategy for *Miracle on 34th Street* specifically. Without even acknowledging the actual plot or subject matter of the film, the studio and distributor marketed the subplot to attract viewers. As will be seen below, the film itself does the same thing with the surface-level plot and messaging of the film that becomes much more complex and even sinister

---

279 For an exploration of more Santa imagery on screen, see: Max A. Myers, "Christmas on Celluloid: Hollywood Helps Construct the American Christmas", in *Christmas Unwrapped: Consumerism, Christ, and Culture*, ed. Richard Horsley and James Tracy (Pittsburgh, PA: Trinity Press International, 2001), 39–54.

with deeper analysis. The ostensible image of the Santa figure in the film as anti-commercialist, the image of him as a "decontaminator of manufactured items," very quickly becomes manipulated by 1947 commercialist needs for the character.

Miracle on 34th Street

George Seaton's *Miracle on 34th Street* is a film about a sweet old man who believes himself to be the real Santa Claus and the lengths he goes to convince a young girl and the city of New York that truly knowing is not as powerful as believing. Kris Kringle (Edmund Gwenn) is hired by Macy's to be the store Santa Claus after a drunken imposter is fired on the spot for being inebriated while presiding over the Thanksgiving Day parade. His hiring manager, Doris Walker (Maureen O'Hara), her daughter Susan (Natalie Wood), and their lawyer neighbor Fred Gailey (John Payne) become central figures in Kringle's life between Thanksgiving and Christmas as accusations against Kringle's mental health emerge. Kringle enacts a goodwill policy at Macy's, telling customers to go to another store if the price is better or a toy they want is only in stock elsewhere. His policy causes a complicated stir at Macy's and prompts a legal battle in which it ultimately is decided on a technicality delivered by the US Postal Service that Kringle is in fact Santa Claus and his goodwill policy shall remain.

The film has many complex layers and leans into manipulations of ostensibly innocent scenes. For instance, young Susan does not believe that Kringle is truly Santa Claus as he claims. She expresses her distrust by being quite vulnerable and telling him that: "That's what I want for Christmas ... a real house. If you're really Santa Claus, you can get it for me. And if you can't, you're only a nice man with a white beard, like mother said." This ultimatum is not a traditional request for Santa Claus. A house is not something that can be made in the North Pole and put under the Christmas tree. Instead, Susan is picking up on a different mode of materialism in the identity of the American Christmas: commercialism. If he cannot provide her with the house she truly wants for Christmas, then there must be no Santa Claus and Christmas must not be the "magical time of year" some of the adults around her claim it to be.

This connection between Kris Kringle and the commercialization of Christmas is the driving force of the plot. Susan's insistence that Kringle can only acquire the house of her dreams if he is the real Santa Claus is deeper than a child's ultimatum. Susan's mother Doris is a single, working divorcee who allows her previous relationship with Susan's father to spoil her own imagination and hope for fairy-tale endings and love. In asking for the house, Susan is expressing a desire to move out of the city and into the suburbs with the symbol of the American family at the heart. If Kringle cannot deliver a happy American ending, then he has no role in her life. Specifically, if he cannot purchase the exact house in the listing Susan showed him, his magic is not real. Susan's request and ultimatum equate the magic of Santa Claus and the Christmas spirit with the purchasing power of commercialism and underscore a more sinister idea: that a happy American ending can, and ideally should, be purchased.

This equation of the Christmas spirit with commercialism is also more emphatically made in the central plot of the goodwill policy. The goodwill policy causes Kringle to clash with his superiors as he independently introduces this honesty policy for helping parents get their children the gifts they *want* instead of the gifts their parents *think* they want. The goodwill policy works by encouraging shoppers to find the best deals for the items they are looking for, even if that means buying from a rival. In response, Macy's customers are shown becoming more loyal, ultimately driving profits up for the store. As one customer exclaims, "Imagine a big outfit like Macy's, putting the spirit of Christmas ahead of the commercial. It's wonderful. I never done much shopping here before, but from now on, I'm going to be a regular Macy customer."

In crafting this idea of the goodwill policy to promote good publicity for department stores, the film forefronts the consumer rather than the customer. The consumer of the toy section at Macy's is not the buyer necessarily but, especially at Christmas, the children receiving the toys as gifts. The film first has the store manager explain to Kringle that the job of the store Santa Claus is to suggest certain toys that are harder to sell, toys or items that happen to be overstocked, hoping to push these products onto a child consumer who will then inform their parents that they want that particular item for Christmas. Kringle becomes irate at the manipulation of a child's desires, scoffing, "Imagine, making a child take something it doesn't want just because he [the store manager] bought too many of the wrong toys. That's what I've been fighting against for years. The way they commercialize Christmas." Kringle's on-screen acknowledgement and disgust at the premise of commercializing Christmas masterfully sells to the audience the idea that Christmas is not about buying anything for the sake of buying it, but rather about buying precisely what a child wants, all the while maintaining the outward appearance that the commercialization of Christmas is a negative interpretation of the holiday. *Miracle on 34ᵗʰ Street*, in a paradoxical way, ostensibly condemns the commercialization of the holiday while also promoting this goodwill policy, suggesting again that not only can you commercialize Christmas, but also that you should, by manipulating the role of Santa from generous toy bringer to business savvy salesman.

In one scene, a child on Kringle's lap asks for a toy fire engine while his mother attempts to discourage this request. Kringle promises the boy he will get a fire engine and then calms the angry mother by telling her she can get the exact toy at a rival store, giving her the location and price while assuring her they are still in stock. When she expresses disbelief at his honesty, Kringle quips that he keeps a close eye on the toy market and says, "Well the only important thing is to make the children happy and whether Macy or somebody else sells the toy doesn't make any difference. Don't you feel that way?" Bewildered, she responds that she certainly feels that way but didn't know Macy's did.

This exchange exposes one of the most apparent adjustments *Miracle on 34th Street* makes to the Santa Claus image. As mentioned above, the image of Santa prior to his twentieth century's rampant commercialist exploitation – and the reason for it – was as a "decontaminator of manufactured items," as one who does not purchase his toys and who is free of market considerations.[280] In popular mythologies around him, Santa Claus has a workshop at the North Pole in which elves make the toys that he delivers. However, in *Miracle on 34th Street's* Manhattan, Santa Claus isn't producing the toys, but rather relaying customers to department stores to purchase them while he keeps "track of the toy market pretty closely." This portrayal of Santa as a moderator of well-priced toys is a dereliction of his role up until this point. He had been used in earlier advertising to sell a company's own products, but never before had Santa been such a public agent of general commercialism promoting any sales as long as profits were made for Christmas. Santa here is no longer the decontaminator of manufactured items, but rather their direct dealer.

Relegating Santa Claus to the role of keeping track of the best deals on commercial goods removes him from previously established myths of Christmas and places him as nothing more than a signifier denoting that it is the season of buying. In key, brief instances, audiences are treated to the "real Santa Claus" character Kris Kringle is portraying. In the first scene of the film, Kringle walks past a shop clerk decorating a window display for Christmas on Thanksgiving morning. Here, as Schmidt observes, this opening scene of Kringle looking through a shop window sets up the idea that "commerce frames the story" and symbolically and literally places Kringle directly in the middle of it.[281] Kringle, stopping to admire the display, notices that the reindeer are out of order as he would have them. Addressing the shop clerk, Kringle corrects his placement of the reindeer with such lines as "Dasher should be on my right-hand side," and "I don't suppose anybody would notice except myself." This quick scene establishes for the audience in the opening sequence that whether he truly is or not, Kringle believes he is Santa

280 Waits, *The Modern Christmas in America*, 25.
281 Schmidt, *Consumer Rites*, 171.

Claus and, further, that he is willing to use his identity to help vendors properly and accurately commercialize Christmas.

This portrayal of Santa Claus as an economically wise market-watcher giving cost-effective advice to parents is a stark deviation from the publicly-accepted version of Santa as the toymaker and gift-giver. To normalize the actions and behaviors of Kringle's deviation from the "traditional" depictions of Santa Claus, the film makes a concerted effort to portray Kringle as the real mythical figure complete with a certain magical quality. At one point, when a young, newly-immigrated Dutch girl sits on Kringle's lap in Macy's, her adoptive mother apologizes profusely that the girl doesn't speak English, yet she insisted on meeting him regardless. Kringle waves the woman off and speaks perfect Dutch to the bemused girl, learning exactly what she wants for Christmas. This moment feels as though it is magical, giving a glimpse of the more traditional "Sinter Claes" as the girl calls him, all witnessed by Susan who begins to believe that Kringle may truly be the real Santa Claus.

Immediately following this magical scene, Doris asks Kringle definitively to tell Susan that he is not Santa, which he refuses to do. Doris decides to discreetly fire him but is subsequently praised in another meeting with her superiors for hiring him in the first place, as Macy's customer loyalty and, more significantly, profits have gone up as a result. These three scenes happen in quick succession: Kringle displaying perceived "Christmas magic," his firing for proclaiming himself to be the true Santa, and his rehiring for increasing profits. The film seems to be signifying that the real Santa Claus is no longer marketable if representing such traditional, magical elements, but *is* marketable when turning a profit for the company.

The film endorses a complex message rebranding not only Santa Claus but also commercialism through him as positive American forces. The film mixes traditional Santa Claus iconography – bestowing gifts, embodying kindness, being worldly and welcoming – and the for-profit commercialist structure of the post-war department store. By abandoning the traditional Santa and literally firing him for believing in the ideals and existence of the holiday's more "magical" aspects, Macy's hires the version of Santa they wanted in the first place: the one who will inspire better sales, higher profits, and more loyal customers by exploiting those innocent associations with his name and image.

Playing Santa Claus in *Miracle on 34th Street* is not only for Kringle. There are two other Santas in the film: the drunk Santa whom Kringle replaces in the Thanksgiving Day Parade and subsequently at the store; and the young Macy's janitor, Alfred (Alvin Greenman), who dresses up as Santa for the children at his local YMCA. The first, drunken Santa, is immediately scorned as he fits neither the traditional Santa myth nor the role of the good commercialist icon that Kringle will later fill. The second, Alfred, is a parallel character experiencing the same changes to the holiday that are affecting Kringle without the added element of potentially being the true Santa.

Alfred and Kringle form a relationship around both of their interests in the Santa figure. Alfred claims that he loves playing Santa for the look on children's faces when he gives them gifts, reassuring Kringle that he also disapproves of the commercialist angle of Christmas. As cited at the start of this chapter, Alfred states, "Yea there's a lot of bad -isms floating around this world, but one of the worst is commercialism. Make a buck, make a buck. Even in Brooklyn it's the same. Don't care what Christmas stands for; just make a buck, make a buck." Despite the first line's possible pass at communism, Alfred is affirming to both the audience and Kringle that, even outside of the department store, he believes in the goodness of the traditional role of Santa Claus: giving gifts for the joy of children. Shortly after, however, Alfred informs Kringle that he will no longer be playing Santa at the YMCA because the store's mental examiner, Mr. Sawyer (Porter Hall) has diagnosed him with a guilt complex and subconscious hatred of his father, as discussed in Chapter 2. Sawyer contends that the only reason someone would want to give gifts to strangers for free would be that he must have done something bad in his childhood for which he is trying to forgive himself. Mr. Sawyer also interviews Kringle and diagnoses him with "latent maniacal tendencies." This diagnosis is used later in the film to set up the climactic court hearing to decide whether Kris Kringle is insane or truly Santa Claus.

Sawyer's diagnoses on behalf of Macy's are complex reflections of distrust towards generosity. In both instances, Sawyer, as a representative of Macy's, cannot fathom the desire to do something selfless, especially when it pertains to giving material possessions away for free. Macy's executives, likewise, do not understand the goodwill policy as an intrinsically honest policy, but see it rather as a way to exploit customers from an emotional angle. Adding the external storyline of Sawyer misdiagnosing Alfred, an average person with a kind heart, brings in a deeper layer of not only the more understandable challenging of the mental state of an old man who claims to be Santa, but also challenging anyone's desire to give gifts solely for the purpose of giving without any added incentive. Centralizing this concern in Sawyer also allows the film to introduce this idea of the absurdity of selflessness in juxtaposition to the Macy's executives who are using that selflessness to increase profits.

In a meeting concerning Kringle's performance, Mr. Macy himself applauds the new policy. He exclaims that over 500 parents, including the governor's and mayor's wives, expressed their gratitude for the new "merchandising policy." He suggests that every department should employ the strategy, proposing "No more high pressuring and forcing a customer to take something he doesn't really want." Macy continues, realizing the profitable potential of this scheme should they lean into emotional manipulation: "We'll be known as the helpful store, the friendly store, the store with a heart, the store that places public service ahead of profits," before adding with a snide smile, "and consequently we'll make more profits than ever before." This misuse of the goodwill created by Kringle is an exploitation of the Christmas spirit, and it is never condemned within the film because it is, in the film's estimation, a good commercialist practice.

To the point, other department stores in the film – namely Gimbel's, Macy's fiercest competitor both in the film and reality – also employ the same strategy, and both expand the policy nationwide. In one scene, Santa is literally stood between Mr. Macy and Mr. Gimbel as they shake hands for a photo-op. In front of the photographers and journalists, Macy gives Kringle a sizable Christmas bonus with which Kringle says he will purchase an x-ray machine for a doctor friend, leaving Macy and Gimbel to argue over who will cover the rest of the costs. Again, the film is displaying the notion that the department store only gives value to the monetary benefits of performative philanthropy, concerning itself principally with the publicity of grand gestures. This performative philanthropy is not criticized in the film.

Alternatively, Sawyer's character is rebuked. The film is very careful in who is made the villainous character, not wanting to frame the department stores negatively. While the department store executives embracing the goodwill policy are superficially engaging correctly with the commercialization of Christmas, following Kringle's own lead, Sawyer is the embodiment of the critiques Kringle makes of the rampant commercialism he is supposedly challenging. Later in the film, Kringle is admitted to a mental hospital and says openly to Fred – his lawyer and friend – that Sawyer is "contemptible, dishonest, selfish, deceitful, vicious," continuing, "yet he's out there and I'm in here. He's called normal and I'm not. Well, if that's normal, I don't want it." Fred reminds Kringle that "what happens to [him] matters to a lot of people" and offers hope that one day things may change with the Sawyers of the world being "in here, instead of out there." Ultimately, the inclusion of this scene commits the film to the message of the correct approach to commercializing Christmas. Framing Sawyer as the villain, the character who cannot fathom kindness and selflessness, as the antithesis and threat to Santa reinforces the idea that giving gifts is good, and that those gifts can and should be purchased from "the store with a heart." What happens to the film's Kris Kringle happens to the real world's Santa Claus: he and his myth are co-opted by the department store for an exploitative commercialist scheme to sell more products and increase customer loyalty without rebuke.

This ostensibly positive portrayal of commercialism in the film creates a paradox of acting selflessly for the sole purpose of driving one's corporate profits up. Despite acknowledging it is the right thing to do to be honest with customers and help them get the right toys for a good price, the department store executives admit alternative motives. The executives explain how embracing the goodwill policy will boost customer loyalty and ultimately manipulate the consumer into thinking a selflessly generous approach to commercialism is what Macy's and other stores are striving for. As in the evasive trailer, promotional materials reflect the reality of the manipulation within the film. In the pressbook material for *Miracle on 34th Street*, there are instructions detailing how real store owners could capitalize on the goodwill policy as portrayed in the film. The pressbook reads:

NOT JUST FOR MACY AND GIMBEL, BUT FOR ALL STORES

WHY? BECAUSE THE DEPARTMENT STORE IS DEMONSTRATED AS A COMMUNITY INSTITUTION – WITH A SOUL! STORE PERSONNEL ARE NATURALLY AND HUMANELY PORTRAYED, AND THE PART PLAYED BY DEPARTMENT STORES IN THE LIVES OF CHILDREN AT CHRISTMAS CARRIES A MIGHTY PUBLIC RELATIONS MESSAGE ...

THE PICTURE DOES A POTENTIAL PUBLIC RELATIONS JOB FOR ALL STORES EVERYWHERE.

... even though this benefit is really part of the entertainment and was not planned that way.[282]

This pressbook section explains that all stores in conjunction with 34th Street in Manhattan would be participating in the tie-ins for the film with window displays, perpetual showings of the trailer for the film, and themed histories of their stores to show the humanist side of the shops themselves.

This approach to the tie-ins possible for *Miracle on 34th Street* is exploiting the same Christmas "spirit" shown in the film. By enlisting the real-world department stores in this "public relations" campaign of advertising, the stores are hoping that the good press from the film's portrayal of Macy's as the "store with a heart" will increase their own profits and customer trust. The added insistence that this positive portrayal of department stores is a happy by-product of the film's story echoes the words of the film's R. H. Macy quoted above, delivered with a snide grin and chuckle: "We'll be known as the helpful store, the friendly store, the store with a heart, the store that places public service ahead of profits. And, consequently, we'll make more profits than ever before."

Miracle on 34th Street's surface-level disdain for commercialism while advocating for consumerism at Christmas became common among Christmas films that were released subsequently. The commercialist urge to emphasize profits is crass, but the consumerist requirement to purchase gifts is integral to the celebra-

---

282 *Miracle on 34th Street* Pressbook, Twentieth Century Fox, 1947, microform, Reuben Library, British Film Institute. All font and underlining from original source.

tion of the holiday. This dichotomy of spending money on the right gift but declaring an aversion to the discussion of such spending can also be seen in a film from two years later, Don Hartman's *Holiday Affair* (1949).

Department Stores and Commercialism in *Holiday Affair* (1949)

Holiday Affair follows a single mother and war widow, Connie Ennis (Janet Leigh) and her love-life predicament at Christmas. Connie is a comparative shopper for department store Fisher & Lewis, meaning she engages in corporate espionage, purchasing products from different stores to compare quality, price, and other product information that is then reported back to Fisher & Lewis to surveil their competition's retail business practices. In the film's opening scenes, Connie interrupts a conversation store clerk Steve Mason (Robert Mitchum) is having with a young boy about a toy train Steve is operating on display. The two exchange a frigid back and forth in which Connie asserts herself as a "real customer" who "actually want[s] to buy" a train. Steve remarks that he has no reason not to believe the young boy is intent on purchasing the train as his floor manager shoots him a look encouraging him to make the sale. Already evident is the dichotomy between the customer who purchases the item and the consumer who will actually use it. Here, the child desiring the toy is the consumer who will be gifted it once an adult customer purchases it. Much like *Miracle on 34th Street*'s Kris Kringle, Steve insists on helping the children who will actually play with the toys to understand them and ensure they are asking for what they really want at Christmas.

Connie, impatient and unwilling to wait for a response on the price, hands Steve exact change for the item, "$79.50 plus tax", abruptly shuffling off while rejecting the complimentary Christmas gift-wrapping. Immediately, Steve assumes she must be a comparative shopper, and when she arrives the next day to return the train after having gathered the relevant information, he gives her a refund and is fired on the spot for allowing her corporate espionage. Steve is largely unperturbed by the firing and even assists Connie in purchasing the next item on her list while asking her out to lunch.

These exchanges set up the personalities of the two characters. Steve is unbothered with the corporate side of the department store experience, caring much more for the child consumers who will actually be using the products than for their parent customers who purchase them. Gradually, through the film, Steve's character is revealed to be a vagabond, traveling from hostel to hostel as he works odd jobs to collect enough money to follow his passion of boat building to the West Coast where he plans to buy into a company in Southern California. On their first outing together, Steve takes Connie to Central Park where he remarks that the seal in the zoo is "the happiest guy in New York" because "he'll never be the president of the First National Bank." His disdain for the monotony of everyday life and for the consumerist-led existence so many New Yorkers live is evident in most of his dialogue and facial expressions.

Later in the film, however, Steve buys the same toy train from the beginning of the film with the last of his money for Connie's son Tim (Gordon Gebert). Tim had seen the train the night Connie brought it home from work and assumed it was his Christmas present. With his heart set on this particular train, Tim is shattered when Connie scolds him for assuming it was his, only to rejoice later when the same train arrives from Steve. With Steve's act of purchasing the expensive gift for Connie's son, knowing that opening the gift on Christmas morning will bring the boy joy, Steve's hard exterior of personal disdain for the commercialist way of life softens. Despite his repeated displays of disaffection for the profit-driven department store ethos, Steve purchases the train in a selfless act to make Tim happy. Steve's actions in the face of his disdain for the cold, corporate commercialism that Kris Kringle is also fighting against in *Miracle on 34th Street* parallel much of Kringle's own attitudes and actions as Santa Claus.

Conversely, Connie's character, as built from her initial exchanges with Steve, is indicative of the negative aspects of commercialism. Her role as an agent of corporate espionage is to pose as an unassuming customer, an average woman out for the day shopping in other department stores so as to inform her store on the competition's pricing, product display, product quality, and customer service. Multiple times, Connie is presented as bad at her job of being a customer. Steve mockingly gives her tips on how to pretend to be a better customer, suggesting she's "much too professional". Connie's stern and detached shopping habits for her job and her refusal to purchase the toy train her son truly wants for Christmas represent everything Steve dislikes about the commercialist sector, especially at Christmas.

Here again, however, as in *Miracle on 34th Street*, the department store executives are not made out to be the villains. When Tim receives the toy train from Steve on Christmas morning, the rest of the film revolves around what to do with it. Connie's boyfriend Carl (Wendell Corey) is uncomfortable with the gesture Steve has made and suspects that Steve is trying to get in close with Tim so as to win his mother's affection. Steve asserts that he just wanted to give a young kid the gift he really wanted, leaving Connie torn over the happiness of her son, the suspicions of her partner, and her own unexpectedly warm feelings towards Steve. Ultimately, Tim decides he wants to return the gift so that the adults in his life will stop arguing over it and that he may give the money back to Steve because Connie makes it clear Steve needs the money more than Tim needs the train.

On his own, Tim runs away to return the train to Crowley's department store and meets with Mr. Crowley himself to explain the economic troubles Steve is in, asking for a refund on the $79.50 Steve spent on the toy. Mr. Crowley gives the 6-year-old a refund and drives him home to Connie who is worried sick over Tim's disappearance. This scene firmly suggests, as *Miracle on 34th Street* does, that the department store executives are the heroes with hearts of gold while simulta-neously throughout the film villainizing Connie's corporate shopper role. Connie's employment in the film represents the cold, corporate side of the department stores as Mr. Sawyer's does in *Miracle on 34th Street*, while also depicting depart-ment stores as a safe haven when they employ empathetic, sentimental, and hu-manist consumer-focused commercialist tactics.

Steve and Connie, at the start of the film, are polar opposites. Steve is sponta-neous and fun, living only within his means and despising the corporate system; Connie is kind and pleasant, but rigid and structured in her life, feeling the need to control everything so as to maintain order in her single-parent household. By the end of the film, Connie softens and runs away with her son to catch Steve on his midnight train to California, presumably leaving her job at Fisher & Lewis for a more spontaneous lifestyle. Steve, on the other hand, seems to maintain his dispo-sition throughout the film. His disdain for all of the things Connie represents at the start remains throughout the film, even as he engages in consumerism when buy-ing the toy train for her son.

Connie's boyfriend, Carl, is also rigid, not spontaneous, and awkward around Tim. Connie and Carl have an uncomfortable multi-year relationship in which Carl has proposed marriage numerous times, only to be told by Connie that they should wait. Tim doesn't like Carl very much and is visibly upset when Connie finally tells him that she has made up her mind and is going to marry Carl on New Year's Day only a week later. With the introduction of Steve into their lives, Carl notices small but distinct changes in Connie's behavior and the ways in which Tim immediately takes a liking to Steve. Carl begins to fear for their relationship and lashes out to-wards Steve with cynicism, voicing suspicions about his generosity that parallel Mr. Sawyer's diagnosis of Alfred in *Miracle on 34th Street*. Similarly, this accusation of impropriety and the instigating gift-giving itself become the turning point for the rest of the film. By spending the money he has been saving for his next adventure on her son and showing him the affection he does not receive from either Connie or Carl, Steve becomes a Santa figure to Tim, putting all else aside for the sake of a child's joy at Christmas.

On Christmas morning, Tim wakes Connie and races to the living room to open presents. He has saved up all year to buy Connie her favorite perfume. This sweet moment is cut short when he begins thanking Santa for the train, and Connie re-alizes Steve must have purchased it for him. Carl calls to wish the pair a merry Christmas ahead of coming round for dinner later and becomes irate again when he hears about Tim's train. Carl accuses Steve of trying to make a pass at

Connie by buying her son gifts, claiming that no man would have done that out of the kindness of his heart for a stranger's son without an angle of wanting to get close to the boy's single mother. As in *Miracle on 34th Street*, the characters who cannot fathom someone wanting to do a kindness for a child with no reciprocity are indicative of the cold, distant, and negative sides of commercialism at Christmas. Selflessness is seen as a ploy, and here Carl's fears become a self-fulfilling prophecy as Connie does ultimately choose Steve for the kindnesses shown to her son as well as her own sudden attraction to him.

When Carl accuses Steve of having a self-interested angle in buying the train, Connie is confused and concerned about what to do. This is the moment her character begins to change and be influenced by Steve's. She states that Steve didn't have the money to spend on this expensive train and that she is determined to get the money back to him. Carl offers to pay for the train, so as to act as though he saved the day with the pretense that, ultimately, he is the one who paid for it and so Tim should be thankful to him. Tim sees Connie's despair and offers to return all of his other gifts to the department store to raise the money to give back to Steve for the train. Tim's consumerist mentality is the same as that which Kris Kringle exposes in *Miracle on 34th Street:* giving a child the gift he or she wants for Christmas is more important than giving just any gift. Tim's willingness to return all of his other gifts solely to be able to keep the one he actually wanted shows further that Connie is disengaged from what her child actually wants.

The commercialism of Christmas in these two films revolves around the department store as a source of goodness while condemning the people who see shopping as a means to a selfish end. Any character who takes issue with giving a gift for the sole purpose of a child's joy on Christmas morning further suggests a personal selfishness or even alleged mental illness for doing so. This attack on those characters who would give selflessly is further supported by the department store executives, namely R. H. Macy and Mr. Crowley, who embrace – so as to exploit – the Christmas spirit. The films' suggestion that there is a good reason and specific way to commercialize Christmas – by putting the children's wants first and being "the store with a heart" – as opposed to the negative, more selfish reasons of profits and personal gain, come together to shape the consumer's experience as an activity that should be embraced and enjoyed. The films in this study not only instruct businesses on how to portray a positive commercialization of Christmas but also instruct shoppers on how to be good consumers during the holiday.

Consumerism and How to Shop, on Film and in Print

Shopping in department stores, as explored above, was an integral part of the metropolitan culture many Americans enjoyed. The ways in which people shopped in these Palaces of Consumption are documented both in the films of this study and in magazines and women's chronicles such as *LIFE, Ladies' Home Journal, Redbook, Women's Day, Seventeen*, and more. Frequently in these publications, shopping tips and advice were conveyed through sponsored content advertisements and stories of women going about the family shopping or making personal purchases. These shopping guides and sponsored suggestions give insight into not only how people shopped, but also the ways in which print media wanted people to shop as compared to how Hollywood movies presented shopping.

A primary focus of the advertisements and shopping tip guides in women's publications was the raising of young girls to be smart shoppers, something Connie had not mastered in *Holiday Affair*. This training included hunting for the best bargains, learning about the shops themselves, and making shopping decisions on their own while supervised by their mothers. One SWAN soap advertisement from a 1946 issue of *LIFE* is entitled, "How to Bring Up a Young Daughter: Tips from a Teen-ager's Smart Mama!"[283] The by-line of the advertisement – itself structured as a photo-essay – begins, "Lucy's mother has big dreams for Lucy: She wants her 13-year-old daughter to have the fun of being pretty and popular right now. And she knows ... that this just leads up to the day Lucy will leave to start a home of her own." The advertisement continues to present six tips with accompanying photos, the first of which is "learning to be a smart shopper." Part of the process of learning to be a smart shopper, according to *LIFE*, is Lucy's abilities to learn "to compare. And know a thrifty value when she sees it." The final tip of the section for raising a daughter correctly as a woman is "choosing her own wardrobe," emphasizing that, "Mother lets Lucy buy some of her clothes – with just a word of advice," and while promoting the soap in the sponsored content, the tip reminds its readers "pretty clothes must be *clean*." This photo-essay collection is not rare among the pages of women's publications. Rather it perpetuates a common view that learning how to shop and, equally as importantly, what to purchase is a key skill in a young girl's development into a woman who is ready to be a wife.

The emphasis on learning to be a discerning shopper who hunts for bargains and compares the quality of products against the price is evident throughout both printed publications and the films in this study. In another advertisement from

---

283 "How to Bring Up a Young Daughter: Tips from a Teen-Ager's Smart Mama!", *LIFE*, March 11, 1946, ProQuest.

LIFE in a 1951 issue on the importance of smart shopping to buy luxuries with the savings, A&P Super Market boasts that, "My food budget bought the bouquet – thanks to A&P!" while showing the various ways a "test shop" at their stores would help women find the best prices around for their weekly shop.[284] With the development of supermarkets as a form of department store in which all the groceries could be purchased at once without needing to attend various shops or pay at each counter – e.g. the grocer, butcher, baker, etc. – women were incentivized to become acquainted with their shopping experience as a single trip with one receipt, making tallying and saving easier.[285] *Redbook* in 1960 included an article entitled "How to Avoid Being Cheated By the Pound, Gallon or Yard: How to Make Sure You Get What You Pay For" in which the authors provide tips for being a better shopper anywhere, but specifically addressing the issues of "housewives" in New York City who "were complaining bitterly about meat markets which failed to give them full weight."[286] There was a considerable variety of articles in women's journals from the post-war period and throughout the 1950s addressing women's concerns of how to shop and advising them on the best shopping practices.

Throughout both *Miracle on 34ᵗʰ Street* and *Holiday Affair,* there is much emphasis on the ways people, and particularly women, participated in consumerism. Their shopping habits were key to the plot of *Miracle on 34ᵗʰ Street* with Kris Kringle marketing the commercialism of Macy's directly towards mothers seeking the best prices for their children's gifts and citing the customer who, bewildered by the goodwill policy, praises Macy's for making it so much easier to engage with the shopping season. The same constructions of women being good, smart, calculating shoppers that are used in sponsored content advertisements and articles in women's journals are used in *Miracle on 34ᵗʰ Street*, pointing towards the desired perception both in print media and in Hollywood's portrayal that shopping is not only an activity performed by women, but also one perfected by them.

This idea of women perfecting the art of shopping is used as the punchline to a recurring joke throughout *Holiday Affair.* Connie is a corporate comparison shopper and notoriously bad at her job. Steve immediately recognizes her as such, saying "[you] didn't ask me a lot about the train; didn't ask me the price, but you had the exact amount all ready, including the tax. You didn't want me to send it. You didn't want Christmas wrapping," adding, "It didn't take the greatest brain in the world to spell out 'corporate shopper'." This exchange not only moves the plot

284 "A&P Super Markets Advertisement", *LIFE*, July 9, 1951, ProQuest.
285 Gordon, *The Rise and Fall of American Growth*, 341.
286 Ruth Brecher and Edward Brecher, "How to Avoid Being Cheated By the Pound, Gallon or Yard: How to Make Sure You Get What You Pay For", *Redbook*, August 1960, ProQuest.

along in getting Steve fired for not reporting Connie to his employer, but it also sends the message to the audience that a good, smart, discerning shopper would inquire about the product and its quality, ask about the price, and then make a value judgement for herself instead of knowing ahead of time what she wanted and how much it would cost.

The film makes an even clearer assessment of women shopping when Steve gives Connie tips on how to be a better shopper, saying, "you're much too professional. A customer doesn't know what she wants until she sees it, and then she doesn't want it." Throughout the film, Connie is teased for her bad judgement when purchasing gifts and her terrible taste in men's neckties. Her character's inability to shop seems to parallel her inability to decide on whom she wants to be with, Steve or Carl, and adds to the presentation of her primarily as a mother and widow more than as a woman in her own right. The fun the film pokes at her poor shopping habits is a character judgement on her confidence in her womanhood, a joke that would likely land well with an audience of women primed to be good shoppers from the time they first started reading women's magazines and journals.

In other articles, women were taught to want to shop, and more exactly, how to want to shop. In the same 1946 issue of *LIFE* in which the SWAN advertisement explored above was featured, appeared the article "Naked at Bergdorf's: A Shopper's Dream Takes Place in New York Store." This photo-essay follows model Stasia Linder as she starts "practically naked" and wanders through the store accompanied by a photographer to capture her living "every shopper's dream – of starting from scratch on a shopping binge with unlimited funds and nothing to 'match.'"[287] The article advises that Bergdorf Goodman's department store is the ideal place to live out this fantasy, describing it as "an elegant place with carpeted floors, crystal chandeliers and refined but not supercilious salesgirls." It continues: "In it one can buy all the beautifully useful and silly things women like. It has $45 panties, $75 shoes, $50,000 sables and swansdown powder puffs for 25¢."[288] Following Stasia around the shop, *LIFE* documents all the finery she picks out starting in a slip and building her outfit from nothing while taking careful consideration about what luxury items she might want.

"Naked at Bergdorf's" is projecting multiple ideas for women readers to internalize. Firstly, the photo-essay is informing women that shopping to match items they already own is burdensome, and it instils the idea and desire to build a ward-

---

287 "Naked at Bergdorf's: A Shopper's Dream Takes Place in New York Store", *LIFE*, March 11, 1946, 85, ProQuest.
288 "Naked at Bergdorf'", 85.

robe from scratch. This insistence that women want to shop from lingerie up challenges the fashion concept of "staple pieces", the garments women would be trying to match while shopping. Instead, it projects the idea that to be a real shopper, one must fantasize about building a wardrobe of outfits rather than a cohesive set of interchangeable garments. This mentality about the wardrobe is designed to convince women to shop regularly and in larger quantities. Secondly, the article is defining the atmosphere of a proper shop being one of grandeur and fanciful, ornate design in which a woman of any class could shop for anything from a cheap powder puff to an elaborate fur and still experience the shopper's dream of elegance and luxury. Thirdly, "Naked at Bergdorf's" undercuts all of this by reasserting that the things women want to buy are either useful or silly, tapping into the idea that shopping should be both a practical and a fun experience. Linking these two ideas frames shopping as an activity one can do in most moods, from serious to jovial, while also telling women how to behave and how to want to behave while performing the activity.

The print media's instructions on how to shop are echoed in the films in this study. *Holiday Affair*'s Connie, as explained above, is repeatedly told she is a bad shopper, that she doesn't know how to play the part of a shopper well enough. She buys bad gifts, and she knows what she wants when she walks in a store. Stasia Linder shopping in Bergdorf's doesn't know what she wants from the experience, so instead wanders the departments staged in photos with shoes of all sorts scattered around her as though she has tried them all, with elegant floor length gowns draped over chairs that she'll get to next. The prescriptive ideas in both *LIFE* Magazine and *Holiday Affair* suggest there is a correct way to engage with the shopping experience that is expounded on further in some women's publications and Hollywood films in this era.

The Bishop's Wife (1947) also plays with this idea of how a woman should shop properly. In the film, Julia (Loretta Young) is shown repeatedly admiring a hat in a store window. She knows she should not spend the money on it, but her admiration for the ornate hat draws her in repeatedly. The relationship between this hat and this presentation of a woman shopping offers a more overt link between Hollywood's messaging and its shopper audience than any other of the films, as this hat was used as a tie-in for department stores upon release of the film. Following an industry fashion as established and perfected in the 1920s and 1930s, *The Bishop's Wife* uses Loretta Young's fame to encourage department stores to recreate the hat and use promotional material from the film to sell it.

Loretta Young, in 1947, would have been no stranger to film tie-ins and exclusive fashion recreations of her filmic outfits in department stores. As Charles Eckert notes in his analysis of Hollywood's commercial tie-ins, Loretta Young was a starlet used for her fame as an advertising model throughout the 1930s to promote

Hollywood fashions with the "aura of exclusivity" that surrounded her.[289] The hat in the pressbook materials, designed to encourage the tie-in, works in the same ways Eckert identifies from the earlier Hollywood commercial practice. As the pressbook states, "In gay relief to the decorous costumes Loretta Young wears in Samuel Goldwyn's 'The Bishop Wife' is an ultra-feminine, breath of spring bonnet."[290] This section of the pressbook continues to outline how to present a re-creation of the hat by a local department store or millinery club and advises that the advert must acknowledge that the hat is a re-creation and not directly from the film.

The language used in the pressbook material functions in the same way *LIFE* Magazine comments on women's shopping as both "useful and silly". By describing the hat as a "gay relief" as juxtaposed with the "decorous costumes" of Loretta Young, the intention is to convince the shopper that the hat is a fanciful luxury as opposed to the practical, restrained clothing the character, and likely the shopper, dons on an average day. Describing the hat as "ultra-feminine" and a "breath of spring" additionally underpins the selling point of perceived luxury. With the film release dated for November 1947, the language of the promotional material was intended to inspire thoughts of spring during a cold late-autumn and to highlight the "ultra-feminine" quality of the hat in opposition to practical, restrained clothing. This smart marketing tactic was intended to attract shoppers who may be wearing less-fashionable cold-weather coats or dreaming of warmer weather. The promotional materials for the film, as well as the shopping scenes in which Loretta Young's character interacts with the hat, are engaging in the same marketing technique as the "Naked at Bergdorf's" article and Hollywood's tie-in practices in informing women what they want to buy, why they want to buy it, and how they want to shop for it.

While shopping, the place in which a thing is purchased and the experience had while purchasing it are portrayed on screen and in print as integral aspects to the cultural practice, especially as part of Christmas, the gift-giving holiday. The items chosen to be purchased in the films, however, can indicate economic and social changes in the wider world when scrutinized more closely. With these portrayals from how to be a good consumer and customer in *The Bishop's Wife* and *Holiday Affair* as well as in the women's journals of the day, and with the added condemnation of overt commercialism emphasizing profits from *Miracle on 34th Street*, this chapter will now turn to the items that were actually pur-

---

289 Charles Eckert, "The Carole Lombard in Macy's Window", in *Stardom: Industry of Desire*, ed. Christine Gledhill (New York: Routledge, 1991), 34.
290 *The Bishop's Wife* Pressbook, RKO Radio Pictures, 1947, microform, Reuben Library, British Film Institute, 16.

chased with a case study on the changing social perceptions throughout the 15-year period of one item in particular: mink.

Gifts

Gifts at Christmas are a fundamental part of the holiday's observances for many Americans and have been for centuries. The tradition's increasing growth and the linking of gift-giving with consumerism can be seen as reflective of the strength of the American economy through the nineteenth and twentieth centuries.[291] The gift-giving aspect of Christmas as portrayed in the films of this study, therefore, offers a unique perspective on Hollywood's attitudes towards the health of the economy over the period. The portrayal of gift-giving simultaneously offers insight into the reasons people use to justify giving presents and also expectations with regard to the gifts themselves.

Material commodities transferred as gifts throughout the films are sometimes key plot devices – such as the above-mentioned toy train in *Holiday Affair* or the house Susan asks for in *Miracle on 34th Street*. Some gifts are more symbolic gestures, however, such as another prominent gift in *Holiday Affair:* the tacky neckties. Connie, already characterized as a poor shopper, is the punchline of a recurring joke throughout the film focused on her equally poor taste in buying neckties. Connie is known for buying loud, garish ties as gifts for both her late husband and her boyfriend Carl, and this becomes a symbol of her romantic interest. When she gives a necktie intended for Carl to Steve as a gift of reciprocity for Tim's train, Carl becomes irate and concerned, knowing the gesture means that she is open to finding love again and remarrying, only not to him. Similarly symbolic, Steve's gift of the train seems to suggest that Steve would be an attentive, caring, well-communicative father-figure to Tim, having taken into consideration what the boy actually wants for Christmas.

Commodities in these Christmas films take on specific meanings and are used as devices to further story development. Some commodities are also used to convey social status and character growth depending on the interactions characters have with them throughout the film. One such item that is present in several of the films and portrays a variety of meanings and usages is the mink coat. The use of mink in films over the 15-year period offers an interesting focus for a case study to explore the changing attitudes towards one specific area of the market: luxury items. Focusing on the category of luxury goods shows an important

---

291 Restad, *Christmas in America*, 123.

aspect of wider attitudes concerning commodities. Luxury by nature is something that is not essential for basic comforts, but rather has connotations of extravagance. Mink coats and other fur clothing were once consumed as an absolute necessity to keep warm in bitter winters. However, as that need diminished with better-heated homes, public spaces, and automobiles, mink slid up the spectrum from need to want to luxury.[292] From the immediate post-war period through the early 1960s, there were marked changes in the social attitudes towards furs. This case study will examine how that change was received by consumers and reflected in Christmas films released in the 15-year period from 1946 to 1961.

Case Study: The Cultural Life of Mink

Mink clothing has a long history in the United States. Originally, fur clothing was used, as it was for centuries before, as a source of warmth and survival against harsh weather conditions. In the early twentieth century, these survival needs were no longer as ubiquitous, and fur clothing, particularly mink, evolved into a status symbol as a piece of luxury fashion by the mid-century.[293] This development in the uses and perceptions of mink is best seen in the 15-year period of this study and evident in several of the Christmas films within it. Mink, in this period and these films, was used as a status symbol, a political statement, a personality trait, and an indicator of the cultural capital one had in a metropolitan space. Mink's use as both fashion and political statements and its repeated appearances on films from 1946 to 1961 offer a balanced case study to examine the changing attitudes towards not only mink, but also the growing affluence throughout these 15 years. By examining the portrayals of mink across these films and also the fashion and political atmospheres in the real world, it is possible to trace the changes in some market attitudes towards consumption and conclude that Hollywood's cultural media was capturing and reflecting the changing tones in American public attitudes throughout the period.

In the immediate post-war period, fashion designers such as Christian Dior saw a need to bring luxury back to women's wardrobes. With his spring line of 1947 debuting in Paris, Dior later recounted that "We were leaving a period of war, of uniforms, of soldier-women with shoulders like boxers," and sought to

---

292 Ruth Turner Wilcox, *The Mode in Furs: The History of Furred Costume of the World from the Earliest Times to the Present* (New York: Charles Scribner's Sons, 1951), 162.
293 Wilcox, 162.

bring femininity back to women's fashion.[294] His line ushered in fashions that would not hit mainstream American consumers for a few years, but introduced women to the notions of luxurious suits, extravagant hats, and broad, full skirts. On 1 March 1948, *LIFE* magazine ran a five-page story on the man and his new fashion trends dubbed "The New Look."

The article claimed that a nation-wide organization of 300,000 women, the Little Below the Knee Club, "succumbed to the overwhelming pressure of events and admitted that its valiant fight to preserve America from the New Look had ended in defeat" after nearly a year by early 1948. Dior's New Look featured low-cut dresses, higher hems, padded hips, exaggerated hour-glass figures, and sensuous designs for women that ultimately won many admirers in the US.[295] After years of the Depression and war rationing, the post-war period was ready for a change – a move towards luxury and finery, albeit at affordable prices. Women, according to Marling, "learned to covet ensembles in which shoes, bags, and even perfume were carefully coordinated by a designer to achieve an artful totality."[296] Gradually, from Dior's Parisian debut of the New Look through protests against the trend's immodesty, the American public learned to embrace this lavish, if not excessive, consumer expense as a new necessity of the 1950s.

As the introduction and appropriation of Parisian fashion made its way into the nation's average fashion, the political sphere began to weigh in on the trends. On September 23, 1952, six weeks ahead of the presidential election Republicans Dwight D. Eisenhower and Richard Nixon would win, Nixon as the prospective Vice-President gave a televised speech concerning his personal finances. Five days prior to the speech, allegations were published in the *New York Post* claiming Nixon was being financed by a private trust fund that kept him "in style far beyond his salary" and accused the candidate of misappropriating campaign funds for personal purchases.[297] To confront this fund crisis, Nixon delivered the speech claiming that all private fund contributions were accepted appropriately and legally and explicitly used for political matters. The speech was later dubbed the "Checkers Speech" after his black and white cocker spaniel whom Nixon mentions his family received as a gift after winning his first election as a United States Senator in 1950. In mentioning Checkers, as well as discussing his personal and family finances, Nixon successfully diverted attention away from the political implications of his fi-

294 Karal Ann Marling, *As Seen on TV: The Visual Culture of Everyday Life in the 1950s* (Cambridge, MA: Harvard University Press, 1994), 9.
295 Jeanne Perkins, "Dior", *LIFE*, March 1, 1948, 85, ProQuest.
296 Marling, *As Seen on TV*, 10.
297 *New York Post* article quoted in John W. Malsberger, "Dwight Eisenhower, Richard Nixon, and the Fund Crisis of 1952" *The Historian* 73, no. 3 (2011): 526.

nances and towards the sentimentality of his wife, children, and family pet.[298] This diversion towards his personal relationships, among other deceptions, helped to mislead the public and shift focus from the questionable details of the accounts and funds, while politicizing certain purchases and gifts including the allegation of his wife owning a mink coat.

The speech was seen by an unprecedented 58 million people and garnered overwhelming support of the candidate after near 8,000 telegrams were sent backing Nixon.[299] After this outpouring of support, Eisenhower was convinced to keep Nixon on the ticket for the ensuing election; however, many historians believe this crisis to be a turning-point in the relationship of the president and his Vice-President. Eisenhower's trust in his running mate was diminished from then on, leaving the two men with a tense and even hostile relationship.[300] The Checkers speech was a significant moment in the election campaign not only for the eventual President and his Vice-President, but also for the framing of morals in the Republican party. In this speech, Nixon opened his personal accounts to scrutiny and made a crucial but poignant joke on the stance of the Republican party: "Pat doesn't have a mink coat. But she does have a respectable Republican cloth coat, and I always tell her she'd look good in anything."[301]

Following the war, the American economy had recovered slowly. There was a housing crisis in the late 1940s, a slow decrease of the unemployment rate, and a return to some sense of what could be considered a new normal economic status after decades of fluctuation, depression, and world wars. This recovery opened the US to a new form of purchasing power that shifted economic priorities and the definition of what some would label as "essential".[302] As Nixon remarks, his wife Pat had a "respectable Republican cloth coat". In the years leading up to this speech, there is evidence from the films in this study of the idea of the cloth coat as a respectable alternative to luxurious, expensive mink. These films, as well as Nixon's remarks, frame mink and furs as a symbol of ill repute and undeserved wealth, a view that would change considerably across the films from the 1950s.

In *It's a Wonderful Life* (1946), Violet (Gloria Grahame) comes to George in her hour of need and asks him for a loan so she can start a new life in New York City.

---

298 "The 'Checkers Speech' (September 23, 1952)", in *Richard Nixon: Speeches, Writings, Documents*, ed. Rick Perlstein (Princeton: Princeton University Press, 2008), 76.
299 James Devitt, "Tokens of Deception in the 'Checkers' Speech", *Political Communication*, 15, no. 1 (December 1998): 1.
300 Malsberger, "Dwight Eisenhower, Richard Nixon", 527.
301 "The 'Checkers' Speech", 76.
302 Nigel Whiteley, "Toward a Throw-Away Culture. Consumerism, 'Style Obsolescence' and Cultural Theory in the 1950s and 1960s", *Oxford Art Journal* 10, no. 2 (1987): 8.

Violet feels shamed and disgraced in Bedford Falls owing to her overt sexuality and inability to fit in with the small-town life; she feels living in an urban setting would be more appropriate for her personality and character. While this scene, and the alternative world sequence in Pottersville in which Violet is manhandled and disrespected as a loose woman, can be read as commentaries on the juxtaposition of urban versus small-town life, George makes an offhanded joke that also highlights the disparity between Violet's character and the respectability portrayed by others. George hands Violet money from his own pocket for her move to New York and, in her hesitancy to take it, he asks, "what do you want to do, hock your furs, and that hat?" George's comment is a quick joke but embedded within it is the view many Americans had towards fur and young single women: that furs could represent a part of a woman, be it her personality or physical body.

Clothing in general is often used as a symbol of a person's character, personality, social class, gender, or other outward presentation of the self. Theories around clothing and fashion sense are particularly helpful for analyzing filmic representations of characters. As Patrizia Calefato writes, in cinema "every sign on the body of a character has a precise meaning, linked to social characterization, historical identity, grotesque emphasis, transformation in terms of personality or feeling, and so on."[303] The signs on the body often transcend a scene's audio and offer a new avenue of visual interpretation for the characters portrayed, allowing one to read how the characters present themselves. Calefato continues, "in the great sense-making machine of cinema, costume represents yet another signifying system, the signs of which become distinctive features, functioning as linguistic units that are often more important than script or soundtrack."[304] Violet's furs are indicative not only of her fashion sense, but even more so of her personality and the person she presents herself as.

In a study on mink in film noir, Petra Dominkova discusses the use of furs strategically on screen. She writes that fur in this period was often used as a point of personality for a character and as a juxtaposition between two women: films can "differentiate between the woman in mink as a rotten, selfish dame and an unpredictable force, and her mink-less antithesis, the maternal 'good' woman who cares about her child and household."[305] In the scenes involving Violet, she is distinguished from characters such as George's wife Mary (Donna Reed) not only due to her personality but also explicitly due to the furs she wears. Mary

---

303 Patrizia Calefato, *The Clothed Body*, trans. Lisa Adams (Oxford: Berg, 2004), 91.
304 Calefato, 91.
305 Petra Dominkova, "I Want That Mink! *Film Noir* and Fashion", in *If Looks Could Kill: Cinema's Images of Fashion, Crime and Violence*, ed. Marketa Uhlirova (London: Koenig Books and Fashion in Film Festival, 2008), 140.

is always dressed in plain, sensible clothing, never overtly glamourous. Violet, on the other hand, is repeatedly referencing her own clothing with her on-screen presence dominated by acknowledgements of the way she looks.

In one scene at the beginning of the film, Violet, in a beautiful seemingly satin day dress and matching hat, stops to say hello to George who is speaking with Bert the cop (Ward Bond) and Ernie the cab driver (Frank Faylen). George comments on her appearance saying "Hey, you look good. That's some dress you got on there" to which Violet responds with a hair flick, "Oh, this old thing? I only wear it when I don't care how I look." This is the first introduction of an adult Violet in the film, immediately objectified for her outward appearance and enjoying the attention it attracts. One man stops in his tracks in the middle of the street as she walks by, stopping traffic to watch her walk away. George, Bert, and Ernie are visibly flustered by their own sexualizing of her, taking a moment to snap back to reality. This scene introduces the sexualizing of Violet that will continue throughout the rest of the film and was initially perceived as such, so much so that the Production Code Administration (PCA) flagged it as "unacceptable because of its offensive sex suggestiveness."[306]

In her moment of vulnerability, when she asks for help from George in starting over, Violet drops the pretense of the confident, strong woman she has portrayed thus far. That George jokes that she would sell her furs or hat with fur on it is indicative of her options: she may either change her personality and powerful presence by selling the furs, or she can take his money and continue living with the air of glamorous superiority. This moment of vulnerability is an intense one for her, bringing her to tears, as she recognizes she is not comfortable in the small town under the reputation by which she has come to be known by her neighbors. When George delivers this joke, he frames it as absurd that Violet would even consider selling the furs, knowing her outward presentation as confident, ambitious, sexual, and powerful is important to her sense of self.

With this theoretical view of the importance of clothing, and furs specifically, as tied inherently to filmic characters' personalities, this line from George can be read as almost metaphorical of Violet selling part of herself to start her new life in New York City. Repeatedly, in the PCA files for *It's a Wonderful Life*, there are notes regarding the "characterization of Violet as a prostitute" through allusions and unfinished sentences in the script that sparked concern within the PCA.[307] These files do not note the use of fur as part of Violet's over-sexual behavior. However, the

---

306 Correspondence from Joseph I. Breen, "Page 4: March 6, 1946", *It's a Wonderful Life*, Motion Picture Association of America – Production Code Administration Records, Margaret Herrick Library Digital Collections, digital ID 102_074357_p003.
307 Breen.

choices made in dressing Violet, the use of furs in the final cut of the film, and the joke made by George about selling her furs – a part of her personality – in order to start her new life in metropolitan New York do fall in line with contemporary portrayals of fur in other films from the decade as analyzed by Dominkova. Violet's furs and George's comments point to the familiar ill-repute and negative connotations of fur that audiences in the immediate post-war period may have brought to the film.

In the following year, 1947, two films make mention of furs in more substantial ways. In *Christmas Eve*, Michael (George Brent) is courting a wealthy woman, Harriet (Molly Lamont), with the intention of proposing to her. Michael does not love this woman and has a girlfriend on the side. However, he feels he must marry Harriet, claiming the marriage is "destiny", to gain her family's fortunes so he may pay off his own overwhelming debts. In order to propose, he purchases on credit a $32,000 sable coat, a blue sapphire, and other expensive gifts far exceeding his own finances. Harriet rejects his proposal, but keeps the coat and jewelry, leaving Michael broke and helpless without the option of returning the coat for a refund. He believed the fur and other expensive gifts would solve his financial problems by securing him a rich wife, but the coat damages him further and is referenced multiple times throughout the film as a needless waste of money. This representation of a fur coat as a meddlesome, wasteful garment echoes the negative connotations surrounding fur in this period as confirmed five years later by Nixon in his Checkers speech.

Likewise, *It Happened on 5ᵗʰ Avenue* (1947) has a more sentimental portrayal of mink that directly supports Vice-Presidential candidate Nixon's later views. When Trudy (Gale Storm) returns to her father's mansion to find an outfit for a job interview, she discovers Mac (Victor Moore) and Jim (Don DeFore) squatting in the house. She disguises herself as a thief and says she only needs to borrow a coat, promising she will return it after the interview. Mac allows her access to a coat on the condition she does not take the mink, "but something less expensive." Later in the film, for Christmas, Jim gives Trudy a cloth coat and says, "It may not be mink, but you sure make it look like it." Trudy says she cannot accept the gift because he does not have the money for it to which Jim replies, "well, it's Christmas." In this exchange and the former comment on mink's expense, Dominkova's observation that mink is a personality indicator is confirmed. Trudy begins the film as a wealthy and errant teenager who owns and wears mink coats, but through the course of her humbling character arc, she becomes more compassionate, more endearing, and more sensitive to the luxuries she enjoyed in her former life. Trudy cries and leaves the room, touched by Jim's gift of a cloth coat, embracing the shift towards respectability and her newfound desire to marry Jim and settle down in a way she earlier resisted. By not giving Trudy a mink coat for Christmas, Jim allowed Trudy to complete her character arc into a more domestic, "maternal 'good' woman".[308]

Nixon's remarks on mink coats and the contrasting idea of a respectable Republican cloth coat are reflective of a prevalent view within his contemporary culture on the subject of mink. Prior to World War II, throughout the 1920s and 30s, mink was a staple in many people's wardrobes for its practical usage; however, due to the war effort demand on resources, this style of coat became scarce.[309] The later 1940s witnessed years of a post-war economy working its way back to a sense of normalcy and meeting the fresh demands of a peacetime market, including recovering products, such as fur garments, back from the scarcity they had experienced during the war. This reintroduction of mink and other furs to the market stabilized throughout the 1950s while maintaining the perception of fur as a luxurious status symbol. From the early 1950s onwards, however, as the economy stabilized and grew healthily, popular attitudes towards the acceptability of owning and wearing mink for classes below the wealthiest did begin to change with help from one person in particular: First Lady Mamie Eisenhower.

By 1952, the American fashion business had turned to cheaper imitations of Paris's most popular new trends. This greater accessibility for the lower-income general population, combined with the economy beginning to recover from the post-war housing crisis and income inequality, helped to garner widespread support and appreciation among American shoppers. One such admirer of Dior's New Look, the arguable pioneer of the New Look in mainstream America, was Mrs. Mamie Eisenhower, First Lady of the United States from 1953 to 1961. Mamie Eisenhower's love for fashion was well-known and she was herself well-photographed, appearing in both national and international publications even before her husband became president. No stranger to hunting for a good bargain, Mamie gleefully recounted stories of shopping in Macy's and Bloomingdale's department stores for the mass-produced American versions of Parisian vogue.[310] As a fashion icon for the American market during the booming consumer culture of the 1950s, the First Lady's style choices set a standard for the American woman with many accessories and ensembles. One accessory that gained historic renown and signified a newfound American obsession with fashion essentials was the mink coat.

In a publicized tour of the executive mansion in December after the 1952 election, three months after Nixon's Checkers Speech, soon-to-be-former First Lady

308 Dominkova, "I Want That Mink!", 140.
309 Dominkova, 138.
310 Marling, *As Seen on TV*, 20–23.

Bess Truman and First Lady-elect Mamie Eisenhower posed under the portico for a picture, with Mamie in a floor-length mink coat. When prodded by the press about the material of the expensive-looking coat, she replied, overjoyed, "Mink, of course."[311] Mamie's pleasure in revealing that she owned a mink coat fewer than three months after Nixon's smart remark about the respectability of a "Republican cloth coat" is indicative of a shifting sense of acceptability in terms of owning mink. As one fashion writer, Ruth Turner Wilcox, wrote in her 1951 book *The Mode in Furs* concerning the state of fur in fashions worldwide, "A truly wonderful fairy tale is the saga of furs." That saga recounted the new ability for men and women in the modern world to wear furs not out of a necessity for warmth and survival as primitive peoples did, but rather for luxury. She continues: "We have come a long way from the severe sumptuary decrees of olden times in which only aristocracy was permitted to own and wear fine furs and when even nobility, if not of royal blood, was told what width their fur trimming might be."[312] While some of her points are contentious – including one in which she writes that "the luxury of the fur garment is available to people in all walks of life" – her words in 1951 are representative of a growing change abroad that would make its way to the United States in the ensuing years. This change of more people gaining access to the luxuries that once belonged only to the highest social classes and aristocracies around the world was made even more evident by Mamie Eisenhower's mink in 1952.

That the First Lady of the United States could own a mink coat in the early 1950s – and proudly wear it – was an important moment for the visibility of the health of the American economy. Mamie Eisenhower was, as noted above, both a fashion icon and also, as one historian describes her, "an avatar of 1950s consumption-oriented US society, that society that had been so recently scarred by the depredations and collective trauma of the Great Depression and World War II."[313] This consumption-oriented society was made possible by the growing health of the economy throughout the 1950s and the dawn of what John Kenneth Galbraith termed in 1958 "the affluent society".

In *The Affluent Society*, Galbraith maps the ways in which American society had changed economically since WWII and how those economic changes impacted American culture. He concludes that the growth of consumption and the current

---

311 Marling, 31.
312 Wilcox, *The Mode in Furs*, 162.
313 Anthony Rama Maravillas, "Overrated Pleasures and Underrated Treasures: Mamie Eisenhower, a Bridge between First Lady Archetypes", in *A Companion to First Ladies*, ed. Katherine A. S. Sibley, Wiley Blackwell Companions to American History (Chichester, UK: Wiley Blackwell, 2016), 492–502.

direction of American capitalism in overproduction was not necessary, as goods were being mass produced to a point of abundance and waste. Galbraith's argument is that the overproduction in the US was due to a "highly irrational emphasis" on an ever-increasing economic growth.[314] This needless production, he concludes, needed immediate attention so that the abundance could be redistributed to areas and peoples who need it more than the increasing "New Class" – a class above working poverty but below any perceived aristocracy. Overproduction of frivolous products, ultimately leading to waste, allowed for the emerging middle class, the New Class, to engage with consumerism on a personal level without thinking about the utility, or lack thereof, of the abundance of goods and misuse of resources in society that could be redirected "to eradicate remaining pockets of poverty" in the US.[315] This apparent call to socialist action was a difficult message to persuade Americans of, as the "extra production was adding nothing (or almost nothing) to well-being" for many once they were within the New Class.[316]

The New Class, as Galbraith writes, emerged from the disappearing leisure class in the United States. The New Class was not exclusive, but rather was growing exponentially; according to Galbraith, "while virtually no one leaves it, thousands join it every year" with the primary prerequisite qualifications being education and the desire to enjoy one's work.[317] This class was different from the leisure class because it focused on "earned income" and the perception that working an enjoyable job in a surplus society rewarded the worker with comfortable wages with which to buy luxuries. The emphasis on "earned income" replaced the aristocratic ideals of an older leisure class with the perceived new moral superiority of working for one's comforts and luxuries. Here, in this idea of earned income affording luxuries, is how Mamie Eisenhower's statement affirming her coat was "mink, of course" aided in shifting popular American perceptions of mink as no longer a garment of ill-repute to be disrespected, but rather a new kind of luxury status symbol: luxury that was earned.

Mink in the mid-1950s was a cultural signifier of opulence and desire rooted in this culture of the New Class, as opposed to the earlier view of it as disreputable as expressed by then-Vice-Presidential candidate Nixon and in the earlier films discussed. In the 1954 film *Susan Slept Here*, for example, Mark (Dick Powell) gifts a mink stole to Susan (Debbie Reynolds) as she is expressing her wishes to be beau-

---

314 Galbraith, *The Affluent Society*, 93.
315 Robert M. Whaples, "Why Didn't Galbraith Convince Us That America Is an Affluent Society?", *The Independent Review* 24, no. 4 (Spring 2020): 582.
316 Whaples, 584.
317 Galbraith, *The Affluent Society*, 219.

tiful and desirable with "clothes that are really with it." Her first reaction is to say that she cannot accept it, and when Mark insists that she take the mink, Susan's demeanor changes as she asks incredulously, "a mink? A real mink?" The conversation continues:

Mark: Mhmm. That's for being a good cook.

Susan: Imagine me in a mink. You know, Mr. Christopher, some girls would do anything for a mink.

Mark: I heard. And now, Susan, you're the perfect combination for any man: beauty within and beauty without. [*Wolf whistles at her*] There you got your whistle. Now go look at yourself in the mirror.

Susan: Mr. Christopher?

Mark: Yes?

Susan: I can't look in the mirror.

Mark: Why not?

Susan: If I see myself in it, I'll never take it off.

Mark: Then never take it off.

The mink stole for Susan is a symbol of desire and elevates her appearance and, therefore, perceived value to men. Captivated by even the *idea* of herself wearing a mink, she refrains from looking in the mirror knowing the moment can only be a fantasy in her current financial situation. In response to Mark's insistence that she keep it, Susan asks if he would like her to kiss him, explaining "because you gave me a mink." Mark responds, "absolutely not – [it] wasn't that kind of mink" implying that mink itself can take on certain characteristics depending on the context in which it is given, with the most common and expected characteristic one of a sexual transaction, as heavily implied in *It's a Wonderful Life*. This portrayal of mink in *Susan Slept Here*, however, is not connoted as disreputable or particularly depraved. It merely underlines the fact that, in the mid-1950s, mink began to take on multiple characteristics with one of them still carrying the sexual connotations from earlier times.

Views of mink throughout the rest of the 1950s continued to foreground opulence and desire. Some women did still harbor views of mink and other fur garments as indicative of the wearer's overt sexuality, according to an investigative marketing report by the *Chicago Tribune* in 1958. The social scientists producing the report interviewed 128 women from Chicago and the surrounding suburbs inquiring about their attitudes towards furs and concluded that some apprehension towards wearing mink publicly was still evident due to these older concerns from the 1940s connecting fur with immorality; however, women with these views were predominantly older middle-class housewives. Younger women from the working world and upper middle class and above were far more comfortable with the idea of wearing furs, either extravagant ones for the wealthier or within their means for the lower-income women.[318] For most women in the study, however, mink specifically was seen as a desirous, even aspirational commodity despite any concerns about sexually charged connotations. This conclusion is also supported by the answers to a Gallup poll question from December 1958 asking women "If you could have your choice, what one present would you most like to have for Christmas?", in which a mink coat (though unranked) was among the most common answers.[319]

Three years after those Gallup answers highlighting mink as a most preferred gift for Christmas and the *Chicago Tribune*'s marketing study concluding most younger women across economic classes interviewed were either comfortable with the idea of wearing furs or saw them as aspirational commodities, Frank Capra released *Pocketful of Miracles* (1961). The final film in this study, *Pocketful of Miracles* offers an interesting perception of luxury in 1961 that will be treated more fully in Chapter 5. The mink coat in this film is a part of a larger makeover from rags to riches and shows this gradual emergence of mink from scornful in the 1940s to aspirational in the early 1960s. Such a coat not only exudes luxury as an abstract concept, but also buys the wearer access to spaces she would not have been welcome in before as part of a juxtaposition of two extremes of the social and economic spectrum.

Capra's *Pocketful of Miracles* shows very clearly the distinctions between the lowest and poorest class and the highest wealthy class. In his 1961 remake, Capra expanded on the 1933 version of the story and added modern dimensions to the portrayal of the rags-to-riches motif that would elevate Annie to the status acceptable for engaging with "society" by contemporary 1960s standards and granting her access to the wealthy spaces in New York City. Annie's transformation is more than solely through her clothing, encompassing her appearance, posture, mannerisms, speech, and more to play the part of the noblewoman. However, the articles chosen to make her appear to be wealthy are crucial and cannot be taken for granted. The furs Annie dons as Mrs. E. Worthington Manville are integral to convincing the Count and others that she is the noblewoman they assume her to be. Furs, by 1961, had become so acceptable in the mainstream vision of the

---

318 "Women's Attitudes Toward Furs'"(Chicago Tribune, 1958), 15, Hathi Trust.
319 Gallup, *The Gallup Poll*, vol. 2, 1584.

upper classes that the transition from poverty to nobility was best articulated on screen through the addition of them to the main character's wardrobe.

Conclusion

The quotation opening this chapter – "A lot of bad 'isms' floating around this world, but one of the worst is 'commercialism'" – begs the question of whether commercialism was truly commonly seen as critically as projected by Alfred's character in *Miracle on 34th Street* (1947). This chapter has examined the critiques of commercialism and consumerism across the Christmas films in this study, as well the real-world connections drawn between those on-screen and off-screen stores and shoppers. In the late 1940s, suspicion around commercialism is represented in the films, with shoppers and businesses to some degree being shown how properly to engage with each other. Throughout the 1950s, attitudes towards consumption began to change as the "age of affluence" grew and consumerism adapted to the average customer's increasing spending habits.

These early projections of commercialism and consumerism in the films of the late 1940s show how Hollywood tackled the pressures of a post-war economy now on the verge of recovery in films such as *Miracle on 34th Street* (1947), *The Bishop's Wife* (1947), and *Holiday Affair* (1949). Macy's is depicted as "the store with a heart" for allegedly putting humanity before profits while also exploiting that humanity *for* profits. Ultimately, the good deeds accomplished through the goodwill policy are meant to leave the audience with a positive view of department stores and shopping altogether. In *Miracle on 34th Street*, there is a paradoxical dichotomy drawn between commercialism and consumerism that emphasizes that profits are crass and selfish while also arguing that maximizing profits is decidedly good if secured by listening to the consumer. This view of commercialism as potentially moralistic – offering a moral judgement on how commercialism should be injected into Christmas traditions – echoes the debates in *It's a Wonderful Life*, emphasizing the moralistic alternative to monopolistic capitalism as explored in Chapter 1.

Holiday Affair similarly can be mapped onto this dichotomy of commercialism and consumerism. Despite being set up as a rugged individualist who hates all aspects of commercialism, Steve is selfless with his money and buys Connie's son the toy train he truly wants for Christmas. Connie, as a comparative shopper, is presented as representative of the negative profit-driven side of department stores and also ridiculed for her poor shopping habits in general. This ridicule is reflective of the instructional stories and articles in women's publications of the late 1940s and early 1950s educating women and girls about how to be good consumers with various tips and tricks as well as advise on how they should feel about shopping. Hollywood's inclusion of this ridicule of Connie as a bad shopper reflects such attitudes from the wider culture about how properly to engage with consumerism and commercialism as the economy grows.

Social attitudes towards the rebuilding economy are helpfully seen in these films through the examination of luxury items, notably mink. As the economy strengthened in the 1950s, social attitudes towards luxuries became more favorable. In this period of growth and economic development spurred on by increased consumption, mink gained in popularity and shed some of the negative connotations that had been attached to it in the 1940s. These changing attitudes towards mink are evident in at least five films spanning the 15-year period from 1946 to 1961. When taken together, the films show a changing wider cultural perception towards this luxury item culminating in 1961 when mink is increasingly socially acceptable, now understood as a glamorous status symbol but without its more critical connotations from earlier times. The furs worn by Bette Davis's Apple Annie in *Pocketful of Miracles*, although they set her apart from the lowest classes, were not explicitly discussed in the film, an implicit acknowledgement perhaps of the growing social acceptability attached to wearing a fur by 1961.

Commercialism and consumerism in the 1940s and 1950s went through many different iterations. The sentiment of Alfred that commercialism was one of the worst "isms" was quickly undercut by the uses made of it in *Miracle on 34th Street*. As the post-war economy expanded into the age of affluence, films no longer showed commercialism as something which needed to be policed and consumers were no longer portrayed as needing instruction on how to engage with shopping as an experience. The Christmas films in this study do not stand alone in reflecting these changes. However, they do offer a unique perspective through which to explore the pressures and economic changes of the post-war period.

In showing how Christmas films adapted due to wider cultural and social changes in this 15-year period, this chapter highlights a consistent theme in the genre. Emphases on commercialism and consumerism are mainstays in the Christmas film genre as an integral part of how Americans celebrate the holiday. The next chapter will take a similar overarching perspective on the same 15-year period but in place of a theme, it will follow the evolution of two filmmakers: Walt Disney and Frank Capra. Having in previous chapters established the changing tone of the genre as a result of the many political, economic, social, and cultural factors throughout this post-war, early Cold War period, Chapter 5 will examine the consequences those factors had on each filmmaker and their 1961 productions, *Babes in Toyland* and *Pocketful of Miracles*.

Chapter 5
Christmases Past and Future: Walt Disney and Frank Capra, 1940s–1961

Toyland, Toyland,
Dear little girl and boy land
While you dwell within it
You are ever happy there

Childhood's toyland
Wonderful world of joyland
Wouldn't it be fine if
We could stay there forevermore
- "Toyland" Theme, *Babes in Toyland* (1961)

In December 1961, Walt Disney Studios released *Babes in Toyland*, their first feature-length Christmas film. The movie is, in essence, a live-action musical of Mother Goose nursery rhyme characters in a fantastical land and follows Mary Contrary (Annette Funicello) and Tom Piper (Tommy Sands) through their fraught romance as it is threatened by the villain, Barnaby (Ray Bolger). The light-hearted Disney movie follows many of the tropes established for Christmas films in the decade prior: it is a bright and colorful musical that abstains from direct commentary on the world outside of the film and presents a simplistic storyline with a happy ending for all but the villain. In these ways, *Babes in Toyland* is similar to the Christmas films of the 1950s with its exuberance, musical numbers, and simplified plots transporting the audience to the wonderful world of Toyland via effective escapism. However, there is simultaneously a darker subtext of murder, celebrated traditional gender roles, and threats of automation to the workforce within the film that makes it so appropriate and so poignant in 1961, matching the contemporary popular mentality of not only Hollywood but also the wider cultural moment in the United States. The film's success can be attributed to Walt Disney's profound connection with the moment and specifically with his audience whom he had consciously and carefully manufactured over the course of the previous decades: a mass target audience of children.

Later in the same week, United Artists released Frank Capra's *Pocketful of Miracles*, his final feature-length film. *Pocketful of Miracles* is a direct remake of his earlier 1933 film *Lady for a Day* stretched to be 41 minutes longer. A Damon Runyon Cinderella story, *Pocketful of Miracles* is about a homeless woman who sells apples to survive on the streets of New York, Apple Annie (Bette Davis), and her estranged daughter to whom she has lied about her real life. Annie told Louise (Ann-Margaret) that she is a noblewoman in the upper echelon of New York society, and when Louise announces she is coming to visit from Spain to introduce her fiancé to her mother, Annie must enlist the help of her gangster friend Dave the Dude (Glenn Ford) to make her over with illusions of grandeur. The charade only lasts until her daughter leaves the city and Annie returns to the streets. In many ways, *Pocketful of Miracles* was a flop and an echo from an earlier time, out of place in a more cynical 1961, not unlike its director Frank Capra.

Neither of these films engages directly with the world of 1961. However, both of them are indicative of the cultural changes that occurred from the start of this study's 15-year period of Christmas films beginning with Capra's *It's a Wonderful Life* (1946) to the release of his final film *Pocketful of Miracles*. Disney's film was an overt success and was the culmination of careful progress towards building a cultural empire with the Walt Disney brand while simultaneously including that radical messaging about automation, workers, and women. *Babes in Toyland* prioritizes escapism into a literal other world where the villain is a fantastical and exaggerated caricature of real capitalistic traits and radical ideologies. *Pocketful of Miracles*, on the other hand, is a remake from a Depression-era film based on a short story about nostalgia for the Prohibition era. The success of *Babes in Toyland* and failure of *Pocketful of Miracles* lies in this distinction: the former looked away from reality to cultivate an escape from the current world's overwhelming complexities, and the latter looked backwards to herald a woman in dire straits whose circumstances are alleviated for but a week before she returns to a difficult life in a harsh city.

Thus far, this book has argued that the political pressures on Hollywood to lean into conservative messaging, as well as the cultural changes that facilitated that shift rightward, had a significant impact on the films released in this period as especially evident in the Christmas films of the time. Ideologically, the films went from the traditional American Christmas with Dickensian themes addressing real-world social problems and Santa figures espousing the virtues of honesty, trust, and generosity in 1946 and 1947 to a new American standard of musicals, comedies, and romances that centered the individual's troubles without much mention of the outside world at all between 1949 and 1954.

By 1961, the emotional needs of the audience had shifted even further as the Cold War heated up, and the light-hearted escapist fare expected from these seemingly innocuous Christmas films required something of a grittier edge to compete with the mounting pressures of the outside world. A gentle romantic comedy in which the biggest problem was the complicated feelings of the woman who can't choose which man to love no longer had the appeal *Holiday Affair* did in 1949. Likewise, a film about structural inequalities and highlighting the plight of the homeless such as 1947's *It Happened on 5th Avenue* was far from the type of film that would come to be acceptable as Christmas fare after the 1950s dip into romances. Instead, a film with darker interpersonal drama – such as the 1961 Best Picture winner, Billy Wilder's *The Apartment* (1960), a comedy about management staff exploiting a subordinate's apartment for extra-marital affairs leading to a suicide attempt by the primary love-interest, Fran Kubelik (Shirley MacLaine) on Christmas Eve – was the exact right pitch. While Disney did not go as far as to portray extramarital affairs and a suicide attempt, he did create a children's fantasyland in which the primary villain plots to kidnap, murder, and replace a young girl's fiancé so that he instead may marry her and acquire her inheritance.

The Christmas films released in 1960 and 1961 mark the final phase of these dramatic developments in the genre's culture and outlook. The Christmas film genre had developed from social problems embedded in the Christmas themes themselves to light-hearted romances, comedies, and musicals dictated by the politics and cultural needs of the time. By the 1960s, the genre began to encapsulate an edgier middle ground, uncommitted to representing structural problems in society but willing to portray far more serious interpersonal issues between individuals than the 1950s films allowed. This drastic change over the 15-year period is most evident in the juxtaposition of Disney's and Capra's releases in the same week of 1961. With Capra looking back to the filmic Christmases of the past to his earlier 1946 film and Disney looking forward with his eye on profitability and finger on the pulse of the audience's needs for escapism in the turbulent, heated Cold War present of 1961, the antiquated "Yuletide theme" of *Pocketful of Miracles* falls short of meeting the moment and ultimately costs Capra his career.[320]

By examining each director's experiences throughout this 15-year period and the trajectories of their careers as they individually navigated the same political and cultural pressures both in and outside of the motion picture industry, this chapter will deviate somewhat from the previous four chapters in foregrounding the contexts surrounding these final two Christmas films as the primary focus ahead of textual analysis. Exploring Disney's and Capra's motivations and career moves in this period shows how the pressures on the industry were not disconnected abstractions for filmmakers, but rather had direct influence on the filmmakers themselves that translated into their cultural outputs. Disney carefully crafted his brand, testified as a friendly witness to HUAC, and showed shrewd awareness of his audience throughout this period, ultimately producing a successful Christmas film at the end of the 15 years. Capra, on the other hand, was forced to defend himself against accusations of communist sympathies, questioned the

---

320 Frank Capra, *The Name Above the Title: An Autobiography* (New York: Da Capo Press, 1997), 482.

American values he modelled in his earlier filmic successes of the 1930s and 1940s, and struggled to make the types of simplistic, romantic comedies and musicals asked of him in the 1950s, ultimately producing an unsuccessful, unremarkable Christmas film at the direction of several studios that had refused his more politically-charged and socially challenging passion project, *Ride the Pink Cloud.*

This is not the first time Capra and Disney have been compared in film scholarship. In his *Movie-Made America*, Robert Sklar dedicates a full chapter to the ways in which each director read the moment in the 1940s. Sklar writes,

> The government had confidence in Capra, and in Disney as well. They had demonstrated remarkable skill at infusing social myths and dreams with humor, sentiment, and a sense of shared moral precepts and responsibilities. No one in Hollywood was better equipped than they to convince wartime audiences that America was worth fighting for, that there were pleasures, satisfactions and rewards in store for those who followed their leaders.[321]

As cinema during World War II started to be regarded as a serious artform through which political messaging could be conveyed, the US government was able and willing to enlist the help of such prominent directors whose famous works on building social mythologies had garnered such clout and reward.[322] During the war, Disney and Capra worked to create propaganda for various departments of the US government and military, raising funds and awareness with their work. Building on Sklar's foundation, this chapter explores how the careers of these promising directors developed after the war, how one lost the confidence of the US government, and how the other became the leader he inspired others to follow.

After analyzing each directors' experiences in the 1950s, this chapter will discuss these final two Christmas films in relation to the others in this study and another 1960 movie with a Christmas background – *The Apartment* – evidencing the more general shift from gentle romances and comedies to darker messages dressed up as whimsical comedies. To understand the mental pressures that led to this "world faced by grimmer problems," as one reviewer wrote on the failure of Capra's *Pocketful of Miracles* to capture the 1961 moment, the chapter will first highlight the political turbulence of the late 1950s and early 1960s as the Cold War heated up.

---

321 Sklar, *Movie-Made America*, 214.
322 Sklar, 197.

Turbulence

Between 1954 and 1961, there were significant changes in domestic and foreign policy as well as changes in the period's cultural outputs. Focusing primarily on the external pressures that affected the culture, this section will give a brief summary of politically significant domestic and foreign events in the late 1950s. These events did not have as direct an impact on Hollywood as HUAC, the FBI, and the Supreme Court of the United States did in the late 1940s and earlier in the 1950s. Instead, these events provided context for some of the cultural changes in American cinema. This context suggests a correlation between the criticisms Capra received – such as not reflecting the moment in the "grimmer" context of the 1960s – and the success of films with darker messaging or undercurrents released around the same time – such as *The Apartment* in 1960 or *Babes in Toyland* in 1961. As the Cold War began to heat up and the perceivable period known as the "postwar" drew to an end when President Dwight D. Eisenhower left office, the challenges of the 1960s began to set in and American society and culture began to experience the first intimations of the immense changes that would occur later in the decade.[323]

As noted above, in the mid- to late 1950s, the Cold War began to heat up considerably, particularly with US involvement in foreign territories explored more fully below. Simultaneously, extreme domestic suspicions of communist infiltration popularized by Senator Joseph McCarthy were gradually replaced in the mainstream public consciousness by perceived threats of nuclear war from abroad. This shift in the public consciousness – from individual fears of others' politics to collective fear of national annihilation – is crucial to understanding the context for filmmakers in the late 1950s. Mainstream culture and public consciousness are never singular, but acknowledging the different threats to and fears of the average American in this period provides that backcloth to why the Christmas films released in 1960 and 1961 were so different from those released earlier.

McCarthy was effectively ruined by his televised performance at the Army-McCarthy hearings between April and June 1954 and was censured by the US Senate for contempt of the Congressional subcommittee in December 1954, with his influ-

---

323 Gary W. Reichard suggests that the Truman and Eisenhower administrations constitute the cohesive historical period understood as the "post-war" period. This categorization is justified by periodizing the New Deal years, the war, this post-war, and the ensuing 1960s as distinct categories with the Cold War running consistently throughout the post-war and beyond. Reichard, *Politics as Usual*, xiv.

ence dwindling dramatically.[324] Anti-communism was still a prevalent concern for many Americans; however, with the simultaneous gradual progression of foreign intervention in Asia and South America explored below, internal tensions largely turned into nuclear fears. Since the political history of the years from 1954 to 1961 has been written about extensively elsewhere, this section will highlight a selection of the larger concerns that, when taken collectively, illustrate crucial factors in this period of increasing fears, concerns, and cynicism that ultimately would translate to the screen.[325] Specifically, this section will focus on developments within or as a result of the Eisenhower administration's responses to global affairs that escalated the Cold War between 1954 and 1961.[326]

During a press conference on April 7, 1954, Eisenhower reintroduced and named the Domino Theory, the geopolitical theory popularized earlier by Truman that if one nation fell to Communism, its neighbors would fall under its influence and create what, from the US's perspective, would seem a global crisis.[327] As Eisenhower simply summarized: "You have a row of dominoes set up, you knock over the first one, and what will happen to the last one is the certainty that it will go over very quickly. So, you could have a beginning of a disintegration that would have the most profound influences."[328] The Domino Theory effectively dominated US foreign policy for much of the early Cold War studied here, from Truman's administration through John F. Kennedy's in the early 1960s. As the Korean War that began in 1950 receded into the distance by 1953, the US slowly started to turn toward intervention in Vietnam – the next "domino". According to David Anderson, historian of the Eisenhower administration, "to withhold support [to France and

---

324 Jeff Broadwater, *Eisenhower & the Anti-Communist Crusade* (Chapel Hill: The University of North Carolina Press, 1992), 165.

325 For more on the political events of 1954 to 1961, see: Broadwater, *Eisenhower & the Anti-Communist Crusade*; Allen J. Matusow, *The Unraveling of America: A History of Liberalism in the 1960s* (New York: Harper & Row, 1984); Reichard, *Politics as Usual*; Isidor F. Stone, *The Haunted Fifties: 1953–1963*, 2ⁿᵈ ed. (Boston: Little, Brown & Company, 1989); Isidor F. Stone, *In a Time of Torment: 1961–1967* (Boston: Little, Brown and Company, 1989).

326 For more on Eisenhower's administration, see: Stephen. E. Ambrose, *Eisenhower. Vol. 2, The President* (New York: Simon & Schuster, 1984); Richard. V. Damms, *The Eisenhower Presidency, 1953–1961* (New York: Longman, 2002); William I. Hitchcock, *The Age of Eisenhower: America and the World in the 1950s* (New York: Simon & Schuster, 2018); Chester J. Pach and Elmo Richardson, *The Presidency of Dwight D. Eisenhower* (Lawrence, KS: University Press of Kansas, 1991).

327 David Anderson, *Trapped by Success: The Eisenhower Administration and Vietnam 1953–1961* (New York: Columbia University Press, 1991), 18.

328 Dwight D. Eisenhower, "The President's News Conference", The American Presidency Project, accessed July 10, 2023, https://www.presidency.ucsb.edu/node/233655.

the State of Vietnam] was deemed more dangerous" than intervening as "that would jeopardize US containment strategy in both Europe and Asia."[329]

As Eisenhower's administration came into power in 1953, it adopted Operation Candor. Operation Candor was the conclusion of the panel over which Robert J. Oppenheimer presided under the Truman administration, organized to confront the growing number of atomic and hydrogen weapon capabilities around the world.[330] With the realization that the US government would need to dramatically increase defense spending, the panel concluded that the next administration would have to be candid with the American people about the need for increasing taxes and for a collective understanding of Eisenhower's vision of "national security".[331] This tactic of selective transparency with the American people was a public relations operation marketing a military-centric vision of security over the increasingly unobtainable illusion of peace in a world with nuclear weapons. The campaign effectively instilled in much of the American public fears of large-scale nuclear warfare as Eisenhower promised that an expanded US military would not hesitate to use nuclear weapons if need be.[332] Eisenhower asserted this threat to use these weapons publicly in several speeches throughout the mid-1950s, inspiring fear in enemies, allies, and US citizens alike while attempting to reassure them that America's nuclear weapons would only be used as a deterrent to worldwide nuclear war.[333]

By 1957, nuclear fears, foreign policy, and scientific advancements escalated tensions internationally. In the first quarter of 1957, the Eisenhower administration and Congress adopted the Eisenhower Doctrine, in effect a policy promising that any nation in the Middle East could request military and financial assistance from the US if threatened by "overt armed aggression by any nation controlled by international communism."[334] The doctrine's indirect threat to Russia added to the momentum of the Cold War that was underscored later that year by the Soviet

329 Anderson, *Trapped by Success*, 15. Bracketed text is Anderson's own phrasing.
330 Ira Chernus, "Operation Candor: Fear, Faith, and Flexibility", *Diplomatic History* 29, no. 5 (2005): 781.
331 Ira Chernus, *Apocalypse Management: Eisenhower and the Discourse of National Insecurity* (Stanford: Stanford University Press, 2008), 53–55.
332 James Ledbetter, *Unwarranted Influence: Dwight D. Eisenhower and the Military-Industrial Complex* (New Haven: Yale University Press, 2011), 63–64.
333 Steven Wagner, *Eisenhower for Our Time* (Ithaca, NY: Cornell University Press, 2024), 101 https://doi.org/10.1515/9781501774317.
334 Office of the Historian, Foreign Service Institute, "Milestones: 1953–1960 – Office of the Historian", United States Department of State, accessed July 10, 2023, https://history.state.gov/milestones/1953-1960/eisenhower-doctrine.

launch of Sputnik 1 in October. Sputnik 1 was the first artificial satellite to orbit Earth, and this technological advancement triggered the beginnings of the Space Race and the establishment of National Aeronautics and Space Administration (NASA) in July 1958.[335]

In 1959, American culture became a more overt centerpiece of diplomacy when Eisenhower sent Vice President Richard Nixon as the US representative to the American National Exhibition in Moscow. At the exhibition, Nixon met with Nikita Khrushchev as diplomats guided the two through a model of a "typical" American home filled with recent gadgets, appliances, and commodities.[336] This exhibition sparked one of the period's most important cultural debates and a milestone in Cold War tensions, as Nixon extolled the American way of life and Khrushchev admonished the Western display of excess. In this so-called "kitchen debate", Nixon emphasized the abundance of choice in manufacturers and appliances and the leisure they afforded American housewives.[337] His mission on this diplomatic visit was to instill in the Russian spectators the idea that the American way of life was superior to their own because of the freedoms afforded not only to choose consumer goods, but also in the liberation of time, allowing women a degree of agency in how they spend leisure-time newly afforded by the latest gadgets and appliances.

With the newest appliances, comforts, and luxuries, this model "average" American home was a manufactured ideal, projecting the image of how the American government wanted American homes to be seen by Russians attending the exhibition. Similarly to how Christmas films project a perceived ideal of American identity, values, and attitudes on screen, the model home was a tangible and immersive experience through which Nixon could build a vision of who Americans were, what they stood for, and how they lived their everydays.

With nuclear terror mounting and the cultural and diplomatic tensions between the US and the Soviets rising, Kennedy won the 1960 presidential election. In January 1961, ahead of Kennedy's inauguration, Eisenhower announced a formal severance of diplomatic ties with Cuba after three years of embargoes against the nation. The further deterioration of US relations with Cuba led to the Bay of Pigs invasion in April 1961, a covert mission originally planned by the CIA under Eisenhower. The "unmitigated disaster" of an invasion was led by CIA-backed

335 Zuoyue Wang, *In Sputnik's Shadow: The President's Science Advisory Committee and Cold War America* (New Brunswick: Rutgers University Press, 2008), 88.
336 May, *Homeward Bound*, 155.
337 May, 20.

Cuban counterrevolutionaries who had been exiled for opposing Fidel Castro's revolution.[338]

As international tensions rose abroad and the Berlin Wall was erected in August 1961, social and cultural changes began to emerge in the US, particularly in Hollywood. In the later 1950s, the blacklist began to break. The first major cracks began on television in 1957 with Alfred Hitchcock knowingly hiring actor Norman Lloyd for his show *Alfred Hitchcock Presents*. Lloyd had learned of his blacklisting four years prior in 1953 when he was barred from casting in Joseph L. Mankiewicz's *Julius Caesar*.[339] Gradually, writing credits for blacklisted writers began appearing on other programs over the next few years. In 1960, the film industry began to catch up with the movement to break the blacklist and its lasting stigma when Kirk Douglas demanded screen credits on *Spartacus* (1960) for Dalton Trumbo, one of the original Hollywood Ten whose charges of contempt of Congress had helped instigate the blacklist in November 1947.

The US was experiencing a backlash against the highly pressurized fearmongering of the early 1950s, and Hollywood was poised to confront it. As discussed in previous chapters, Dorothy Jones's research into the impacts of HUAC on Hollywood had identified a resounding lack of communist messaging, propaganda, or subversion in American filmic content between 1947 and 1954. Instead, what Jones found was an increase in comedies, romances, and musicals, that, as examined in Chapter 3, manifested a culturally simple ideology in Christmas films especially. The dramatic decrease in social problem and psychological films that Jones noted in her research continued beyond her study through the end of the 1950s and into the early 1960s. However, the light-hearted nature of the films that replaced them in the 1950s – comedies, romances, and musicals – also began by the late 1950s and early 1960s to reflect the growing tension, bitterness, and rebellion within Hollywood itself. With such renegade acts as boldly and blatantly breaking the blacklist, Hollywood filmmakers rebelled against the pressures to create simplistic works such as the Christmas films produced between 1949 and 1954.

Screenwriter Michael Wilson argued during the blacklist era that films of the 1950s contained "a pervading anti-intellectual quality, an absence of *ideas*, a dis-

338 Huw Dylan, David V. Gioe, and Michael S. Goodman, "The CIA and Cuba: The Bay of Pigs and the Cuban Missile Crisis", in *The CIA and the Pursuit of Security: History, Documents and Contexts* (Edinburgh: Edinburgh University Press, 2020), 112–113.
339 David Hudson, "Norman Lloyd's Long and Triumphant Run", The Criterion Collection, accessed April 25, 2024, https://www.criterion.com/current/posts/7389-norman-lloyd-s-long-and-triumphant-run.

dain for rational motive."[340] With many notable exceptions – *A Face in the Crowd* (1957) or *The Defiant Ones* (1958) among them – it is important to note that while this statement reflects a biased perspective from a blacklisted filmmaker, there was still a truth to it across certain genres, including Christmas films. By 1961, this perceived absence of ideas began to be remedied as Hollywood began to change, reintroducing an intellectual depth to genres that had trended towards more shallow storylines in the wake of the federal pressures impacting Hollywood in the late 1940s and early 1950s. Disney, with his keen eye on the market and shrewd business acumen, reacted to these gradual changes in the culture towards more intellectual depth both within and outside of the film industry in the late 1950s. In remaking *Babes in Toyland,* Disney updated the story to include more complex underpinnings that confirmed – rather than challenged – complexities in the wider world while simultaneously creating an atmosphere of escapism. Capra, on the other hand, ultimately remade a Depression-era film with no engagement with or adaptation for the far more complex world of 1961. The freshness of Disney's ideas in *Babes in Toyland* and Capra's seeming failure of imagination in the production of *Pocketful of Miracles* reflect their experiences in the 1950s.

A Comparative Study: Walt Disney and Frank Capra

As mentioned in the chapter introduction, Disney and Capra have been compared by film and cultural historian Robert Sklar for their successes in constructing national identities and social mythologies on film in the 1930s and into the 1940s. Their positions as mythmakers in American culture at the end of the war were well-established. Disney was on the rise after his first feature-length animation, *Snow White and the Seven Dwarves* (1937), and significant contributions to war bond initiatives. Capra, having dominated the populist cinema of the 1930s, was returning from his wartime service creating films such as those in the *Why We Fight* series on behalf of the US military.[341] Until the anti-communist campaign in relation to the motion picture industry – pursued by the FBI and HUAC federally and the MPAPAI and MPAA internally – Capra and Disney were both professionally well-esteemed while also financially struggling upon their full-time returns to Hollywood.

---

340 As quoted in Alan Casty, *Communism in Hollywood: The Moral Paradoxes of Testimony, Silence, and Betrayal* (Lanham, MD: Scarecrow Press, 2009), 255.
341 Sklar, *Movie-Made America,* 214.

The rest of this chapter will be devoted to a comparative study of how both Disney and Capra experienced the ensuing 15-years from 1946 to 1961 and how those experiences affected their filmmaking. Because Capra's downfall is much more illustrative of the ways in which the social, cultural, and political pressures on the motion picture industry could negatively impact filmmakers, this chapter will spend more time on the nuances of Capra's negative experiences than Disney's positive ones. Based on an analysis of documents in his archival materials from the period as well as his filmic releases and the ways in which he struggled to meet the anti-communist challenges within Hollywood, this chapter will argue that Capra was failed by the industry executives who bowed to those political pressures in the late 1940s and early 1950s. It will also conclude that a significant change occurred in the cultural outputs of Hollywood between 1946 and 1961 as a result of first and foremost the political turbulence in the industry, together with the ripples of cultural and social changes happening in the wider US throughout this period. These changes were so profound that Frank Capra, the former populist film icon, decided to retire as his old style of messaging had failed and his new ideas had been rejected from ever being put to film.

Disney's Escapist Empire

Disney's brand throughout the 1950s grew in line with Walt's personal vision for the company. He expanded it into a multi-media empire specializing in escapism with a key demographic that no other studio to date had successfully exploited: children. This empire grew laterally as Disney acquired other means of profiting off of the characters and films children loved by reaching into the budding television industry, the world of theme parks, print media including comics and books, and merchandising with ruthless marketing strategies and a keen eye for the social and cultural evolutions affecting consumers of entertainment throughout the early Cold War.

Throughout the 1950s, the Disney Company took the lead in marketing to the youngest generation: baby boomers.[342] The post-war baby boom vastly altered the demographics of the US population. In the mid-1930s, the annual American birth rate was as low as 2.3 million, whereas, in 1947, 3.8 million babies were born. These numbers continued to rise with more than 4 million babies born each year between 1954 and 1963. Ultimately, the baby boom resulted in a new genera-

---

342 James Russell and Jim Whalley, *Hollywood and the Baby Boom: A Social History* (New York: Bloomsbury Academic, 2017), 4.

tion of 75 million Americans born between 1946 and 1964.[343] According to historians James Russell and Jim Whalley, the baby boomer generation became the primary focus of the entertainment industry in the 1950s with Hollywood producing epics that would engage "young and old alike", television oriented towards children, and Disney assuming the top position in the children's market. This focus on a singular audience in the late-1950s was an industry-changing phenomenon according to Hollywood scholar Janet Staiger. Staiger writes that by the end of the 1950s, "the goal of aiming a film at a heterogenous audience was no longer standard", as manifested not only in the content of films but very specifically in their advertising.[344]

Disney's ability to capitalize on the changing industry and anticipate the marketing needs that would accompany it separated him and his company from competitors in the 1950s. On this phenomenon, Russell and Whalley write: "In fits and starts, the child audience – which is to say the boomers – became one of the industry's most lucrative audiences for the first time in its history, although only one company really recognized their commercial power at this time: Disney."[345] Historian of the Disney Company Amy Davis supports this assertion in claiming Disney's projected brand of "wholesome, high-quality, family-friendly entertainment" emerged during the 1950s when baby boomers were children. According to Davis, the brand's logo recognition and guarantee of family-friendly content was then solidified in the 1960s when other filmmakers increasingly began challenging aspects of the Hays Code, meaning there was no reliable guarantee of the content of a film available for the audience prior to viewing it. Davis suggests that the Disney logo assured audience members in the Production Code era – which ended in 1968 with the establishment of the new age-related Ratings System – that a film was "safe" for their children.[346]

After suffering a total accrued $4.2 million bank debt by the end of the 1940s, the Disney Company gradually recovered financially with the success of *Cinderella* (1950), which earned a gross rental of nearly $8 million.[347] The same year, Disney released its first wholly live-action film *Treasure Island*, which grossed $4.8 million.[348] *Cinderella* was distributed in conjunction with RKO Studios and *Treasure*

---

343 Russell and Whalley, 6.

344 Staiger, "The Package-Unit System", 333.

345 Russell and Whalley, *Hollywood and the Baby Boom*, 4.

346 Amy M. Davis, ed., *Discussing Disney* (Bloomington: Indiana University Press, 2019), 3.

347 J. Michael Barrier, *The Animated Man: A Life of Walt Disney* (Berkeley: University of California Press, 2007), 205; 221.

348 Barrier, 221; 223.

Island was both produced and released in collaboration with RKO Studios. However, the gross earnings were enough, even when shared, to get Walt Disney Productions out of its debts and poised to lead the industry in children's media as its brand recognition grew throughout the 1950s.

Disney had also begun plans for his amusement park, Disneyland, in the late 1940s. The earliest recorded notes for the park, according to Cynthia Read Miller, curator at the Henry Ford Museum, are dated August 31, 1948.[349] These plans would develop further in the 1950s culminating in 1955 with the opening of Disneyland in Anaheim, California. Simultaneously, Disney moved into television with a Christmas Day 1950 debut of a special entitled *One Hour in Wonderland* broadcast on NBC.[350] *One Hour in Wonderland* was effectively an hour-long advertisement offering the first look at the anticipated *Alice in Wonderland* (1951), hosted by Walt Disney himself – joined at a tea party by familiar cast members – and showing shorts including familiar characters such as Mickey Mouse, Pluto, Br'er Rabbit from *Song of the South* (1946), and a scene from *Snow White and the Seven Dwarfs* (1937). Interestingly, this special had nothing to do with Christmas at all, save for the date it aired.

These forays into live-action films, amusement parks, and television helped develop the well-rounded child-centric brand of Disney throughout the 1950s, and all of them grew in popularity because Disney understood very well how to market to his target demographic. In October 1954, Disney brought television and Disneyland together nine months before the park even opened with the debut of the television show *Disneyland* (1954–58) on ABC.[351] *Disneyland* featured teaser clips introducing the sections of the then-unopened park – Frontierland, Tomorrowland, Adventureland, and Fantasyland – as well as behind-the-scenes footage of animators working on films, previously seen musical numbers, occasional animated sequences, and appearances by Walt Disney himself. This anthology variety show was used to further promote the cohesive synergy of the various Disney products and familiarize audiences with the parks before they even opened.

Harrison Price, a member of the Stanford Research Institute and Walt's lead consultant on Disneyland, produced a site study entitled "Analysis of Location Factors for Disneyland" in August 1953. Within his analysis, Price considered "a large number of factors, including likely population growth patterns, freeway construc-

349 Cynthia Read Miller, "Walt Disney Visits Henry Ford's Greenfield Village", The Henry Ford Museum, February 22, 2014, accessed July 1, 2022, https://web.archive.org/web/20140222100833/http://www.thehenryford.org/exhibits/pic/2005/september.asp#more.
350 Davis, *Discussing Disney*, 4.
351 Davis, 4.

tion, and 'the effect of terrain on television transmission'." According to Walt Disney biographer Michael Barrier, Price was aware "that TV '[would] play an important part in the promotion and development of Disneyland.'"[352] Disney and ABC then established a deal in which ABC would pay $500,000 and guarantee a bank loan of $4.5 million to invest in the park and the television show extension of the park that would be filmed prior to its airing, as opposed to most of ABC's competition's live broadcasts.[353] Simultaneously, in 1953, as Disney was gaining a television distribution partner in ABC, his company broke ties with RKO Studios and established its own distribution subsidiary, Buena Vista.[354]

Both Roy and Walt Disney planned for the television show to be a supportive enterprise to promote their theatrical releases and amusement park plans. Walt secured in the contract with ABC that he had "complete say" over what was to be produced and so incorporated the park into the show both as visually and literally as possible, interacting with it in every episode. The show therefore included the four "lands" that mimicked those in Disneyland itself and began with a sequence leading in through the front gates of the park. By May 1954, Disneyland, Incorporated was its own separate company with Walt as the CEO and President and a board of directors comprised of representatives from both ABC and the Western Printing and Lithographing Company. The latter had at that point been responsible for Disney's print media including books, games, puzzles, and comic books for over twenty years.[355]

All facets of Walt Disney's companies, media, and products across film, television, theme parks, and print were designed to work in conjunction to target children successfully as their primary customers. With the addition of Buena Vista, Disney evolved from an independent to a studio on a par with the other major production companies in Hollywood, elevating not only vertically within the film industry but also laterally with all the subsidiaries of other media and the parks.[356] All of these advantageous evolutions of the Disney brand and company happened when the largest generation to date, the baby boomers, were at the oldest 8 years old, having been born between 1947 and 1955. In addition, Barrier also noted that the youngest parents of baby boomers would themselves have been children in the 1930s and thus quite likely had memories of seeing *Snow White and the*

---

352 Barrier, *The Animated Man*, 240.
353 Barrier, 244.
354 Richard Schickel, *The Disney Version: The Life, Times, Art and Commerce of Walt Disney* (New York: Simon & Schuster, 1968), 302.
355 Barrier, *The Animated Man*, 245.
356 Schickel, *The Disney Version*, 303.

Seven Dwarfs (1937) as an escape from the troubles of the Great Depression.[357] Both parents and their children, therefore, would likely have had some comforting association with the Disney brand by the mid-1950s and a possible aspiration, as child or as parent, to visit Disneyland when it opened.

In the late 1950s, Disney continued making television shows that would target child audiences, such as *The Mickey Mouse Club* (1955–59). *The Mickey Mouse Club* averaged 25 million viewers a week while *Disneyland* amassed 50 million viewers weekly.[358] The Disney brand's mass marketing poised the company to take advantage of the age brackets of both baby boomers and their parents, leveraging nostalgia to introduce new and younger audiences to Disney's offerings. With this context, it is unsurprising that *Babes in Toyland*, a film that is essentially a feature-length advertisement for Disneyland with its whimsical fantasy-land feel and sets that very much reflect the theme park aesthetic, was produced in 1961 after the television show *Disneyland* ended.

During the 1940s and 1950s, Disney dedicated himself and his businesses to building a multi-media empire. This empire catered to children as the primary consumer and also understood that their parents had the actual purchasing power. By getting Disney products – be they parks, films, merchandise, comics, books, etc. – in front of children in as many ways as possible, Disney effectively cornered the market in children's popular culture. Additionally, he used these outlets to keep up with the changing times and, by the 1960s, his films were reflecting a darker cultural messaging than before – messaging that was to some degree detached from the cognizant realities of his audience of children and rather more mature in nature.

This grittier edge to Disney films was particularly evident in 1961. In another Disney release from that year, *One-Hundred and One Dalmatians*, the story follows an increasingly deranged, evil woman, Cruella de Vil, hunting anthropomorphized dalmatian puppies to make a coat from their skin. It is clear this woman is the villain from the start, not only because of her name but also as a consequence of the lyrics to the song sung about her in anticipation of her introduction claiming that she is "a vampire bat/ an inhuman beast". The song, character, and plot suggest far more misogyny and villainy than Disney's earlier animated releases. *One-Hundred and One Dalmatians* as a whole has a darker edge that takes the scarier scenes of a film such as 1959's *Sleeping Beauty* a step further into a grittier world of harsh, life-like individuals. While there is distance between the animated London of *One-Hun-*

357 Barrier, *The Animated Man*, 248.
358 Cher Krause Knight, *Power and Paradise in Walt Disney's World* (Gainesville: University Press of Florida, 2014), 15.

dred and One Dalmatians with its talking animals and extreme villain, there is a life-like quality to Cruella that separates her from the shape-shifting dragon of *Sleeping Beauty*'s Maleficent.

Simultaneously, however, *One-Hundred and One Dalmatians* extols family values above all else, showing the lengths a family will go in order to rescue their children and restore order in the home. While embracing these family values that are not dissimilar to the socially conservative messaging of the earlier 1950s films in this study, *One-Hundred and One Dalmatians* emphasizes other socially conservative perspectives such as misogynistic views on women and complex presentations of class dynamics. This balance in *One-Hundred and One Dalmatians* of a distanced world with an identifiable but exaggerated villain and socially conservative values is the same balance that Disney strikes in *Babes in Toyland*, for instance with manifold discussions of work ethics – or the lack thereof – within this fantasy land.

The overemphasis on labor in *Babes in Toyland* could reflect Disney's past relationships with unionization and strikes within the entertainment industry. One significant factor to Disney's success in building this escapist empire was his cooperation with and conformity to pressures on the industry. Disney, as a shrewd, almost obsessive studio head had many issues with labor unions in the 1940s and 1950s and came to see anti-communist investigations and eventually HUAC as an opportunity to oust the troublemakers in his organization. As early Disney historian Richard Schickel quotes him saying about the fraught period of the 1940s from the start of the labor strikes in defiance of his studio through the anti-communist investigations of the period, "it was probably the best thing that ever happened to me ... I didn't have to fire anybody to get rid of the chip-on-the-shoulder boys and the world-owes-me-a-living lads. An elimination process took place I couldn't have forced if I'd wanted to."[359] Disney's relationship with labor unions and repeated attempts to secure an advantage for his own company against them led to his "friendly witness" testimony before HUAC in October 1947.[360]

Disney Studios had screened anti-communist sentiments as early as 1925. In one short, entitled *Alice's Egg Plant* (1925), the titular Alice receives an order for five thousand eggs, and in order to meet this demand, she and her cat Julius must break the strike organized by a Bolshevik Rooster named Little Red Henski. Disney historian Joshua M. Hollands acknowledges that this short is "a deviation from the rule" of early Disney shorts in that it has a narrative arc and contrasts with the more frequent messages of social liberation portrayed in this period.

---

359 Schickel, *The Disney Version*, 255.
360 John Wills, *Disney Culture* (New Brunswick: Rutgers University Press, 2017), 16.

However, the anti-communist sentiments boldly depicted in this short, as Hollands also notes, are significant in the social context of the aftermath of the First Red Scare and would come to foreshadow later labor disputes between Disney and his animators in the 1940s.[361]

Walt Disney was a micromanager within his company, especially with the animators and directors bringing his visions to life. Additionally, by the end of 1940, the studio had become so large that management could not keep up with the number of animators employed, and the Disney brothers distanced themselves further from those workers by setting up animation boards of senior animators to oversee the work in the studio.[362] When the studio was in financial crisis in 1941, and with pressure from Bank of America, Disney began laying off animators, prompting the animators' strike of 1941 in conjunction with the Screen Cartoonists Guild.[363] Walt refused to negotiate with the unions and left the arbitration to his brother, Roy, and their attorneys, holding a grudge against the strikers and union leaders and members for worsening the company's existing financial crisis by several hundred thousand dollars, with debts topping $3.5 million by August 1941.[364]

In 1944, Disney became a founding member of the MPAPAI. The MPAPAI, as discussed in Chapter 1, was responsible for the Ayn Rand pamphlet *Screen Guide for Americans* that comprised a list of the things not to allow in one's film to prevent it from being accused of communist subversion. When called to testify, Disney was a friendly witness for HUAC and specifically its principal witness on October 24, 1947. His testimony recalled the animators' strikes, labeling them as "a Communist group trying to take over [his] artists" and he pointedly accused Dave Hilberman as the orchestrator of the strikes, alleging him of being a communist.[365]

The overemphasis in *Babes in Toyland* on industrial child laborers working with their hands and avidly wanting to work could be a deliberate commentary on these prior relationships between Walt Disney, his company, and the Hollywood unions he clashed with repeatedly. Contextually for Hollywood, these 1961 perspectives on a perceived reluctance to work came just after the settlement of the Writers Guild of America and Screen Actors Guild (SAG) strikes in the first

---

361 Joshua M. Hollands, "Animating America's Anticommunism: Alice's Egg Plant (1925) and Disney's First Red Scare", in *Discussing Disney*, ed. Amy M. Davis (Bloomington: Indiana University Press, 2019), 37.
362 Barrier, *The Animated Man*, 164.
363 Barrier, 170.
364 Barrier, 171–172.
365 As cited in Barrier, *The Animated Man* 201. Barrier believes there is little evidence for a "vendetta" against Hilberman but acknowledges that Walt held grudges against those who disrupted his work.

half of 1960. These strikes won significant residuals for actors and writers for films shown on broadcast television and were led by another friendly HUAC witness and returning SAG president, Ronald Reagan.[366] The repeated portrayal of shock and awe over the desire to work in *Babes in Toyland* seems very much a reflection of Disney's own complicated history with Hollywood labor movements and HUAC in the mid-century.

Throughout the 1940s, Disney was leveraging his position politically within the motion picture industry's business practices so that in the 1950s he could focus heavily on building his brand into an empire. This empire thrived with multi-media options for engagement with the brand's properties, familiar characters, and tangible escapist land akin to a Foucauldian heterotopia that was separate from the dangers of the actual world, but real and immersive as an idealized sim-ulacrum by design. This chapter will next explore Frank Capra's radically different experiences in the 1950s before turning to a comparative analysis of the two direc-tors' 1961 Christmas releases, *Babes in Toyland* and *Pocketful of Miracles*.

Capra's Not So Wonderful Life

While Walt Disney astutely leveraged his political position in Hollywood, carefully built his brand, and vastly expanded his filmmaking operations into a multi-media empire of escapist fare, Frank Capra experienced a very different 15-year period after the release of *It's a Wonderful Life* in 1946. His final film in this period, *Pocketful of Miracles* (1961) ushered in an early retirement for the director after a grueling production and disheartening reception left Capra even more bitter and disillusioned than ever. Throughout this period, Capra felt himself ostracized from the film community with his American identity and loyalty called into ques-tion by federal organizations as well as mounting public disinterest in more clas-sically Capra-esque films.

This chapter argues that, while there is a confluence of factors as with all Hol-lywood changes and developments, one frequently dismissed factor contributing immensely to Capra's decline is the changing political landscape in Hollywood. His experiences over the 15 years between 1946 and 1961 led to an increasing cyn-icism and questioning of the American values Capra had espoused throughout his earlier film career.[367] By the late 1950s and early 1960s especially, Capra's growing

---

366 Iwan W. Morgan, *Reagan: American Icon* (London: I. B. Tauris, 2016), 76–77.
367 It is important to note that there are few biographies about Frank Capra. His autobiography and fullest biography, Joseph McBride's, are both written from highly personal perspectives that

discomfort with the degradation of American values, as he saw it, was deemed un-conscionable for Hollywood screens and he ultimately was pressured by the studios to rehash a film through an extended remake that would end his career entirely.

In analyzing the films Capra released between 1948 and 1961, finishing with an examination of the extant pages of a never-made passion project, it is evident that there was also a fundamental change within Capra himself. As Sklar wrote of both Capra and Disney and their influences in the 1930s, both directors, "shared the acclaim of all three significant audiences for movies: the ticket-buying public, the critics and the commentators on films, and their Hollywood co-workers."[368] By the 1950s, as explored above, Disney escalated these relationships and connections with his audiences by working within Hollywood's changing political landscape and enjoying the privileges afforded to him for that cooperation. Capra, however, accustomed to making more straightforwardly political films that challenged Hollywood's political landscape, struggled to compromise with and adapt to the new expectations.

Across these films, there is a sustained degradation of the qualities that made Capra's earlier films what they were in the classic populist sense. While his earlier films about politics were critical of US political institutions and harbored a sense of cynicism towards the government, they also had a balance of optimism. After experiencing real political consequences for his 1948 film *State of the Union*'s even more intense cynicism towards the US political establishment, Capra's faith in his freedoms as an American filmmaker faltered. Ultimately, Capra's experiences in the 1950s both in and out of Hollywood lost him the profoundly positive relationships he once had with all three of the audiences Sklar names. By not adjusting to the influence of HUAC even after having been named in the FBI's 1947 report as producing potentially subversive material in *It's a Wonderful Life*, Capra also compromised his relationship with his Hollywood co-workers to the detriment of his ability to produce films. Having lost their trust and support already, after *Pocketful of Miracles* Capra also lost the goodwill of the critics and, with them, the ticket-buying audience. Due to his noncompliance with the changing culture and federal pressures, Capra was pushed out of Hollywood by the studios, the industry, and the cinema-going public. This drastic fall from grace was a

---

are heavily criticized when referenced in other works. Most other biographical information in other scholarly accounts of his life is imported from interviews with Capra, personal writings from him, or inferred alongside film criticism. What can be known more definitively about Capra's life will be cross referenced between these accounts and supplemented with the evidence in the Frank Capra Archives at Wesleyan University.

368 Sklar, *Movie-Made America*, 197.

personally painful end to one of the most iconic and leading directors in Hollywood's history, who would now be derisively remembered mainly for making sentimental hogwash critics had dubbed "Capra-corn."

The argument that the studios and industry failed Capra – as opposed to the idea that the director had simply lost touch with the people – stands in contrast to the views of many commentators on his life. For instance, his most famous and controversial biographer, Joseph McBride, argues it was a lack of "courage" that ended his career mixed with other factors explored below.[369] Likewise, critic Matthew Gunter argues that Capra "had simply run out of things to say" while Raymond Carney refers to the decline of Capra's career as "the greatest possible imaginative sellout or compromise."[370] These critics put the blame squarely on Capra himself for the misguided *Pocketful of Miracles* while ignoring both the influence of the studios and producers funding the film and the drastically changing cultural landscape of the early 1960s.

However, one film critic and quasi-biographer, Leland Poague suggests that much like the politics of Capra's films, there are many more nuances to the director's ultimate decline. The postscript to Poague's *Another Frank Capra* is dedicated to addressing the aggressive approach McBride takes in his *The Catastrophe of Success*. In the postscript, Poague challenges McBride's faulty logic in some of his conclusions, particularly concerning the involvement of Robert Riskin.[371] Riskin was a close collaborator of Capra's and worked almost exclusively as his writing partner throughout the 1930s.[372] Some of the films the duo worked on together include *Lady for a Day* (1933), *It Happened One Night* (1934), *Mr. Deeds Goes to Town* (1936), and *You Can't Take It With You* (1938). According to Riskin's biographer Ian Scott, after Riskin began feeling the two had nowhere left to go artistically and when Capra signed a contract for a film as director alone without Riskin attached in 1941, the two parted ways and never directly worked together again.[373] McBride in particular credits Riskin with the entirety of the political heart of Capra's films, going so far as to argue that Capra's only successes without Riskin were

369 Joseph McBride, *Frank Capra: The Catastrophe of Success* (New York: Simon & Schuster, 1992), 547.

370 Matthew C. Gunter, *The Capra Touch: A Study of the Director's Hollywood Classics and War Documentaries, 1934–1945* (London: McFarland & Co., 2012), 205; Raymond Carney, *American Vision: The Films of Frank Capra* (Cambridge: Cambridge University Press, 1986), 488.

371 Leland Poague, *Another Frank Capra*, Cambridge Studies in Film (Cambridge: Cambridge University Press, 1994), 228.

372 Ian Scott, *Robert Riskin: The Life and Times of a Hollywood Screenwriter*, 1st ed. (Lexington: The University Press of Kentucky, 2021), 3.

373 Scott, 158.

not because of Capra at all, but rather were due to the narrative formula Riskin had developed and perfected out of his own political thinking and personal connection with the audience.[374]

While the narrative structure Capra and Riskin developed was of particular success in the 1930s while they worked together, Capra was not devoid of his own political views nor incapable of asserting them in his art. As explored in Chapter 1, while *It's a Wonderful Life* did have elements reminiscent of earlier Capra films, it was both unique and simultaneously a product of the post-war period looking backwards over the 1930s and early 1940s. Riskin certainly influenced Capra's early career and the two made excellent cinema together; however, McBride's assessment that Capra had no political heart without Riskin attached is a bold and inaccurate exaggeration about Capra's filmography. In fact, Capra's political messaging in two of his 1940s films (*It's a Wonderful Life* and *State of the Union*) twice caused problems for him by attracting federal interest and scrutiny over their potentially "un-American nature". This scrutiny of his political ideas in the 1946 to 1961 period – not his lack of a political heart in his films – is one of the most significant factors in his declining prestige and ultimate retirement.

One critic, Michel Cieutat, argues that there were wider political nuances at play and agrees to an extent with this chapter's argument that Capra was coerced into making *Pocketful of Miracles*, the film that ultimately ended his career. Cieutat argued in 1988 – in a book published in France and not the US where Cold War tensions were still very much present – that Capra left Hollywood in 1961 "plus ou moins contraint et forcé, en tout cas à contrecœur" [more or less by constraint or force, or in any case reluctantly].[375] Cieutat explains these constraints and forces pushing Capra out:

> Il dut céder la place, dépassé qu'il était par l'évolution de Hollywood, déplacé qu'il se sentait par rapport aux changements des temps (de Hiroshima à la guerre froide, l'Amérique était passée successivement, sur le plan international, de la désillusion au cynisme, et au niveau domestique, de la joie à la fureur de vivre).

> [He had to give way, overwhelmed as he was by the evolution of Hollywood, displaced as he felt compared with the changes of the times (from Hiroshima to the Cold War, America had successfully passed, on the international level, from disillusionment to cynicism, and at the domestic level, from the joy to the fury for life).][376]

---

374 McBride, *Frank Capra*, 238.
375 Michel Cieutat, *Frank Capra* (Paris: Rivages, 1988), 11.
376 Cieutat, 11.

This assessment is very much in line with the critiques explored in this chapter, which will go a step further than Cieutat to consider more fully the changes within Hollywood as a direct result of mounting Cold War political pressures on the cultural industry. Additionally, this chapter explores the more personal political experiences Capra endured throughout the 1950s that forced him out of Hollywood.

Cieutat also acknowledges that Capra, a famous micromanager much like Disney, had lost control over his films and was forced by Hollywood politics and economics to relinquish effective power over his work. All four of Capra's final films between 1950 and 1961, according to Cieutat, "étant dominés par les exigences de leurs interprètes principaux" [were dominated by the demands of their principal performers].[377] This chapter explores these films in the context of Capra's own recounting of his experiences in the 1950s and how they ultimately spelled the end of his career as he gradually lost control over his directorial direction.

Capra's 1950s

Between 1946's *It's a Wonderful Life* and 1961's *Pocketful of Miracles*, Capra released four feature-length Hollywood films: *State of the Union* (1948), *Riding High* (1950), *Here Comes the Groom* (1951), and *A Hole in the Head* (1959).[378] These films very much align with the changes in filmic content identified by Dorothy Jones in the period between 1947 and 1954 and the extension of those changes examined in this book. *State of the Union* is the last of Capra's films to engage directly with politicians and Washington D.C. with an even more direct and cynical look at the political landscape than his earlier films such as *Mr. Smith Goes to Washington* (1939).

As the influences of HUAC and the pressures on Hollywood to move away from social problem films mounted, Capra's films from 1950 and 1951 are both distinctly different from much of his earlier, more politically-minded work. Both musicals starring Bing Crosby, the tone of those early 1950s films and their simplistic romantic narratives do not fit comfortably with the majority of Capra's filmography, at least of the two decades prior to their release. This abrupt tonal shift suggests that Capra, whose micromanagement style fed his obsession with perfecting fine details and maintaining control over his productions, had been swayed by the pressures facing the whole industry that led to the decline in social problem and psychological films and the rise in light-hearted romances, comedies, and musicals, both trends that Jones identified.

---

377 Cieutat, 11.
378 Alongside these films, Capra directed three documentaries for Bell Laboratories: *Our Mr. Sun* (1956), *Hemo the Magnificent* (1957), and *The Strange Case of the Cosmic Rays* (1957).

State of the Union is a mostly typical populist Capra film concerned with corruption in Washington DC and expressing apprehensions of the unchecked power leaders may exert over the people. A businessman Grant Matthews (Spencer Tracy), with lofty ideals about the promise of the American people, is hand-chosen to seek the Republican nomination for president due to his popularity, exploitable personal relationships and, above all, his ostensible dedication to morality. Throughout the film and the course of his campaign, Grant allows himself to be consumed by corrupt practices including false campaign promises and backdoor deals with agricultural, union, and business leaders to win delegates at the convention. His wife Mary (Katharine Hepburn) reminds him of the honesty he began the campaign with and the intentions he had to stay above the deceit in Washington in order to better the country. Ultimately, Mary delivers a shaming speech that drives Grant to announce on a national television and radio broadcast that he is dropping out of the race due to the contempt he believes politicians hold for the American people. The film finishes with Grant's raucous decision made over the airwaves to leave politics behind entirely in favor of trying as a private citizen to convey to the American public the dangers of Washington's corruption.

Early on, Grant arrives in Washington to hear the plans of his former – and future – mistress, Republican newspaper magnate Kay Thorndyke (Angela Lansbury) as well as Republican strategist Jim Conover (Adolphe Menjou). In this scene, there is a very clear personal temptation Grant has towards Kay, introducing the notion that she is willing to exploit their relationship in order to further her own career ambitions to become a top political consultant. Grant has already developed inner turmoil about seeing her when he delivers a speech to the pair of them espousing his very negative views of politicians:

> You politicians, instead of trying to pull the country together, are helping pull it apart just to get votes. To labor you promise higher wages and lower prices. To business, higher prices and lower wages. To the rich, you say let's cut taxes. To the poor, soak the rich. For the veterans, cheaper housing. To the builders, uncontrolled prices.[379]

His contempt for politicians begins and ends the film, slamming the system of backdoor deals for its disregard of the American people in choosing their own leaders. Throughout the film, Capra's own political evolution from 1939's *Mr. Smith Goes to Washington* can be seen, as Grant begins – like Jefferson Smith – with the classic populist tour of Washington, inspired by the architecture and leaders invoked along the way. However, unlike Smith or even George Bailey, whose

---

[379] These sentiments about labor and veterans' housing difficulties echo those social problems emphasized in the films from 1947 explored in Chapter 2.

lapses in judgement and temptations last only a moment, for the majority of the film's second half Grant becomes seduced by the corruption that promises a road to the White House. The populist hero ultimately is not Grant but rather his wife, whose conscience and morals keep her from compromising the film's ultimate moral message.

State of the Union is a more cynical film than many of Capra's previous ones. There are several reasons why this could be the case, including that the film is based on a 1945 play of the same name by Russel Crouse and Howard Lindsay. Capra and his writers stuck closely to the play but updated it to be more accurate to the moment, emphasizing its connections with present politics. For instance, instead of a general businessman reminiscent of Wendell Wilkie and his unexpected 1940 Republican nomination for president, Grant was specifically changed to be an aircraft tycoon – probably an allusion to Howard Hughes.

Another influence on the cynicism within *State of the Union* concerns the contextual politics within Hollywood around its production. As mentioned in Chapter 1, in 1947, upon the announcement of HUAC's intentions to hold hearings into Hollywood, *The Best Years of Our Lives* director William Wyler, director John Huston, screenwriter Philip Dunne, and actor Alexander Knox among others formed the Committee for the First Amendment (CFA) to fight back against what they saw as egregious federal oversight and a violation of First Amendment rights. Capra himself was among the signatories of the first statement delivered by the CFA. That statement read in part:

> We are tired of our industry, and our professions, and of our family and friends, eternally being placed in a defensive position by every group seeking notoriety at Hollywood's expense. We have faith that the great majority of the elected Congressional representatives of the American people resent equally with us abuses of powers of the Congress.[380]

The CFA and many individuals in Hollywood sympathetic to the cause, including Capra, were concerned with this overreach of power into the film arm of the cultural sector.

Political factions in Hollywood were now deepening beyond labor disputes and union organizing and becoming more ideological and abstract as the concerns over communist subversion became more rampant. As political ideologies and the process of filmmaking overlapped more and more, productions had to navigate differences of character and opinion on sets. Adolphe Menjou, as noted above, played the part of a corrupt politician in *State of the Union*. Menjou, in Capra's own words,

---

380 Gabriel Miller, *William Wyler: The Life and Films of Hollywood's Most Celebrated Director* (Lexington: University Press of Kentucky, 2013), 298.

was "a flag-waving super-patriot who invested his American dollars in Canadian bonds" and had "a manic thing about Communists."[381] Menjou was also one of the first to testify before HUAC in 1947 as an eager friendly witness alongside Disney and Ayn Rand.[382] Tensions on the set of *State of the Union* consequently ran high and, as Capra recounts, Menjou butted against his more liberal co-stars including Spencer Tracy and Katharine Hepburn. Capra also wrote retrospectively of his experiences producing a film in this period:

> The year 1947 was a time of vicious intra-industry political war; returned service veterans and others were trying to root out the entrenched reds. Bitter arguments, loud shouting matches, even blows filled the air.
> ... But despite the presence and war-created popularity of reds in Hollywood, red propaganda in films had been miniscule in importance or dividends.[383]

These pressures and tensions on set, as well as in the political landscape of Hollywood surrounding it, influenced Capra. He made a stand in 1947 to sign his support for the CFA's cause and he certainly allowed his views of the federal government's overreach into cultural media to become a major point of interest in *State of the Union.*

As Capra's politics were always nuanced, *State of the Union* offers a strong and compelling case against Washington corruption, while supporting both socially conservative ideas of the family and more liberal ideas of women in the public sphere. The film emphasizes the promise of power not for the betterment of the nation, but rather for the sake of power itself. Grant does eventually put an end to the charade of his presidential campaign and sees the light, but not without his wife's steadfast challenges to the political fixers who are determined to secure Grant's nomination and therefore power for themselves. The film is quite progressively pro-women with multiple scenes suggesting that women have a true power over men's minds and that a woman should even be president, while also foregrounding the importance of a woman's place in the home raising her children. It straddles social conservatism for traditional roles while at the same time empowering women to positions of moral influence in society, for better or for worse as shown with Kay's role in the plot.

The beginning of Capra's own increasing disillusionment with the US government is evident in *State of the Union.* In many respects, it is a classic Capra film. Through Grant and Mary's speeches, Capra's populist ideals have ample opportu-

---

381 Capra, *The Name Above the Title*, 391.
382 Miller, *William Wyler*, 301.
383 Capra, *The Name Above the Title*, 390.

nity to shine. Much of the film, like several of its predecessors, becomes Capra's own diatribes on the state of the nation, its people, and the growing divide between communities played against one another for the sake of votes. Several times, the equation of Democrats and Republicans is suggested, that both are as good and as bad as the other and that both are highly orchestrated charades involving supposed democratically decided leaders but in fact without any say from the people. Capra had always been cynical of political elites and challenged the extent to which they upheld the ideals of the US, but *State of the Union* takes this cynicism a step further and allows the hero to become obsessed with pursuing delegates rather than speaking on truths he knows are right. Additionally, the film takes many cracks at Communism within the US and abroad, making it clear that while criticizing the US establishment, the film is not an endorsement of Communism, but rather a cry for help to save the American union from itself.

However, the film offers a wide departure from Capra's earlier populist classics in allowing the main protagonist to be seduced by the corruption for so long and then leave politics entirely at the end. When Grant walks out of the broadcast after giving his speech, he is giving up any opportunity to reform the government from within. Previous films, particularly *Mr. Smith* which addresses Washington corruption directly or *It's a Wonderful Life* with George working from within the banking system to correct Potter's corruptions, have the protagonist identifying the corruption and working within the system to fix it. Grant leaves entirely, deciding that his energies are better spent organizing individuals outside of the federal government as the structures of power inside US institutions are too corrupt to fix from within as an individual. This is a departure for Capra and one that will be seen again below when the protagonist of his *Ride the Pink Cloud* – a film that was never made – leaves the New York media scene because the corruption within it is too great for one man to change.

Capra, whose previous films supported the American exceptionalist idea that any individual American can do anything even in the face of a large and crooked system, leaned into the cynicism of the moment in *State of the Union*, questioning the effectiveness of the individual in making a difference against such organized and systemic corruption. Further, Grant's introduction with his moving speech about seeing the corruption in Washington for what it is encourages the audience to think of him at the start as a classic Capra populist hero. The film then follows this populist hero as he is seduced by not only the corruption and backdoor deals but also his former mistress Kay, and it underlines the message that any individual, even those most ardently advocating for their political principles, may succumb to the temptations of promised power, fame, and apparent reverence. It is self-evident that Capra connected to this film in a personal way from the way he wrote in his autobiography about the production and the Hollywood moment, his own support of the CFA against HUAC, and retrospectively looking back at his career's trajectory over the next 13 years as it declined and ultimately ended with *Pocketful of Miracles.*

Interestingly, however, to borrow Sklar's three-audience framework, Capra's work still had a fairly strong resonance with movie audiences. *State of the Union* was the 14th top-grossing film of 1948 at approximately $3.5 million.[384] However, his relationship with colleagues within Hollywood was beginning to fracture as factions began to take hold in the industry on either side of the HUAC investigations. And with regard to critics, Capra had already begun to lose favor. One review by Lee Mortimer of the New York *Daily Mirror* alleged that *State of the Union* was in itself communist subversion and joked about how Menjou, as the staunch anti-communist he was, had allowed Capra's subversion to slip past him. This review, as will be explored further below, would come back to haunt Capra three years later in 1951 when he had his national security clearance formally revoked by the US Defense Department, for whom he was working at the time.

Capra's next films after *State of the Union* were two unremarkable musicals with notably no direct political commentary. *Riding High* (1950) is a musical remake of Capra's earlier comedy-drama *Broadway Bill* (1934), and *Here Comes the Groom* (1951) is a light-hearted musical romantic-comedy, both starring Bing Crosby. These films were a far cry from his previous two in the late 1940s, both of which attracted critical and federal concerns about his political leanings. What is notable here is that Capra made these two musicals and showed his willingness to bend to industry pressures and not make such straightforwardly politically challenging films as he had earlier. These new films were also consistent with Jones's findings of an increasingly higher rate of Hollywood romances, farces, and musicals in place of the declining number of social problem films of the kind Capra himself had been making for over a decade prior.

This willingness on Capra's part to comply with Hollywood's new priorities, however, was not rewarded which he blames on Mortimer's 1948 review of *State of the Union.* Capra recounts in his autobiography that he was invited to join the Committee of Psychological Warfare for the Defense Department's think tank Project VISTA, organized under the Truman administration in April 1951. In December 1951, however, Capra's security clearances were abruptly revoked, and he was handed a letter detailing seven charges levied against thousands of suspected communists in Hollywood and two direct charges against Capra himself based on Mortimer's earlier review in the *Daily Mirror.*[385] According to Capra, he re-

---

384 "Top Grossers of 1948", *Variety* (Los Angeles, January 5, 1949), ProQuest.
385 Capra, *The Name Above the Title*, 427.

sponded urgently, spending the next ten days through Christmas 1951 devising a 220-page defense of himself and his work against these allegations of un-American activity. But after this vehement defense, Capra received no reinstatement of his security clearance or position on Project VISTA. Instead, he writes that he was invited by the State Department to travel to India in an official capacity as a US Delegate for India's first international film festival. His role was apparently to serve as a cultural ambassador sent on the premise of foiling an alleged "Soviet plot" to infiltrate the global film community.[386]

In the same section of his autobiography, Capra refers to this time of his life as "self-exile", a period when he removed himself from Hollywood. The more likely view of the situation, however, was that a man who dedicated his life to the portrayal of the American Dream, American ideals, and American identity on film from the perspective of an immigrant who chose this life, who defended the US, who was instrumental in the war effort, who worked for the government, and who created their propaganda, was then branded as un-American and subsequently used as a pawn, allegedly sent abroad to be an asset of the US government while serving to root out communists on their behalf, something he signed the CFA letter in defiance against in 1947.

As few sources for Capra's life exist and his autobiography cannot be fully trusted, it is important to remember that this confusing account of what happened in 1951 and his "self-exile" are reflections from two decades later. Whether these events truly happened as he says is not easily verifiable, but the fact he wrote them this way reveals that he was still bitter about them. He asserts ownership over his departure from Hollywood for the eight years between 1951 and 1959, when he would release his next feature-length film. He emphasizes what he saw as his importance to the US government and the respect he felt he should have been afforded as an integral architect of American identity and morale in the 1930s and 40s, as Sklar likewise contends.[387]

It can then be surmised that Capra, who had produced two films that were criticized as potential communist subversion and two subsequent films that sought not to engage with anything opinionated enough to draw such criticisms, felt the sting of those allegations of pro-communist views from the US government. He likely resented the fact that his willingness to make those musicals, that departed so widely from the kind of films he had been accustomed to making for decades prior, had not been appreciated. Even after all his service to populist American patriotism on screen, he could still be labeled a disloyal person and have his Amer-

---

386 Capra, 429.
387 Sklar, *Movie-Made America*, 214.

icanness questioned. This treatment, the allegations of communist subversion for the second time in only four years, and the pressure to confront his own identity as an American citizen forced a "bitter realism" on Capra that he brought into his final film of the decade, *A Hole in the Head*, as well as a film he had been working on for years but never made, *Ride the Pink Cloud.*[388]

A Hole in the Head, starring Frank Sinatra, was released in 1959 to moderate box office success, earning $3.04 million.[389] This film is a less characteristically Capra film from this period that does end on a very Capra-corn note, similar to *State of the Union.* The resounding positivity at the film's end, however, does not necessarily convey Capra's idealistic and positive view of Americana as many of his previous films had. Instead, *A Hole in the Head* has a much bleaker outlook on life in the late 1950s, embracing the cynicism understandably troubling Capra in those later years.

A Hole in the Head is about a widower, Tony (Sinatra), who runs a hotel in Miami, and his 11-year-old son, Ally (Eddie Hodges). Tony is served eviction papers and must find the $5000 for rent to keep his home, hotel, and son. When Tony turns to his brother Mario (Edward G. Robinson) for help one too many times, Mario and his wife Sophie (Thelma Ritter) travel to Miami intending to take Ally home with them and leave Tony to his expensive tastes and empty bank account. Tony, meanwhile, is concocting a plan to find investors to buy up land outside of Miami on which to build a "Disneyland" – a plan that is laughed at repeatedly and seen as incomprehensible years prior to the opening of Disney's own Disneyworld in Florida in 1971. Ultimately, Tony gets the money he needs for the rent, gambles it away, and loses the investors for his property. His brother bails him out again, expressing his love for Tony and taking Ally to live with him. Ally jumps out of the taxi and runs to his father and the two sing "High Hopes" as they walk down the beach. Sophie cries "they're so happy and so poor" to which Mario responds, "No, Sophie, they're broke but they're not poor."

The ending is very reminiscent of a classic Capra film with the reassurance of love, support, and family rallying around an individual whose love is his strength. However, the characterization of Tony as a gambler, a failed businessman, a womanizer, and a man who prioritizes the aesthetics of success and "being on easy street" towards financial success above hard work are not reminiscent of a traditional Capra hero. These aspects make for a grittier, more complex character with redeeming qualities and also flaws and misplaced confidence that put his young

---

388 Capra, *The Name Above the Title*, 460.
389 The full amount grossed is noted as $3,047,296 in a letter to Capra from James Velde, Vice President in charge of Domestic Sales at United Artists dated January 24, 1962 found in the Frank Capra archives at Wesleyan University.

son in jeopardy multiple times. From this film, it is clear that Capra was having more complex feelings about the world than his earlier 1950s musicals with Bing Crosby would suggest.

Capra also had a complex relationship with this film and saw it as indicative of the changing times. Reflecting on *A Hole in the Head* in his autobiography, Capra writes:

> The other major news item about *A Hole in the Head* was the answer to this personal question: Could I evoke heart and humor out of a "sex and violence" entry, a story with no hero, no Mr. Deeds or Mr. Smith; a story about hard, unpleasant characters? Bitter "realism" was the trend. Could I leap a seven-year hiatus, dive into the pool of cynicism, and come up with laughs? Or, was my courage too worn and my legs too stiff to run with the times?[390]

Capra's reflection in *A Hole in the Head* of this awareness of the changes in the seven years since his last feature film project, as well as the reasons for that hiatus, are crucial to understanding why *Pocketful of Miracles* failed. In Capra's words, the "bitter realism" on trend was a reading of both the movie industry and contemporary culture and also a personal reflection of his experiences throughout the 1950s.

Capra's disillusionment with not only Hollywood but also the US government and his experiences of being an Italian-American in the 1950s hardened him. Despite his disillusionment, Capra engaged with the time as best he could upon his return from exile – and a brief stint making documentaries for Bell Laboratories – in making *A Hole in the Head*. Even he was aware that this film failed to be a perfect comedy or even a classic Capra film, though he did count it as a success. In his view, "there was a seventeen-year comedy dry spell (1944–60) between McCarey's *Going My Way* and Wilder's *The Apartment* – two great motion pictures that dramatized and epitomized the seventeen-year growth of cynicism in our national attitudes and in our Hollywood films." He goes on to characterize protagonists of this period as "non-heroes" with "daring villainy" and continues "*A Hole in the Head* was filled with what we used to call unpleasant characters. The leading man was a grandstanding, dame-chasing wastrel; rearing a ten-year-old son in an atmosphere both sinful and phony."[391] These characteristics are a wide departure from the Mr. Smiths or George Baileys of previous decades and paint an interesting contextual framework for the Capra film that never was, *Ride the Pink Cloud.*

---

390 Capra, *The Name Above the Title*, 460.
391 Capra, 462.

Ride the Pink Cloud

While making *A Hole in the Head* and the Bell Laboratories documentaries, Capra was ruminating on another script. He had been approached in 1956 by Columbia to remake *Lady for a Day*, but Capra wanted to write something new and compelling that matched his growing dissatisfaction with the contemporary world. Capra's most critical biographer, McBride, wrote of this potential remake:

> The Frank Capra who returned to Columbia to remake *Lady for a Day* in 1956 was a shell of the man who had made the original in 1933. Like most of the other projects he worked on in his later years, the remake foundered at Columbia because of "script problems," a euphemism for his increasing incoherent socio-political ideas and for his inability to cope with the changing times in a meaningful way.[392]

These "script problems" McBride references are a seldom discussed and underknown project of Capra's that never progressed beyond the script. The project had several titles but is officially underscored as *Ride the Pink Cloud* on Capra's own original pages. Only seven pages of the script exist in the Frank Capra Collection at the Reid Cinema Archives housed at Wesleyan University in Connecticut, but from them the opening of the film, the setting, and the characters are made clear.

Dated April 15, 1957, Capra started the first draft of his never-produced script *Ride the Pink Cloud*.[393] The cover page has typed – and crossed out – the title "The Mustard Seed", a second illegible and scribbled title beneath it, and written above in pencil "Ride the Pink Cloud" above "(Lady for a Day)". It is unclear what Capra meant by these titles and whether *Ride the Pink Cloud* was actually intended to be a remake or adaptation of *Lady for a Day*, but from the script's first seven pages, that does not seem to be the case.

Set in Goshen, Washington, on the apple farm of Dave and Betty Smith, the film would have opened on a welcoming ceremony that "should lift the hearts of Americans and of the world." In these opening pages, Dave has traveled to Korea and adopted ten war orphans whom he is bringing home that day to the fanfare of a local holiday that had closed the community's banks and schools "to honor a simple American couple for an act of human kindness that has fired the imagination and kindled the hearts of humanity everywhere." A Mr. Briggs of the State Department, commenting on the festivities, remarks that the event "just grew and grew and grew! What with all the trouble, cold wars, etc. the

---

392 McBride, *Frank Capra*, 627.
393 "First Draft by Frank Capra April 15, 1957." Frank Capra Collection, Box 30, Folder POCKETFUL OF MIRACLES, "Ride the Pink Cloud draft, notes" April 15, 1957.

world is hungry, hungry for human kindness." When pressed whether this mass adoption was organized by the State Department as propaganda, he wholeheartedly answers in the negative and profusely praises the good nature of Dave. In the margins of the script next to this section, there are comments that do not appear to be in Capra's own handwriting. One reads, "to my mind, the best speed on world affairs I've heard this year" with "year" underlined.

Mr. Briggs wants to invite the local paper to record the events but the head of the local Chamber of Commerce tells him that they would not cover such a story as there is nothing to "blast out here." Red Neenan, the editor of the local paper is described as a "tough but civilized Mick" and then, when he is introduced, openly criticizes Dave Smith's adoption of the orphans saying, "it's either a publicity stunt, or else he wants some cheap apple pickers." Marginalia that appear to be from Capra himself read "either way, it's tough on those orphans."

Red then returns to a conversation in progress about a store wanting a story about a Mexican girl being found innocent of shoplifting pulled from the paper. When he refuses, the store threatens to pull advertising funds to which Red responds that they ought to because the story of the girl being declared innocent of the store's implied racial profiling is going on the front page, "pictures and all." Red's wife Mary, having witnessed his heated exchange, announces that this is the final straw: their telephone had been repossessed that morning and they cannot afford to feed their children. It is clear they are in financial straits due to Red's moral code and pursuit of journalistic integrity putting his income in jeopardy.

In a final plea, Mary begs her husband to come back with her to New York where he can return to being a big city editor and give up the small-town news to which he is clearly not suited. She says to him, "Come down to earth. This idea you're another Ed Howe or a William Allen White might have sounded big in the men's bar at the Waldorf, but it doesn't even make a murmur out here in the sticks a million miles from nowhere," adding later, "when the dream's over, come on back, Mr. Galahad."[394] The pages end with Mary telling her husband that chasing his dream has soured him and made him "hate people who adopt orphans."

These seven pages of a script do not seem to suggest a remake or even adaptation of *Lady for a Day*. Instead, they introduce a grim look at the world, imme-

---

394 Ed Howe and William Allen White were newspaper editors from Kansas in the latter 1800s and early 1900s. Howe was concerned with writing about what he called "the small affairs of humanity" while White was a more political journalist and both a local editor and a leader of the Progressive movement (see: Philip Mangelsdorf, "When William Allen White and Ed Howe Covered the Republicans", *Journalism Quarterly* 44, no. 3 (September 1967): 454–60).

diately commenting on the Cold War, the harshness of reality, the existence of children made orphans by an American war effort, the very real suspicion that the State Department would stage an adoption of those orphans for pro-American propaganda, the financial challenges of small-town America, distrust of media outlets, commercialists' control over those media outlets, and, most surprisingly for Capra, the death of a man's American dream. This film was never made, but the script's first draft was evidently read and remarked upon by at least one other person who praised Capra's perspective on world affairs and made some editorial suggestions throughout these seven extant pages. McBride suggests that there was a much longer script that Capra presented to Columbia and then shopped around to other studios when rejected.[395] It is unclear how long the final draft was or what stage of completion it reached, but regardless, the ideas within it are far starker than the light-hearted comedies and musicals Capra had been producing throughout the 1950s, echoing his growing distrust, disillusionment, and disdain for the America of the early Cold War.

While the full picture of *Ride the Pink Cloud* does not exist today and much of this analysis is projected from a script's opening scenes, the trajectory of Capra's thinking can be seen in how he chooses to frame the introductions of characters, a consistent trend in his previous films. Capra's concern with the media here highlights a different perspective from that of *State of the Union* nearly a decade prior. In the 1948 film, the concern with the media was that there were dangerous links between establishment politicians using the media in dishonest ways to further their own careers and ambitions, a sentiment also seen in his earlier *Mr. Smith Goes to Washington* (1939). In the opening pages of *Ride the Pink Cloud*, however, Capra's presentation of the media has shifted to focus on a cynical reporter who distrusts the motivations of individuals who are doing ostensibly good things and, especially, those of the State Department. The journalist, Red, is wary of an individual adopting orphans and challenges the inherent worth of doing so for their new father, raising the issue of whether Dave is an intrinsically good person or whether he has staged an event for the positive publicity or even potentially adopted the children to exploit as cheap laborers.

On his introduction, again, Red is having a conversation with a store representative about the store seemingly racially profiling a young Mexican girl. The representative wants the story pulled so as to mitigate any negative press, but Red refuses, adamant that the story remains to protect the girl's reputation. These actions are those of an even more assertive George Bailey-type from *It's a Wonderful Life:* a man willing to put his own personal life on the line – as he does when

---

395 McBride, *Frank Capra*, 627.

his wife leaves with the children – in pursuit of justice and integrity in a small town. Red is wary of the US government for their potential propagandizing – ironically a role Capra himself played for the government during WWII – and of businesses that would willingly and eagerly destroy the life of an immigrant by not publicly retracting false accusations of her alleged crimes – the kind of a position in which Capra had found himself in 1950.

Further, Red is framed as a bitter individual and sarcastically likened by his wife to Galahad, a Knight of the Round Table from Arthurian legend in search of the Holy Grail. This reference is a powerful insight into Capra's own political predicament in the late 1950s as he confronts the unobtainable nature of the American Dream he had so frequently extolled in his own works. The progression of Capra's portrayals of the media – from a tool of corrupt politicians to individuals like Red refusing to uncritically report on the government in pursuit of social justice – is exemplary of his own growing criticisms of the US.

Regarding the title of this seeming self-portrait of a script, it is unclear what the "Pink Cloud" is. It could perhaps be an allusion to the red imagery used for communists or, possibly, an idiom from Alcoholics Anonymous. In September 1955, American psychologist Harry M. Tiebout penned an article for the publication *AA Grapevine* – the journal for Alcoholics Anonymous – entitled "The Pink Cloud and After". In this article, Tiebout describes for the first time in writing the philosophy behind the pink cloud during recovery, a "blissful" state of euphoria just after entering sobriety when "the ego which has been full of striving, just quits and the individual senses peace and quiet within." Tiebout continues, "The result is an enormous feeling of release and the person flies right up to his pink cloud and thinks he has found Heaven on earth."[396] It is possible that Capra became aware of the phrase and its larger philosophy around the time of its conception and related to the idea of euphoria after dropping the pursuit of an unobtainable goal. While it is unclear exactly who the protagonist of *Ride the Pink Cloud* is, Red, his idealistic pursuit of fair journalism that has brought his family to ruin, and the sarcastic reference to him as Galahad – the pursuer of the Holy Grail – seem to fit with this potential understanding of the pink cloud.

If this reference to the euphoria felt after the ego is checked is accurate and if Red is the main character of the proposed film – and both seem likely – it enhances the argument that *Ride the Pink Cloud* would have been the logical continuation of Capra's own politics. In these opening pages of *Ride the Pink Cloud*, it is clear that Capra is attempting to channel the small-town politics of *It's a Wonderful*

---

396 Harry M. Tiebout, 'The Pink Cloud and After', September 1955, https://www.aagrapevine.org/magazine/1955/sep/pink-cloud-and-after.

Life into a connection with the wider world. A local "hero" adopting children made orphans by the US military as the opening scene highlights the importance, to Capra, of a small American town to the wider world. By welcoming immigrants into the small town, Capra echoes the scenes in *It's a Wonderful Life* in which George welcomes and houses the immigrant populations of Bedford Falls and embraces them as a vital part of the local community and economy. Red's concern at the staging of this event by the State Department in *Ride the Pink Cloud* only furthers the divide Capra sees between real American people in small American towns and their government. Having worked for decades on films centered on the experiences of Americans with optimistic messages and inspiration to work hard in pursuit of proclaimed American values, Capra's opening pages here read as a dropping away of the pretenses of positivity in favor of a much more critical distrust of the contemporary world and the motivations within it.

Ride the Pink Cloud had the potential to complete a trajectory of Capra's own politics as captured on film across two and half decades comprising the Great Depression, WWII, the post-war period, and the tail end of the first full decade of the Cold War. His own experiences as an immigrant finding Hollywood fame through his art and his celebration of American values, his critical patriotism, and his gradual disillusionment with all of it as the government and studios began to turn on him are all seen on screen and in the start to this script. *Ride the Pink Cloud*'s portrayals of the media and challenges to the government are not, as McBride comments, "incoherent socio-political ideas" but rather are a distillation of his own experiences and interactions with the US government throughout the 1950s, causing not an "inability to cope with the changing times" but rather an ability to react to his own cynicism about an increasingly out of reach promise sold by the same US propaganda he once made. *Ride the Pink Cloud* was blocked by every studio Capra brought it to.

Capra was not out of touch; the studio heads and other Hollywood executives blocking his very apt reflections on the harsh realities of the Cold War were out of touch. For instance, in 1957, the Academy of Motion Picture Arts and Sciences banned communists' eligibility for winning Oscars, doubling down on anti-communist sentiments years after HUAC left Hollywood. Coincidently, that same year at the Oscars, Dalton Trumbo of the Hollywood Ten won the Academy Award for Best Story under the pseudonym "Robert Rich" for *The Brave One*. This ban was repealed just two years later in 1959 for having been "unworkable" and "impractical."[397] The pressures on Hollywood detailed in this study, both political and social,

---

397 Thomas M. Pryor, "Academy Repeals Ruling on 'Oscars'; Anti-Communist Ban, Voted 2 Years

to oust communism from the movies and create more pro-American content worked in the late 1940s and early 1950s, for critics and audiences alike. By the later 1950s, however, the same Hollywood elites, who established the blacklist and approved of which scripts would be produced and when, were the ones who decided that Capra's timely script *Ride the Pink Cloud* was unsuitable for production and unfit for audiences.

Affording Capra his understanding of the nuances of a complicated moment removes the entirety of the blame for the end of his career on his own inability to read an audience or his perceived "selling out" as his critics have argued. Instead, Capra was led in the wrong direction and allowed himself to be steered there having lost faith in himself as a director over the course of his own turbulent 1950s. Taken in conjunction with Disney's quite opposite experiences up to 1961, the ways in which the two filmmakers reacted to and engaged with the crushing political pressures on their industry in the late 1940s and early 1950s had a clear impact not only on the films they made, but also the relative successes of their own brands and name recognition. To fully explore that duality between success and the willingness to adapt to the moment, the next section will analyze the two 1961 Christmas films from Disney and Capra, *Babes in Toyland* and *Pocketful of Miracles*, with the backdrop of Wilder's 1960 hit, *The Apartment.*

The Apartment, **Babes in Toyland**, and *Pocketful of Miracles*

Thus far this chapter has presented the case for the upwards trajectory of Disney's multimedia empire and the downward spiral of Capra's dwindling career. Both filmmakers had quite similar inclinations when it came to work, demanding obsessive control over their film projects. As Capra spiraled throughout the 1950s, he gradually lost control of his productions and was made to defer to the studio heads, stars, and financiers of his films. Disney, on the other hand, meticulously grew his empire to ensure complete creative control over every aspect of the Disney brand, even films with other directors attached that were produced by Disney. These two filmmakers diverged wildly and to an extent swapped positions from the 1930s and early 1940s versions of themselves that Sklar captures. By 1961, the two have fully embodied opposite ends of a spectrum of influence, prestige, and power in the motion picture industry, and Capra has lost the three audiences Sklar iden-

---

Ago, Is Revoked as 'Unworkable,' 'Impractical'", *The New York Times*, January 14, 1959, accessed May 12, 2023, *The New York Times* Archive.

tifies – "the ticket-buying public, the critics and the commentators on films, and their Hollywood co-workers".[398]

Simultaneously, within the content of films and as a reflection of the growing harshness of the wider world so commonly experienced by Capra himself over this decade, Hollywood proved no longer content with merely the light-hearted fare evidenced in the rise of comedies, musicals, and romances identified by Jones. Even in these genres of film, a darkness had begun to creep in showing the cracks in the perfect performative normalcy of the earlier 1950s and echoing the growing refusal to perform that normalcy as the US committed further to foreign containment policies, culture wars, and the publicly declared willingness to use the atomic bomb. This darker edge manifests in multiple films from this period including Disney's own 1960 *Swiss Family Robinson* in which a family of refugees is marooned on an island after being shipwrecked by pirates. *Swiss Family Robinson* was at the time and still is a much beloved escapist film featuring darker elements of a family fleeing war, facing life-threatening pirates, and becoming stranded. *Swiss Family Robinson* was the fourth highest grossing film of 1960.[399]

Another film in this vein is Billy Wilder's *The Apartment* from the same year. As *The Apartment* was not a family-friendly film produced under the Disney brand, it could include far more adult themes than *Swiss Family Robinson* but still have that darker edge to an otherwise generally comedic or entertaining film. *The Apartment* follows C.C. Baxter (Jack Lemmon) a low-level office worker with aspirations above his station. As Baxter is a single man with his own apartment and knows that the executives in his company are prone to extra-marital affairs, Baxter leverages his property as a private space for those affairs with the expectation of professional quid pro quos. Baxter's boss, personnel manager Jeff Sheldrake (Fred MacMurray) and three other executives exploit this opportunity and have little regard for Baxter himself and even less for the women they bring to the apartment. Fran Kubelik, mistress to Sheldrake and Baxter's crush, realizes that Sheldrake will never leave his wife for her when he leaves her a $100 bill after their Christmas Eve session. Distraught at the implication on her character and not knowing whose apartment they are in, Fran attempts suicide and is found by Baxter when he returns home. Baxter nurses her back to health, trying and failing to convince Sheldrake that he should care about Fran as a human. Ultimately, Fran decides to leave Sheldrake and pursue Baxter romantically as he showed her a kindness no other man in the film seems to possess.

---

398 Sklar, *Movie-Made America*, 197.
399 "Pictures: All-Time Top Grossers", *Variety* (Los Angeles, January 6, 1965), ProQuest.

The Apartment won the Academy Award for Best Picture in 1961. This film is generally a well-structured comedy that maintains a light-hearted tone even in its portrayals of the darkest moments, perhaps due to Lemmon's gentle and positive demeanor throughout. It also carries a biting commentary on the men of the executive class portrayed in the film and addresses misogynistic attitudes towards women directly. Baxter's begging on Christmas Day for Sheldrake to show Fran even an ounce of kindness or remorse or attention fall on a man whose primary concern in that moment is his wife finding out about his actions. He does not see his affair partner as human and has no empathy for the mental position she is in to have hurt herself in this way. Wilder's film is a masterful balance of comedic tones delivering an emotionally devastating plot that carries with it a condemnation of the social inequalities of men and women. It pitches a central villain in Sheldrake and a romantic couple to root for in Baxter and Fran, and it does not address large systemic issues apart from the implied corruption of corporate relationships. Instead, it manufactures a problem that can be dealt with within the confines of the film to deliver a happy ending and a moralistic shaming of misogynistic behavior.

Similarly, *Babes in Toyland* pitches a central villain and romantic couple, manufactures a resolvable conflict, and chides at the murder and kidnapping plots while delivering a picture-perfect happy ending. However, in a departure from *The Apartment*, it not only portrays but actively celebrates misogyny and extreme social conservatism in the portrayal of Mary's character. *Babes in Toyland* is adapted to the moment to fit the audience and the times by delivering those darker plot points in a light-hearted tone popular in this period. *Pocketful of Miracles*, however, misses the target in this way. A comedy in itself, *Pocketful* leans into a Depression-era plot and tone with a depth of sadness throughout much of the film, an overtly acknowledged reality that Annie's escape into her millionairess persona will come to an end and she will have to go back to facing life's hardships when the credits roll. Without a central villain, *Pocketful*'s real conflict is that life is difficult, unfair, and economically unjust. This tone falls entirely too short of matching the expectations of Christmas films at this point, as the culture has changed so drastically in the 15-year period between Capra's *It's a Wonderful Life* and his *Pocketful of Miracles*.

This section will explore these two films more fully and finish with a discussion of how *Pocketful of Miracles* came to be made at all when Capra's obvious preference was the much darker, much more apt for the times tone of his drafted script *Ride the Pink Cloud*.

Babes in Toyland (1961)

Disney's *Babes in Toyland*, directed by Jack Donohue, has a strange narrative arc that departs widely from the earlier Laurel and Hardy 1934 version and the 1903 operetta, both with the same title. Mary and Tom are young lovers who become engaged to be married early on in the film. Barnaby, however, the town's villain, has a dream of procuring the lands of Mother Goose Village, including Mary's inheritance, the existence of which she is unaware. Barnaby sends his two henchmen, Roderigo and Gonzorgo (Gene Sheldon and Henry Calvin) to kidnap Tom and kill him at sea. The henchmen are to tell Mary that Tom has sailed away because he deems himself too poor to take care of her in marriage and that he has advised that, in his stead, she should marry Barnaby. A distraught Mary is then cornered by Barnaby himself who proposes to her in the song "Castle in Spain", telling her:

> In our castle in Spain
> You'll be living rent-free.
> Every capital gain
> You'll share with me.
> From this village below
> Every cent we will drain
> And our fortune will grow
> In our castle in Spain.

Barnaby's proposal revolves around the capital interest and exploitative advantages of combining their assets and raising the mortgage rates for the villagers.

Mary rejects the proposal initially but eventually convinces herself it is the only way for her to survive because she cannot sort out her finances alone either for herself or for the children who inexplicably live with her as wards. The children run off after their sheep into the Forest of No Return when Mary leaves to accept Barnaby's proposal. Simultaneously, in order to profit twice from the kidnapping of Tom, Roderigo and Gonzorgo ignore Barnaby's demand that they murder him and instead sell him to a band of travelers. The travelers then come to town, allegedly to celebrate the engagement between Mary and Barnaby. Making a dramatic entrance with a long song about the art of fortune-telling, Tom reveals himself to be posing as a mystic to thwart Barnaby's plans and expose his villainous plot to the villagers. Once reunited, Tom and Mary escape together to find the children lost in the Forest of No Return. Having found the kids, the group as a whole attempt to leave the Forest, but the menacing, singing trees surrounding them insist that they see the Toymaker as they are now trespassing on Toyland property.

The Toymaker (Ed Wynn) is in dire straits to meet a Christmas deadline of toys after his assistant's fully-automated toy machine breaks, stating that without the toys "the children will have no merry Christmas." Tom, Mary, and the children work on an industrial production line to make the toys and meet the quota, while the assistant introduces his new shrink ray that can shrink anything or anyone down to the size of a doll. After stealing the shrink ray and shrinking both Tom and his henchmen, the latter of whom appear to have grown moral consciences after committing their crimes, Barnaby arrives to try to force Mary into marriage once again with the Toymaker officiating the ceremony in his official capacity as Mayor of Toyland. Tom leads an assault with the toy soldiers in the most consistent musical piece to appear in all versions of *Babes in Toyland,* the "March of the Toy Soldiers." Ultimately, Barnaby is defeated, and the protagonists all live happily ever after in true Disney fashion.

This storyline is simplistic and accessibly presented in sections for children to follow. It also heavily emphasizes the romance between Mary and Tom while keeping the tone generally light with musical numbers and the fantastic vibrancy of Mother Goose Village and Toyland – save for the visible darkness of the Forest of No Return. However, despite the joyous tones both visibly and audibly, the character of Barnaby and all of his actions are heinous. His plan to have Tom kidnapped and killed and his subsequent plan to shrink his adversaries while forcing Mary to marry him are both quite grim for a children's film. Additionally, as the only character who speaks almost entirely in rhyme, his lyrics and dialogue are much darker than the overall tone he suggests.

Babes in Toyland follows from the aesthetics of the Christmas films from the 1950s in its exuberant, fantastic, light-handed approach to a simple linear plot. However, it departs in a crucial direction towards darker elements below the surface. While creating this Disneyland experience for the viewer, a reminder of the purposely constructed otherworldly atmosphere of the park, *Babes in Toyland* subverts that escapism with a gritty villain. This structure works for this film, Disney's brand, and the overall tone of 1961 precisely because it is escapist while not leaving the viewer wanting structural or systemic change. The villain is a defined individual, and when he is dealt with within the film, that is the end of the troubles facing the heroes. This element of a tangible, identifiable villain who is not a stand-in for larger systemic issues in the external world is not seen in any Christmas film in the 15-year period of this study prior to *Babes in Toyland.* By having a single, defeatable villain, a truly happy ending is possible without any lasting concerns or ramifications for the film's heroes.

Other elements of social conservatism in the film point to this change from the earlier films of the 1950s into the early 1960s, carrying the lightness of the aesthetics of the earlier films while underscoring harsher realities for the contemporary viewer. These harsh realities are commentaries on the wider world outside of the film; however, they differ from the social problem films of the late 1940s that Dorothy Jones identified in her study "Communism and the Movies". The decline of the earlier films' social problems – i.e. systemic and structural issues in the wider world including poverty, housing crises, and underfunded communities as discussed in Chapter 2 – are replaced with inter-personal conflicts throughout the 1950s. By 1961, these inter-personal conflicts distilled down into an individual villain, painting the picture of a happily-ever-after within the conservatively constructed filmic world beyond the ending. Some of these conservative values such as misogynistic gender norms and harsh commentaries on laborers are evident in *Babes in Toyland*.

The film does have many of the tropes of Christmas films that were developing throughout the 1950s and have since been solidified in the genre. Thinking of the three tropes of Christmas romances identified in Chapter 3 – a woman secretly wanting a traditional relationship, children as integral to the romantic relationship, and a miscommunication that must be overcome – *Babes in Toyland* takes this already socially conservative structure a step further. The musical revolves around the overt romance of Tom and Mary and Mary's responsibilities as a caregiver to children. With the advent of an actual villain, the miscommunication becomes the direct actions and lies of Barnaby to trick Mary into accepting his marriage proposal by convincing her of Tom's death. *Babes in Toyland* includes those hallmark touches of the conflicts in a growing romance while also introducing some genuinely questionable societal ideas on finances and labor alongside the multiple racist and misogynistic sequences and characters. These aspects of the film are not a complete divergence from the earlier films, but they are more overt and more extreme here, seemingly unquestioned because it was part of Disney's children's media, coming from such a trusted brand.

Barnaby and his henchmen are obsessed with profits and equate murder to crimes of capital, singing, "we'll forge a cheque or cut your neck if we can make a dime." Barnaby's obsession leads him to blackmail Mary financially by insisting she "be resourceful" and "take advantage of [his] infatuation" with her lest he "seize [her] home through legal compensation" for debts she owes to him. Mary, likewise, is concerned about her finances. Despite living in the fantasy land of Mother Goose Village, Mary is beside herself when she hears of Tom's alleged death, partly because she has lost her partner, but seemingly more so because she is concerned about making ends meet while "the price of milk and bread and eggs is rising every day." After initially rejecting Barnaby's marriage proposal, Mary sings "I Can't Do the Sum" which includes imaginary, holographic Marys in a chorus behind her and the lines,

All Marys: Picture us inside a tent -, beastly poor, insecure.
We must save the 6% – 6 times X, how complex!
Numbers always stick our brains, why are we so dumb?
This is much too hard for us, we can't do the sum.

Mary: I'm not a great financial whiz, of that there is no doubt.
The outcome of our income is our incomes all gone out.

...

This is much too hard for me, I can't do the sum.
Looks like there's no hope for me, I can't get out of debt.
If I marry Barnaby, that's the end, why pretend?
Am I doing right or wrong? My heart feels so numb.
No use trying any more, I can't do the sum.

This misogynistic song about how Mary as a woman cannot understand the math required to keep a house and therefore must marry Barnaby reinforces persistent gender stereotypes. In line with the discussion of young marriages in Chapter 3, women in the post-war era were still pressured to marry for various reasons including financial security.

According to one macroeconomic analysis of the post-war period and throughout the 1950s, "Younger women who reach[ed] adulthood in the 1950s face[d] increased market competition, which impel[led] them to exit the labor market and start having children earlier."[400] In addition, Elaine Tyler May notes a shift in the mid- to late 1950s among women enrolled in colleges who sought to be taught more fundamentals of home-making, domestic life, and motherhood than intellectual pursuits that, in many cases, would not lead to a promising, stable, and consistent career for those women.[401] The career paths for even educated women in the late 1950s were scarce and turned many women away from education entirely and towards those same younger marriages discussed in Chapter 3. In *Babes in Toyland*, Mary's reluctant concession to marry Barnaby may be read as a reflection of these marriage trends and the promise of financial security for an uneducated teenager.

Mary's song was adapted from the original 1903 operetta, rewritten for the 1961 film in a wholly different context and with these misogynistic overtones by the same lyricist who wrote "Cruella de Vil" for *One-Hundred and One Dalmatians* the same year, Mel Leven. The original 1903 song was sung by a character excised in the Disney version, Barnaby's orphaned ward Jane. The adaptation from the

---

400 Matthias Doepke, Moshe Hazan, and Yishay D. Maoz, "The Baby Boom and World War II: A Macroeconomic Analysis", *The Review of Economic Studies* 82, no. 3 (2015): 1031.
401 May, *Homeward Bound*, 81.

original operetta emphasizes that it is Mary's femininity that makes her so bad at math and is used as a plot device to justify her marrying Barnaby, a man portrayed as much smarter than she who can take care of her finances.

This overt misogyny is carried into another song entitled "Just a Toy" in the Disney version in which Mary sings a verse to a doll about her features and Tom sings the second verse to Mary posing her as his own doll. His lyrics include, "To hold you and keep you forever, and you'll live for the love and the happiness of this lonely boy and each night he will say in a whimsical way, you're just a toy." This song was written for the 1961 version, emphasizing traditional, conservative gender roles and literally objectifying Mary, a more conservative portrayal of a woman than any of the earlier films in this study. The women in *White Christmas* (1954), for example, or even the teenage Susan in *Susan Slept Here* (1954), all exert much more agency than Mary does in *Babes in Toyland*. Those female characters, while still ultimately fulfilling the conservative ideals of family women with intended marriages and normative relationships, were never objectified into being "just a toy" for the heroic male lead to position and play with. Especially in comparison to a film as critically successful as *The Apartment* earlier that year with its almost opposite messaging condemning men for this exact objectification, the misogyny of *Babes* is unquestionably radical.

Another conservative value in *Babes in Toyland* is not explored in the other Christmas films but echoes the politics of Walt Disney himself. In this version, the Toymaker is obsessed with filling his quota and accidentally breaks his assistant's fully-automated toy-making machine. He derides automation and condemns the desire to use technology to do a job, then praises the children for their own labor and work ethic. When the children eagerly beg the Toymaker to let them help build the toys, he remarks "You want to work? Nobody wants to work these days!" and he tells them "My, you're all so industrious!" The children on the factory production line making the toys are overjoyed at being allowed to work for the Toymaker and to work with their hands and not a machine, dismayed when they are told to go to bed because they want to keep working into the night. The inclusion of this bizarre recurring commentary on the children's industriousness may reflect Disney's own contentious history with labor unions and animators in the decades prior, as discussed above.

These socially conservative values and commentaries emphasized in the film do not seem to have alienated the critics, however. The *New York Times* offered a glowing review of *Babes in Toyland* while *Variety* praised the film as "Walt Disney's Christmas present for filmgoers."[402] Both reviews did acknowledge, though,

---

402 "Babes in Toyland", *Variety*, December 1, 1961.

that the film was a wholly transparent advertisement for the Disney parks with *Variety* snidely observing that "some of the more mature patrons may be distressed to discover that quaint, charming 'Toyland' has been transformed into a rather gaudy and mechanical 'Fantasyland.' What actually emerges is 'Babes in Disneyland'."

Marketing

Contextually, these darker elements and socially conservative values of the film worked well for the target audience of children who likely did not notice the overt misogyny or extolling of child labor practices. In 1961, the oldest members of the baby boomer generation would have been 15 years old. For years, many in this generation would have been viewers of Disney television shows and films and/or readers of the many available print media options Disney produced. Reflecting this, the pressbook materials for *Babes in Toyland* are separated into age groups to demonstrate how most effectively to reach the youngest audience members, teenagers, and their parents. For the youngest viewers, the pressbook recommends, with precise instructions on how to implement this marketing strategy:

Magic with BADGES

Sheer MAGNETISM to SMALL FRY!

A collector's item in white and royal purple. Let the children know you have these and they'll come in droves. Use them as incentive offers. Perhaps each child who brings his parents to see BABES IN TOYLAND could receive one, plus a fan card, plus a balloon. Use them in conjunction with other accessories which bear this monogram, such as the rubber stamp and the teaser press-ad block. "This is the sign of entertainment supreme" could be the covering slogan. Order a supply of these distinguished looking badges right away.[403]

The pressbook also gives instructions for engaging teenagers: "KEEPSAKE. Two different, super-quality, real glossy postcard photographs – for the boys, Annette; and for the girls, Tommy Sands." For adults, the pressbook recommends:

HERE'S A SUPERBLY PRODUCED LEAFLET GIVE-AWAY TO ATTRACT ADULTS

Here is a distinguished, yet provoking looking leaflet designed for use as circulars amongst adults. Its all-purple cover contains the BABES IN TOYLAND monogram and the words (in white) "The lights grow dim... The audience is tense, hushed... We look toward the stage expectantly... Music strikes up and the curtains swirl away to reveal..." The inside bears a strik-

---

403 *Babes in Toyland* Pressbook, Walt Disney Pictures – Buena Vista Distribution, 1961, Reuben Library, British Film Institute. All emphases from original source.

ing montage of scenes and the wording continues much as does the wording in the introduction (this page). Order a good supply of these leaflets – they'll sell the picture well to adults.

These recommendations are for cinemas and merchants to help promote the film, but even the language used within them to address specific audiences is revealing. The pressbook highlights certain words and uses shorter, choppier sentences with emphasis on the additional items children can acquire when discussing how to market to them, as opposed to the adult's section that uses words such as "distinguished" and "provoking". The studio's marketing tactics are designed more precisely and thematically than is apparent for any of the pressbooks for any other film in this study.

On the first page of the pressbook materials, Disney includes an introduction to merchants that, using a martial tone, offered instructions for how to read the marketing strategy. In reference to the "March of the Toy Soldiers" number at the end of the film, the pressbook reads, "Toyland has declared war on your town; you've been named the general in charge of operations – IT'S UP TO YOU TO SEE THAT TOYLAND EMERGES THE WINNER IT IS!" This language can be read as simply thematic; however, the militant tone is striking as the soldiers are the pinnacle of the film but referenced nowhere else within it.

Additionally, Disney uses this martial language to encourage cinema owners to facilitate – in their metaphor – the hostile takeover of their town by the Disney Company's invading fictional world, marketing, and film. To facilitate this, the pressbook has multiple suggestions for towns to implement including using "every possible channel and at every opportunity" to "plug the fact" that "THE DEARTH IN HOLLYWOOD OF SUPER MUSICALS IS OVER AT LAST, THANKS TO WALT DISNEY AND HIS 'BABES IN TOYLAND'." In another section, the pressbook details an idea that's "natural for a department store tie-up." The section reads:

> At Christmas the advantage would be none the less attractive as at any other time of the year, when toy departments could welcome an off-season resurgence in toy interest, brought about by BABES IN TOYLAND.
> This is, of course, Walt Disney's BABES IN TOYLAND, and the accent therefore, should be on Disney inspired merchandise, ever popular, always in stock.

The precision of this pressbook in targeting multiple demographics, using language appropriate for each demographic, trying to instill an atmosphere into a whole town, and facilitating cross-promotional tangential advertising for other Disney products is an exceptional marketing strategy. Disney's effect on the Christmas film genre is highly successful and shows the genre's progression to its pinnacle in this period by having a clear strategy of how a Christmas film should be marketed. The most interesting facet of the Disney approach to creating its first feature-length Christmas film is that *Babes in Toyland,* similarly to *One Hour in Wonderland,* is scarcely about Christmas at all, save for one reference to Santa Claus by the Toymaker and the inclusion of the Christmas romance tropes.[404] However, Disney's marketing of the film and the critics reviewing it, as well as the timing of its release – December 14, 1961 – when Christmas films were beginning to be released more frequently in the final quarter of the year than any other time, solidified its perception as a Christmas film.[405]

With *Babes in Toyland,* Disney perfected the American Christmas film structure – that still informs the genre today – while also tapping into a uniquely 1961 attitude of cynical escapism. Disney's approach to the Christmas genre was not only a transparent marketing strategy to promote the theme park, nor simply a film created for multiple generations of Disney fans, but it was also a successful introduction of children directly as a viable and profitable market for Christmas media. The film centered on a young couple in a fantasyland far removed from the real world, whose only troubles were a greedy, violent man, a common enemy for viewers to revile together. The problems depicted in *Babes in Toyland* are largely manageable and individual, easily solved with child labor and luck. The problems are not systemic to the society within Mother Goose Village or Toyland, and so while the overt misogyny and complex perspective on the industriousness of children are real-world issues that reflected the darker, grittier world of 1961, the structure works. *Babes in Toyland*'s success lies in Disney's brand's success that was painstakingly built up over the past two decades of understanding and reacting to its audience. The radical evolution of the Walt Disney Company and Walt's own acumen for micromanaging his filmmakers to produce timely films is what set the model for future Christmas films.

Pocketful of Miracles (1961)

Unlike Disney's upward rise toward Christmases future, Capra's downward spiral would remain looking backwards to Christmases past. Capra's real passion project, *Ride the Pink Cloud,* was deemed unviable by the studios and, instead, the once-

---

404 The Disney version even goes so far as to excise Santa as a character present in the film, as he was in the 1934 Laurel and Hardy version.

405 In order, the films in this study were released: *It's a Wonderful Life* December 1946, *It Happened on 5th Avenue* April 1947, *Miracle on 34th Street* June 1947, *Christmas Eve* November 1947, *The Bishop's Wife* November 1947, *Holiday Affair* November 1949, *The Lemon Drop Kid* March 1951, *Susan Slept Here* July 1955, *White Christmas* October 1954, *Babes in Toyland* December 1961, *Pocketful of Miracles* December 1961.

domineering director was pushed into a straightforward remake of *Lady for a Day*, albeit 41 minutes longer than the original. The studio's idea was to remake a beloved property with big-name stars attached as an easily profitable film sponsored by United Artists; however, this proved to be a mistake from start to finish. McBride calls *Pocketful of Miracles* "a bloated, unfunny, maudlin, miscast, and thoroughly insincere film which, incredibly, [Capra] claimed to prefer to the original."[406] Its production was also a catastrophe in which Capra slowly lost creative control over the film and quickly lost control of the cast and set after Glenn Ford stepped in as an investor and producer. With immense on-set drama between both Ford and Capra, and Ford's girlfriend Hope Lange – for whom he demanded the role of his character's girlfriend, Queenie Martin – and Bette Davis, rivalries and disagreements made for a shambolic production. The whole process had immense impacts on Capra's own health, causing him to have cluster migraines almost daily, and mentally devastated him further after its poor performance at the box office.

Pocketful of Miracles, when analyzed more deeply, is one of Capra's less-optimistic films. In real terms, as with *It's a Wonderful Life*, there is no structural change by the end of the film. There is no real villain apart from the capitalistic society that keeps Annie on the streets save for the week she is pretending to live in a penthouse suite with a butler and husband, surrounded by finery and garish opulence. The film is, on the face of it, a light-hearted 1930s comedy with standout slapstick moments, provided primarily by The Dude's henchman and film's standout, Joy Boy (Peter Falk). This dated comedy was overwhelmingly a period piece and, as McBride writes, "emotionally distant from its audience."[407]

Additionally, the makeover sequence did not land as well one would have hoped. By casting Bette Davis, a highly respected actress whose public presence and demeanor had always been the epitome of Hollywood glamour, as Annie, the shock was not the makeover into a noblewoman clad in golden garments and jewels with a refined accent and vocabulary. Rather, the shock was the opening sequences in which Davis is dressed as a haggard, drunken homeless woman. That portrayal only lasts a few scenes before she is made over into the dame for the remainder of the film. This casting choice, while understandable as Davis was a star – albeit a bit distanced from the screen in later years due to contractual disputes with the studios – was misguided.

Regardless, Annie's makeover sequence is the film's central structural device, depicting the dichotomy of wealth inequality from which everything else follows.

---

406 McBride, *Frank Capra*, 302.
407 McBride, 301.

This dichotomy is made evident first visually by establishing a set of tangible signifiers – clothing, possessions, locations, etc. – of what wealth looks like in this fictional Depression-era New York. These tangible choices are followed by mannerisms that further develop the collective aesthetics of wealth – and the lack thereof – that come to shape the characters and events within the film.

Aesthetics of Wealth

Capra's last film focusses on creating an aesthetic of wealth. Annie, as the drunken leader of a squad of Times Square panhandlers, is repeatedly shown in confrontation with the city's wealthier inhabitants. In one early scene, Annie is shown going into the Hotel Marberry, the place where she has pretended to live in her letters to Louise, even using their letterhead to send them. The stark contrast between Annie and the hotel patrons is exaggerated by the grotesque leers at her in the lobby with dialogue confirming that she does not belong in such an establishment. Nor are her actions of raising her voice and crying regarded as befitting the hotel. Visually, all the women in the hotel are adorned with furs and jewels, save for Annie who is in muted greys, oversized coats, and dusted in dirt. When she finally reads her letter and faints from the news that her daughter will be visiting New York, a woman on the street mocks her saying, "just as I said, with Prohibition repealed, you'll see our streets filled with nasty old drunks like that." This scene establishes two things. Firstly, that this 1961 portrayal of 1933 New York has two types of people: the well-to-do elites and the panhandlers and grifters. Secondly, it underscores that in order for Annie to return to this hotel, as she does later to assume her made-up persona, she will have to transform herself in the image of the well-to-do elite. This scene emphasizes the aesthetic of wealth that will be carried throughout the film as the ruse to fool Annie's daughter becomes more elaborate.

Considering these two types of people – the elites and the panhandlers – Capra distinctly creates two versions of New York for them. Annie's living quarters in a basement apartment are shambolic, dark, dirty, and littered with empty bottles of gin. Juxtaposing this, the Hotel Marberry is grand, opulent, and clean. These distinctions between not only the people but also the spaces with which they interact are important to clearly portray the difference between the New York that is accessible to the lowest classes and that which is accessible to the upper classes. This juxtaposition in the 1961 film is similar to that in Capra's original 1933 film. One key new feature of the later film that emphasizes these class distinctions is the introduction of color. Color ensured that the dark and dreary world of Davis's Apple Annie is starkly contrasted with the grandeur of the Hotel Marberry and her subsequent façade as Mrs. E Worthington Manville.

In order for Annie to be allowed into her daughter's sophisticated, worldly life, and in order to secure her daughter's relationship with the Count's son, she must assume the role of a noblewoman. Annie fears that if the Count were to know the truth about her, that she is a panhandler on the streets of New York, he would forbid the marriage between their children. In her view of Louise's world, Annie does not have a place as herself, but instead must transform into Mrs. E. Worthington Manville, the wealthy, cultured, reception-throwing hostess to politicians, diplomats, and other elites in New York City. She must change her appearance, her speech, her wardrobe, and her marital status to be granted entry into the charmed cosmopolitan life her daughter leads.

If the Hotel Marberry is viewed as a cosmopolitan space, the space of the well-to-do elites, where the aristocrats, diplomats, and a cultured few mingle, then the contrasting street corners and squalid apartments that form the backcloth of Annie's life must be viewed as distinctly not cosmopolitan. The diplomats and aristocrats do not interact with these spaces nor with the people who inhabit them, and the consensus within the film is that only the privileged few who performatively appear to be elites and play the part of wealthy nobility are allowed to enter the Hotel Marberry without rebuke.

In order to gain access to the Hotel Marberry and the upper-class spaces in the film, there are certain traits that Annie must assume to become Mrs. E. Worthington Manville. The first prerequisite to creating and maintaining the illusion of wealth is the acquisition of a suitable living space. The Dude calls on a favor from a friend and borrows his penthouse apartment in the Hotel Marberry for the week of Louise's visit. The apartment is lavish and ornate with trinkets and decorations denoting a well-travelled inhabitant. There are books and a piano, gold-trimmed furnishings, and delicate ornaments, implying an appreciation of art, literature, and music. The penthouse suite serves as the proper setting for the next stages in Annie's transformation into a true Lady.

The second step in this transition, and arguably the most crucial, is her own appearance. Before and after the makeover, Annie is repeatedly derided. Joy Boy states: "You wanna help her? Help her. But you can't palm that crocodile off as society." Queenie introduces the makeover staff as "the miracle workers" including a maid, manicurist, hairdresser, chiropodist, and masseuse. Queenie tells Annie to "stand up and meet [her] makers" and informs the staff that "this has got to be a complete overhaul from top to bottom." In terms of her appearance, in order to be elevated from her position as a panhandler on the streets, to an elite, respectable woman, Annie has a complete transformation including everything from her nails to her hygiene to her posture.

When the makeover is completed, the eight attendants working on Annie emerge from behind closed doors exhausted, sweating, and disheveled as though they were working tirelessly for hours. Annie emerges from the room with a drumroll as Mrs. E. Worthington Manville, in a golden gown adorned with pearls, jeweled earrings, and a golden walking cane to the triumphant music of the March from Tchaikovsky's *Nutcracker Suite.* Immediately, Annie carries herself differently with her shoulders back and gliding elegantly with her walking stick, contrasting with the harsh and slouched strides she took before. The Dude removes his hat to speak to her, affording her respect she did not previously receive. Junior (Mickey Shaughnessy) then refers to her as "a cockroach what turned into a butterfly". This sentence is the film's most revealing evidence of who is allowed to enter the sophisticated class of the elites and how. Only butterflies belong in the Hotel Marberry. Their faces of shock, delight, and adoration at her new appearance contrast hugely with those grotesque leers Annie received in the same building only a day or so prior to her transformation.

The third trait in elevating Annie's status is wealth. The Dude, as soon as she thanks him for his help, gives Annie "some walking around money" to enhance the façade that she is a noblewoman. Offering Annie money here is an addition to the makeover sequence that is not in the original 1933 film. Here, it is clear that it is no longer acceptable for her merely to look the part as it may have been in the 1930s, but rather she needs to be able to perform socially the actions of the wealthy, by having cash with her and possibly spending it to impress the Count.

The fourth and final trait to make the charade convincing is for Annie to acquire a husband. The Dude, feeling compelled to provide for Annie, states, "For a proposition like this we need a guy with class, with dignity, a gentleman of the old school" then suggests a man known as "The Judge" as the perfect husband material. The Judge (Thomas Mitchell) is a billiards hustler with a predilection towards opulence, royal pronunciation, literature, and fine art. His vocabulary is sophisticated, and his charm is overwhelming, convincing the butler he is culturally refined enough for the role by quoting Sir Walter Scott from memory. When the Dude explains the pretense of the ruse to the Judge that he will be Annie's husband, the Judge is disgusted with the thought. He scoffs, "A creature of the pavements, a ... a ... a frowsy hag, with the breath of a dragon. Sir, despite my larcenous impulses, I am a gentleman." Outraged at the proposition to lower himself to Annie's disreputable ways, he begins to storm out of the apartment when he catches sight of Annie post-transformation. Seeing her in her gold regalia, he relents to kiss her extended hand and assures her the pleasure is entirely his adding that she is a "dear kind and charming lady". The disdain shown for the impoverished and the abrupt shift in the Judge's demeanor emphasize the thin veil that is the aesthetic of wealth.

For the rest of the film, Annie is dressed in pearls and furs matching her daughter's expensive clothing and finery, never again shown in her oversized coats and rags. The Judge, upon meeting the Spanish Count played by Arthur O'Connell, welcomes him to America and states how wonderful this moment is for everyone, despite the fact they are surrounded by the Dude's gang to hide them from reporters and Annie's panhandler friends who are watching from a distance. The moment is not for everyone, but rather for the privileged few welcome in the literal inner-circle, guarded from the rest of New York.

As Annie and Louise get acquainted, the charade becomes harder to maintain. Annie and the Judge are compelled to throw an engagement party with their fictitious society friends. To accomplish this, the Dude hires the panhandlers and vagabonds, local swindlers and gang members under his control who all have a collective makeover sequence together. They are coached on how to speak properly, what things to say to be impressive, how to hold a conversation with nobility, how to dance and move with elegance and grace, and they are given costumes to wear to play the part convincingly. Ultimately, the Dude and his associates are trapped by police as the concurrent plot of the Dude's gangster business coincides with that of Annie's ruse.

Simultaneously, the Count's suspicions that Annie is not actually rich or respected have mounted. He is increasingly aware of the inconsistencies in Annie's and the Judge's stories and concerned that he has not yet met any of the noble elites they claim to know. In order to help Annie still have her engagement soirée to finish out the week of tricking the Count successfully, the Dude gives himself up to the police and explains Annie's predicament to the police commissioner and Mayor of New York. The mayor, moved by the story, contacts the Governor, and at the very last moment before Annie can reveal the truth to the Count, the real politicians, diplomats, and New York's society elites enter the penthouse suite of the Hotel Marberry and perpetuate the charade of Annie's noble persona without any coaching needed.

Ultimately, the elites in this film – specifically the politicians donning their own finery and furs – are the heroes. There is a distinct line drawn between those who can pass successfully as cosmopolitan on their own, who can entertain and even trick a European aristocrat, and those who cannot naturally do this, being the panhandlers, swindlers, and the impoverished. The category of nobility is gatekept by the wealthy and cultured characters in the film and it is confirmed that an impoverished person cannot ever truly inhabit the wealthy's world. Even with the most complete makeover, the structures of society are not open to the poor for more than an evening of goodwill from the wealthiest in the city. Without precise training on how to speak and move like an aristocrat, without the trappings of a millionairess, and, crucially, without the support of real nobility, Annie would have been discarded from her daughter's life and possibly have gotten her daughter expelled from it as well.

By the end of the film, the aesthetics of wealth are proven to be just aesthetics, as there is no social mobility within Annie's reach. The moment her daughter is on a ship and out of sight, Annie almost eagerly reverts back to her role as the leader of the panhandlers, advising them to start picking the pockets of patrons gathered at the docks bidding farewell to their loved ones. This lack of substantive change ends the film on a depressing note that Annie has fulfilled her purpose in lying to her daughter so that Louise may live in a fantasy without knowing the hardship her mother faces on a daily basis and might even take delight in. Without a villain, the antagonizing forces in the film are society's class structure and Annie's determination to protect her daughter from knowing the truth of it. These structural inequalities and the shame inherent in Annie's vision of her own life are not resolved at any point in the film and leave the viewer feeling as though they too should feel shame for accepting that they are powerless over their own lives in this Cold War moment.

Misreading the Moment
In his autobiography, Capra writes that *Pocketful of Miracles* was slated for a Christmas release both for its "Yuletide theme" and the proximity to awards season.[408] The Yuletide theme of *Pocketful of Miracles*, however, is antiquated because of its emphasis on the structural inequalities of the day. As analyzed in Chapter 2, the Dickensian tropes of generating a positive ending by confronting the ills of society and using Christmas as a time to put aside selfishness and harness goodwill towards others are excised from Christmas films in the Cold War years after 1947. By invoking those Dickensian themes and making a film from the perspective of a homeless woman who has to beg a wealthy man to help her lie to her own daughter about the hardships of her own reality, Capra's film might have worked in the Depression and probably would have worked in the 1940s, but this type of storyline was long displaced from the Christmas genre by 1961. The Christmas themes are those of Christmases long past and not attuned to the Christmas present that Capra is failing to speak to with *Pocketful of Miracles*.

In 1933, as the Depression wore on, the original film makes sense as a comedy about the fantasy of a week of luxury and the aspirational goal of giving your child what you lack. The aesthetics of wealth as a hopeful symbol that the economic state of the nation would recover when so many in the audience were likely in financial straits might have been moving for viewers. McBride writes on the earlier version, "In updating Runyon's story to the current economic crisis, Riskin stressed Annie's common link with millions of other Americans, old and young, male and

---

408 Capra, *The Name Above the Title*, 482.

female, urban and rural, who had to beg for a living and were torn between sui-
cidal despair and hopeful dreams."[409] This earlier film fit the experiences and audience it was trying to reach in a classic Capra story of aspirational aesthetics for a
depressed period.

In 1961, after several years of general economic prosperity and distance from
the hardships of the Depression, this message does not land nearly as closely for
the audience. The primary issue was no longer a dire economic landscape domestically, but rather the looming foreign tensions of the dramatically worsening Cold
War. Seeing a woman desperate to lie to her child by pretending to be many social
classes above her station without any promise of realizing that upward mobility
did not relate to the mainstream concerns of audiences in 1961. The aesthetics of
wealth that had become more accessible to more Americans by the end of the
1950s due to mass production, economic vitality, and the falling prices of many luxury goods, were not aspirational so much as commonplace for a largely middle-
class movie audience.

Capra knew *Pocketful of Miracles* was not the film he wanted to make. In his
autobiography, he writes that it was the logical step to get back into the swing of
Hollywood productions after his eight-year hiatus and the release of *A Hole in the
Head*, and he even appeared proud of the film after positive audience feedback
from focus groups. After the première of the film, however, the critical response
destroyed any optimism he felt for the film. *Variety*'s review acknowledges that
the film is out of touch:

> Once upon a time, say a quarter of a century ago, a sweet, sentimental fairy tale like Frank
> Capra's "Pocketful of Miracles" would have been an odds-on shoo-in for a happy ending at the
> wicket windows. But today the tracks are faster, the stakes are stiffer, and the pot of gold more
> elusive. Yesteryear's favorite is today's longshot.

However, it does continue to muse on the needs of 1961 and offers some optimism
for Capra's return as potentially triumphant, continuing:

> The question is whether unabashed sentiment has gone out of style? The answer would prob-
> ably be yes, save for the fact that the old master of mellow, firthful [sic] mayhem had not lost
> his unique touch. Hence, the United Artists release should be a satisfactory box office candi-
> date, especially useful as a Yuletide season attraction. And, should it manage to do better than
> satisfactory, it could kick off a renaissance of 30s-type screen comedy.[410]

---

409 McBride, *Frank Capra*, 301.
410 *"Pocketful of Miracles"*, *Variety*, October 13, 1961.

This renaissance would not pan out. The early 1960s were too gritty for the "unabashed sentiment" of Capra's early works. As the *New York Times* reviewer, A. H. Weiler – who had also reviewed *Babes in Toyland* earlier the same week – wrote, the story had "not worn especially well with the years" and the film feels "dated and sometimes uneven and listless." Weiler continues,

> The simple fact is that even an observer willing to go along with the fable of the racketeers, gangsters, muscle men and molls who fix it for a frowzy harridan of an apple vender to play the grande dame for her daughter, should find that time has dulled the point of the jest. Prohibition and repeal, the wacky citizens of Broadway's demi-monde and Runyonesque language were funnier in 1933. Repetition and a world faced by grimmer problems seem to have been excessively tough competition for this plot.
> ... [T]ime has worn this "Pocketful of Miracles" thin.[411]

Both of these reviews, as well as *Harrison's* lackluster commentary that Davis "fails to beget your sympathy", were blows to Capra whose gamble on listening to the studios did not pay off.[412] The overwhelming national critical reception was that the film was fine, not a complete failure but inaccessible for a modern audience and out of touch with their emotional needs. The cultural distance between 1933 and 28 years later was too great for the film to have an enthusiastic audience, especially after the political pressures directly levied against Hollywood in the later 1940s that fundamentally changed how Christmas could be brought to screen for decades to come.

The Decision to Make the Film

Ultimately, the decision to make *Pocketful of Miracles* was Capra's. His involvement with and interest in developing the film was also not an abrupt choice after failing to find a backing studio for *Ride the Pink Cloud.* From his archives, it is clear that a remake of *Lady for a Day* had been on the table since at least November 1952. One document from January 1953 is entitled "Notes on making LADY FOR A DAY into a musical" that casts Annie in a role reminiscent of Norma Desmond (Gloria Swanson) from Billy Wilder's 1950 *Sunset Boulevard.* That version of the film would have been much more light-hearted with Annie as a washed-up Broadway star prevailing upon her gambler friend and current Broadway star to help her convince her daughter that she is still the star she claims to be when she, her fiancé, and his

---

411 A. H. Weiler, *"Pocketful of Miracles"*, *The New York Times Film Reviews*, December 15, 1961.
412 "'Pocketful of Miracles' with Glenn Ford, Bette Davis, Hope Lange, Arthur O'Connell", *Harrison's Reports*, December 1961.

father come to meet her. Annie would not be the haggard drunken women she was in the 1961 version.

Another set of documents concerning a remake of *Lady for a Day* is from December 1956 with a cover letter to a woman named Lillian. In this cover letter, Capra writes about how excited he is to remake *Lady for a Day* as a "modern, fresh, and important picture" in precisely the way he'd like to do it. This letter suggests that Capra had a specific idea in mind that differs widely from the version of *Pocketful of Miracles* that ultimately was made. The document then goes on to outline, in even more detail than the earlier 1953 notes, this integrated story, remaking *Lady for a Day* with the added element of Annie as a former Broadway starlet. In this version, however, Capra wrote about the single most important aspect of how a remake of the film should be approached and to which he had only alluded in the earlier notes. Capra wrote:

> Now the story starts, and just by giving it this modern, today kind of framework, so much of the original can remain without seeming dated and old-fashioned.[413]

It is clear from Capra's own notes that he had a different original vision for this film. The section in his autobiography concerning his final film is named "Pocketful of Troubles" and details the tormenting time he had even getting to the actual production of the it, having to bend to the demands of the studios and his financier Glenn Ford. Capra recounted the drama of the production, writing, *"Pocketful of Miracles* was shaped in the fires of discord and filmed in an atmosphere of pain, strain, and loathing. Hate and fear smirked in the wings."[414] For all of the complications with using Capra's autobiography as a straightforward and trustworthy source, his reflections on and regrets over *Pocketful of Miracles* seem genuine.

While the ultimate decision for Capra to make the film and participate in the process was Capra's alone, it is clear that he was pushed through a variety of complicated factors to make a film he did not feel strongly about. This ultimate decision ended his career and, as many critics have written, regardless of other factors, Capra sold himself out by agreeing to make a film so far out of touch with the contemporary moment. Despite knowing and having written in his own notes that this film would only work if updated for the modern era, Capra made the film he did and also took ownership of its failure. In the final pages of his autobiography, Capra writes:

---

413 Emphasis Capra's. Frank Capra Collection, Box 30, Folder POCKETFUL OF MIRACLES, Outline of "Lady for a Day," Dec. 27, 1956.
414 Capra, *The Name Above the Title*, 474.

Pocketful of Miracles was not the film I set out to make; it was the picture I chose to make for fear of losing a few bucks. And by that choice I sold out the artistic integrity that had been my trademark for forty years. As a consequence, and by some direct perception independent of any reasoning process, those who listened in the dark sensed what my lucky elves, trolls, and leprechauns had sensed when Glenn Ford made me lick his boots — I had lost that precious quality that endows dreams with purport and purpose. I had lost my courage.[415]

Conclusion

In the 15 years between 1946 and 1961, Disney and Capra had vastly different experiences. Disney, a friendly witness to HUAC and shrewd businessman, executed a carefully laid plan for building a cultural empire while maintaining positive relations with the US government. Capra, an idealistic pursuer of the American Dream, inadvertently challenged the federal government and their propaganda efforts within Hollywood and crumbled under the forced acknowledgment that his cinematic, idealized vision of his nation no longer matched its real-world trajectory.

As with Wilder's successes in *The Apartment*, Disney's emotional understanding of his audience and the changing times allowed him to create a simple story with a heinous villain and a happy ending. The significance of leaving an audience feeling good and safe because the threat had been extinguished was in many ways an insightful observation of the nuclear terror felt by many Americans in the early 1960s. Audiences did not want the hope that Capra had previously been able to deliver, but rather they wanted an escapist dream in which the happy ending was not aspirational or imagined or something to work towards but a realized, holistic happiness with peace and prosperity for the heroes. The threat had to be extinguished.

While Disney grasped the need for a singular villain and the ultimate and complete triumph of his heroes, Capra embraced his more ideological worldview and more nuanced approach to cinema. In his autobiography, when recounting these later years, Capra wrote bitterly and retrospectively that it was becoming harder to make quality films due to the audience's sensitivity. Snidely, he quipped, "Only Disney had it licked. His villains were animals and animals don't go to the movies, or else Disney would have been picketed by the 'Wolf's Protective League.'"[416] Capra continued with his retrospective justifications for his follies in *Pocketful of Miracles*, projecting an insecurity about his later films and the Holly-

415 Capra, 486.
416 Capra, 461.

wood shift to the "anti-hero" he had lamented about earlier with regard to *A Hole in the Head:*

> Well, you can't tell film stories *without* villains. So filmmakers rediscovered the ancient, *general* enemies of *all* humanity: Insanity, Poverty, Disease, War. Being hated and feared by everybody, they made ideal villains. The villain began changing from a person to an idea, a state of mind, or a condition.[417]

This analysis from Capra reads disingenuously, as Capra himself seldom ever had a villain who was not a stand-in for the larger structural and systemic issues in society. It was also a miscalculation in terms of the villains in this period, whose influences seldom extended beyond the scope of the film. In fact, Capra's exact fault in making *Pocketful of Miracles*, albeit at the direction and insistence of the studio, was that he had no villain in the film apart from the abstract ideas of class disparities and the tangible inequalities of poverty.

Capra's production of a mistimed period comedy with a questionably hopeful ending with no structural or situational changes for the hero was doomed from the start. His reputation would diminish even further after *Pocketful of Miracles*, as McBride writes:

> The more overtly socially conscious Capra films were no longer in step with the times. Rather than admit that *Mr. Deeds, Mr. Smith,* and *Meet John Doe* were too passionate, too engaged, too disturbing to the status quo to be acceptable in the 1950s, the Hollywood and critical establishments simply ridiculed all of his work, good or bad, past and present, as "Capracorn." It was a designation he fought, then used as a rationalization for his failure to reestablish himself, and finally adopted as a badge of honor when his old films came back into fashion in the 1970s.[418]

The once beloved director whose films carried promises of better times ahead if American values were trusted and honed was ridiculed as old-fashioned and out of touch. This admonishment of Capra is an indictment of Cold War American culture and its projected morality, as the embodiment of much of Capra's earlier catalogue had previously been heralded as the best of American aspirations. The most striking cultural difference between 1946 and 1961 studied within this project is embodied in Capra's disillusionment, not his failure with *Pocketful of Miracles*. The film ended his career because it was not the feel-good fantasy that Disney offered, but rather it was a classic American fairy tale that in an earlier time of aspirational populist optimism would almost certainly have found its audience. In

---

417 Capra, 461. Emphasis Capra's.
418 McBride, *Frank Capra*, 628.

1961, the audience was as disillusioned as Capra, and neither *Pocketful of Miracles* nor the expected direction of *Ride the Pink Cloud* could have made up for his desire to make real films with real stakes and real problems that resonated with his viewers.

Disney, on the other hand, created a new audience for himself, one which was free of many of the intellectual problems of disillusionment with the American promise and which would open a new avenue for other creators in future. For the first time with *Babes in Toyland*, a Hollywood feature-length Christmas film was directly made for and marketed to children in a way that perhaps only Disney could perfect. Christmas entertainments, of course, would themselves continue on this trajectory throughout the 1960s and 1970s outside of Hollywood's cinematic releases with made-for-tv films, such as the Rankin/Bass Animated Entertainment films *Rudolph the Red-Nosed Reindeer* (1964), *Frosty the Snowman* (1969), and *The Year Without a Santa Claus* (1974). The marketing of Christmas to children remained a consistent trend throughout the rest of the twentieth century and into the twenty-first across home video, streaming services, and theatrical releases. Disney's *Babes in Toyland* pioneered this trend of extending Christmas into children's entertainment – not merely family entertainment suitable for children – by how it reacted to the changing demographics of Hollywood audiences in 1961.

Conclusion

Merry Christmas, movie house!
- George Bailey, *It's a Wonderful Life* (1946)

May your days be merry and bright/ and may all your Christmases be white
- Bob Wallace, *White Christmas* (1954)

American Christmas, much like Hollywood, is never a singular entity. To account for the abstract qualities of the concept of a holiday or to capture what is truly meant by the vast connotations of the metonymic "Hollywood", one needs to approach the thing itself in any given instance with the appropriate historical context. This historical context allows one to strip back the layers of political, cultural, social, and economic influences on the holiday or industry and form an argument about what precisely is being conveyed, by whom, and perhaps even why. This book has sought to form two arguments regarding both American Christmas and Hollywood in the post-war, early Cold War period by providing the historical context deemed appropriate.

The first argument pertains to Christmas and starts from the given understanding among American Christmas historians that the holiday in the US has largely been used in cultural circles to present an idealized vision of American values. This manifestation of the nation at its – often exaggerated – best can take different forms. In the Christmas films released between 1946 and 1947, for instance, Christmas was a vehicle for social commentary and even a platform for demanding that the US government abide by its own alleged respect for veterans by enacting legislative change in *It Happened on 5th Avenue* (1947). This act of critical patriotism challenging the US to live up to its self-proclaimed core values is thematically poignant for Christmas, particularly with regard to the Dickensian challenge put to Scrooge of forcing one to look inward while trying to justify immoral practices. As cultural texts reflecting such an American tradition that historically has been imbued with patriotic emblems and sentiments, Christmas films become a lens through which to understand how filmmakers perceive their own times, their relationship with such questions of patriotism, and their ideas on ideal Americana.

As this book also notes, however, Christmas can also be used as a tool of manipulation, such as in *Miracle on 34th Street* (1947) in which the image of the mythological Santa Claus is invoked to launder the less positive images of commercialism and consumerism. This usage of the holiday and all of its trappings of goodwill and happy endings opens up the questions of how and why presentations of Christmas begin to change in mid-century American cinema. This book argues – from this given point of Christmas as an idealizing vehicle for perceptions of American attitudes – that the iteration of the holiday in any form is ultimately indicative of the ideologies of the person, people, or group producing that particular take. That is to say, American Christmas films are subject to the cultural hegemonic powers of, on, and influencing Hollywood.

This leads into the second argument made by this book which pertains to Hollywood specifically. In the post-war, early Cold War years, 1946 to 1961, Hollywood underwent significant changes. Federal interventions including those from HUAC, the FBI, and the Supreme Court all had varying impacts on the external perspectives of Hollywood, its internal affairs, and its financial business practices. Combined with those federal influences were challenges in the tumultuous early Cold War world including US military interventions and escalations in foreign territories such as Korea and Vietnam, existential threats made practical when Russia developed nuclear technologies, and the increasing resistance to communist ideology as a means of protecting the American way of life. Such changes were also present in domestic policy and the public consciousness at a time when a particular sect of intellectuals was revisiting the potentials for conservative ideologies. All of these areas of gradual or, at times, sweeping and abrupt changes form the context for Hollywood in this political, cultural, social, and economic moment in which the Christmas films in this study were made and to which they speak.

This book does not argue that Christmas films represent all of American culture or all of Hollywood in this period. Instead, it argues that American Christmas occupies a unique cultural space that encourages the projection of what those in power believe to be the best of America in an exaggerated, idealized vision of the nation, and that this holiday, therefore, makes for an excellent source base for a case study on the effects of the myriad pressures on the motion picture industry in mid-twentieth century America. Ultimately, the thesis concludes that through examining the pressures on the motion picture industry and all of the contexts around it, Hollywood Christmas films changed dramatically in this 15-year period, as best exemplified in Chapter 5 which analyses the experiences of Walt Disney and Frank Capra throughout that period and their choices as filmmakers that resulted in one's success and the other's career's demise. Within the genre itself, Christmas became more socially conservative and more simplistic than it had been in releases from 1947 and before.

To reach this conclusion, this book employs a multi-directional approach of looking at the film industry at large as well as the political, cultural, social, and economic contexts around it that together form the "moment". Simultaneously, this book engages with a close-reading approach towards the films, examining the context of their productions as well as the film texts themselves, their marketing materials, and the reception of them. By employing such a close reading of the genre, this book offers a consistent set of themes and tropes to follow throughout the period as a control – such as social problems in Chapter 2 or commercialism in Chapter 4 – to analyze how depictions of these concepts in relation to Christmas change over time. Considering a genre as a relatively contained unit allows for the research to consider how the variables – such as HUAC's presence in Hollywood or increasing economic growth – affect the messaging within the films.

Methodologically, the analysis of a genre over time as a part of a larger examination of Hollywood political and/or business practices encourages a holistic approach to media literacy. Genre studies are not new, as can be seen in the vast collections of science fiction and horror film studies alone. What this project does differently from those sci-fi and horror studies, however, is take a genre that is often seen as "innocuous" or ostensibly non-political and analyze its changes in cultural messaging and reflection over a given period of political and social upheaval to expose ideological links across industries, institutions, and influences in that period. If one were to recreate this study in a different period – say the 1980s – and with a different genre – say action films – the researcher would discover similar overarching contexts – such as themes of patriotism, conservative ideologies, industry-changing technological advancements in visual effects, the same nuclear threats from new and old enemies, and fluctuating economic conditions. Yet, the conclusions of that study would expose far more about Hollywood and its contemporary practices, evolutions within the genre, and how American identities and values were constructed on screens than a study of any of those areas individually. The multidisciplinary approach provides contexts far beyond a singular historical or film studies approach and would allow, in that example, for a crossover with this book, questioning the evolution of the Christmas film genre as it intersected with the expanding action genre of the 1980s with John McTiernan's *Die Hard* (1988).

As mentioned throughout the thesis, Christmas films beyond 1961 went through several iterations as a result of their own political, cultural, social, and economic moments. Throughout the 1960s, following Disney's success with *Babes in Toyland* and with the ever-increasing popularity of television, Christmas entertainments left the big screen for the small one. Made-for-tv movies dominated the Christmas genre for nearly two decades with the successes of Dr. Seuss's *How the Grinch Stole Christmas* on CBS in 1966 and the many Rankin/Bass animations including *Rudolph the Red-Nosed Reindeer* (1964), *The Little Drummer Boy* (1968), *Frosty the Snowman* (1969), *The Year Without a Santa Claus* (1974), and *Jack Frost* (1979). The 1980s, as alluded to, saw Christmas's return to Hollywood but this time with a special emphasis on hybrid genres, such as the horror Christmas film *Gremlins* (1984), the action Christmas film *Die Hard*, and the black comedy Christmas film *Scrooged* (1988). *Scrooged* is also notable for being Hollywood's first mainstream Christmas film with a Dickensian focus in over four decades since the likes of the social problem films analyzed in this book.

By the 1990s, the Christmas film genre had developed a nostalgic lens suggested in the 1983 cult classic *A Christmas Story.* While *A Christmas Story* harbored a nostalgia for a pre-atomic age and celebrated mundane experiences as fantastical memories of an American suburban childhood, the 1990s celebrated its nostalgia with updated remakes of films from the 1940s. The 1996 adaptation of *The Bishop's Wife* (1947) was titled *The Preacher's Wife* and executed an even more successful commentary on social problems and their effects on a community than the original. Meanwhile, the 1994 remake of *Miracle on 34th Street* retained the name but drastically changed the ending to one dependent on religious faith rather than that of a child as in the 1947 version.

Beyond these emphases on nostalgia, 1990s Christmas films occupied new spaces in the cultural sphere as a result of technological developments in the motion picture industry. Depending on the production budgets ranging from high to quite low, these Christmas films were distributed as theatrical releases, as made-for-tv movies, and as direct-to-home-video tapes. This distribution model allowed for studios such as Disney to capitalize on Christmas with releases ranging from the 1992 Dickensian and Muppet classic *The Muppet Christmas Carol* starring film icon Michael Caine, to the mid-budget *The Santa Clause* in 1994 and the low-budget VHS release of *Beauty and the Beast: The Enchanted Christmas* (1997), the sequel to the 1991 animated feature, *Beauty and the Beast.*

The 1990s offered many films that are now considered Christmas classics including those listed as well as *Home Alone* (1990), *Jingle All the Way* (1996), and *While You Were Sleeping* (1996). These films helped to broaden the genre leading into the twenty-first century and the profound changes in the industry, nation, and wider world that would soon come, the most impactful of which for Hollywood's business practices would certainly be the advent of the streaming era. With streaming came an alleged democratization of the industry and an even more exaggerated smattering of films across the budget and distribution spectrum. Christmas films were nearly always hybrid, the most successful and prolific of which was and is the Christmas romances with the same formula that was established in the socially conservative era of the 1950s, as explored in Chapter 3. With big-budget films such as *The Holiday* (2006), mid-budget films such as *Christmas with the Coopers* (2015), and the hundreds of low-budget formulaic Christmas romance films released by the likes of Netflix, the Hallmark Channel, and the Great American Family Channel annually, Christmas romances and their largely conservative messaging are thriving.

The purpose of this book is not to dissuade audiences from watching their favorite Christmas films or "ruin" their beloved holiday traditions. Instead, it offers a suggestion that there is more to be considered beneath the surface of these often fun, joyous films that can speak to significant moments in America's history or present. The impulse to want to escape into cinema is a human one, especially in times of uncontrollable strife and fear, but it is imperative to meet that impulse with an active awareness of the media into which one chooses to escape. By thinking about the contexts of how the Reagan administration of the 1980s impacted filmmakers' choices in "innocuous" Hollywood action films or questioning the influences on Christmas releases when the distribution option of the VHS is introduced, this method of analyzing a period of time through a specific genre can open up avenues of thought that connect all of us more deeply with the cultural media we consume. As Dorothy Jones wrote in her 1955 essay "The Language of Our Time":

> The great danger is not that we may overemphasize pictures and neglect the written word, but rather that we may allow the moving picture, which so abounds in potentialities, to remain primarily a medium for supplying diversion and entertainment. [...] For, whether we like it or not, the language of our day is the motion picture; and those who make use of this language and those who control its main channels of distribution will, for better or for worse, be most influential in shaping our future destinies.[419]

Hollywood audiences have everything to gain from developing deeper media literacy that incorporates the contexts of the political, cultural, social, and economic moments in which that media is made.

As we continue on in a moment very much reminiscent of McCarthyism with attacks on intellectualism, political positions, ideas, and identity, it is our duty to be more thoughtful consumers of cultural media. The language of our day has still largely been the motion picture; however, the motion picture is now inclusive of television, video games, and shortform videos shared to millions at a time on social media platforms globally, far exceeding the reaches of Hollywood in Jones's time. It is crucial that we are active participants in parsing the messaging we receive to understand that today's attacks on "woke" are synonymous with 1947's "communist ideology". With the potential for even further unregulated consolidation of power and studio monopolization among Disney, Netflix, and Amazon especially, and with the resurgence of McCarthy era tactics of baseless allegations, aggressive fearmongering, and assaults on individuals' freedom of speech, it is important to view the cultural media being made now with an active and critical awareness of its contemporary contexts.

---

419 Dorothy Jones, "The Language of Our Time", *The Quarterly of Film Radio and Television* 10, no. 2 (Winter 1955): 178.

By presenting the history of one genre as well as the history of Hollywood in the appropriate contexts of their same tumultuous period, this book has sought to provide a case study that exemplifies how this model may be used. By focusing that case study on Christmas films, this book has used a unique genre that is often considered non-political despite being formed around a historically American and patriotic holiday that automatically imports ideas of civic morality and American values. Ultimately, through the cultural power of Hollywood films and with Kris Kringle's words in mind, this book has shown that Christmas is not just a day by any stretch but rather is a frame of mind that has the potential to reflect a moment, challenge a nation, inspire change, and shape our future destinies.

Appendix – COMPIC Files

The following table details versions of reports in the series entitled "Communist infiltration – Motion Picture Industry" made available via Freedom of Information Act requests on the Federal Bureau of Investigation's website. That webpage is accessible at this link: http://web.archive.org/web/20050309061626/http://foia.fbi.gov/foiaindex/compic.htm

PDF Titles	Date of Report's Update	File Number	Serial Number
1a, 1b	February 18, 1943	100 – 138754	4
2, 3a, 3b, 3c, 3d	May 27, 1947	100 – 138754	157x1
4, 5	July 8, 1947	100 – 138754	250
6, 7a, 7b	October 2, 1947	100 – 138754	251x1
8a, 8b, 8c	July 15, 1949	100 – 138754	1003, part 1
9a, 9b, 9c	July 15, 1949	100 – 138754	1003, part 2
10a, 10b	January 3, 1956	100 – 138754	1103, part 1
11a, 11b	January 3, 1956	100 – 138754	1103, part 2
12	May 15, 1965	100 – 138754	1106
13	May 14, 1957	100 – 138754	1118
14	May 20, 1958	100 – 138754	1122
15	November 14, 1958	100 – 138754	1126

*NB: This chart does not include the version of the report dated August 7, 1947. That version is not available in the FOIA releases of COMPIC files. This researcher does have scans of the pages pertaining to It's a Wonderful Life obtained via email.

References

Primary Source Materials

Films

Capra, Frank, dir. 1946. *It's a Wonderful Life.* Liberty Films.
Capra, Frank, dir. 1961. *Pocketful of Miracles.* United Artists.
Curtiz, Michael, dir. 1954. *White Christmas.* Paramount Pictures.
Del Ruth, Roy, dir. 1947. *It Happened on 5th Avenue.* Allied Artists.
Donohue, Jack, dir. 1961. *Babes in Toyland.* Buena Vista Distribution.
Hartman, Don, dir. 1949. *Holiday Affair.* RKO Radio Pictures.
Koster, Henry, dir. 1947. *The Bishop's Wife.* RKO Radio Pictures.
Lanfield, Sidney, dir. 1951. *The Lemon Drop Kid.* Paramount Pictures.
Marin, Edward L., dir. 1947. *Christmas Eve.* United Artists.
Seaton, George, dir. 1947. *Miracle on 34th Street.* 20th Century Fox.
Tashlin, Frank, dir. 1954. *Susan Slept Here.* RKO Radio Pictures.
Wilder, Billy, dir. 1960. *The Apartment.* United Artists.

Contemporary Books and Scholarly Articles

Anderson, Mary. 1944. "The Postwar Role of American Women". *The American Economic Review* 34
    (1): 237–244.
Bell, Daniel. 1955. *The New American Right.* New York: Criterion Books.
Brodie, Bernard. 1948. "The Atom Bomb as Policy Maker". *Foreign Affairs* 27 (1): 17–33.
Calhoun, Don. 1947. "Woman as Log". *ETC: A Review of General Semantics* 5 (1): 58–61.
Capra, Frank. 1997. *The Name Above the Title: An Autobiography.* New York: Da Capo Press.
Cogley, John. 1956. *Report on Blacklisting.* Fund for the Republic.
Ferry, John William. 1960. *A History of the Department Store.* New York: Macmillan Company.
Fish, Carl Russell. 1927. *The Rise of the Common Man: 1830–1850.* Vol. VI. A History of American Life.
    New York: Macmillan Company.
Galbraith, John Kenneth. 1958. *The Affluent Society.* Boston: Houghton Mifflin.
Hofstadter, Richard. 1954. "The Pseudo-Conservative Revolt". *The American Scholar* 24 (1): 9–27.
Jones, Dorothy. 1956. "Communism and the Movies: A Study of Film Content". Fund for the Republic.
Jones, Dorothy. 1950. "Quantitative Analysis of Motion Picture Content". *The Public Opinion Quarterly*
    14 (3): 554–558.
Jones, Dorothy. 1955. "The Language of Our Time". *The Quarterly of Film Radio and Television* 10 (2):
    167–179.
Kahn, Gordon. 1948. *Hollywood on Trial: The Story of the 10 Who Were Indicted.* New York: Boni and
    Gaer.
Lundberg, Ferdinand, and Marynia F. Farnham. 1947. *Modern Woman: The Lost Sex.* New York: Harper
    & Brothers Publishers.

Resseguie, Harry E. 1965. "Alexander Turney Stewart and the Development of the Department Store, 1823–1876". *Business History Review (Pre-1986); Boston* 39 (3): 301–322.

The Board of Directors of the American Psychological Association. 1949. "Across the Secretary's Desk: Board of Directors' Letter to President Truman Concerning Loyalty Investigations". *American Psychologist* 4 (4): 116.

Tibbitts, Clark. 1950. "National Conference on Aging". *Public Health Reports (1896–1970)* 65 (42): 1369–1374.

Turner Wilcox, Ruth. 1951. *The Mode in Furs: The History of Furred Costume of the World from the Earliest Times to the Present.* New York: Charles Scribner's Sons.

Reviews, Documents, and Archival Materials

Arneel, Gene. "'54 DREAM PIC: 'WHITE XMAS'". *Variety,* January 5, 1955. ProQuest.

"*Babes in Toyland* Pressbook". 1961. Buena Vista Distribution. Reuben Library, British Film Institute. Microform.

Brecher, Ruth, and Edward Brecher. "How to Avoid Being Cheated By the Pound, Gallon or Yard: How to Make Sure You Get What You Pay For". *Redbook,* August 1960.

Bureau of Labor Statistics. 2018. "Unemployment Rate and Timing of Changes to Current Population Survey Measurement, 1940–2017".

Capra, Frank. "Breaking Hollywood's 'Pattern of Sameness'". *The New York Times,* May 5, 1946.

Crowther, Bosley. "It's a Wonderful Life". *The New York Times Film Reviews,* December 23, 1946.

Crowther, Bosley. "'Holiday Affair,' Tinsel-Trimmed Trifle With Mitchum and Janet Leigh, at State". *The New York Times Film Reviews,* November 24, 1949.

Crowther, Bosley. "White Christmas". *The New York Times Film Reviews,* October 15, 1954.

Dwyer, Ed. "Greatest Holiday Movies Ever!' *The Saturday Evening Post,* December 2012.

Eisenhower, Dwight D. "The President's News Conference". The American Presidency Project. Accessed July 10, 2023.

Federal Bureau of Investigation, "Communist Infiltration – Motion Picture Industry (COMPIC) (Excerpts)", Federal Bureau of Investigation, http://web.archive.org/web/20050309061626/http:/foia.fbi.gov/foiaindex/compic.htm.

Federal Bureau of Investigation, "Communist Infiltration into the Motion Picture Industry" Report LA 100–15732 (Los Angeles: FBI, August 7, 1947). Courtesy of John Noakes.

Frank Capra Collection, First Draft by Frank Capra April 15, 1957." Box 30, Folder POCKETFUL OF MIRACLES, Outline of "Lady for a Day," Dec. 27, 1956.

Frank Capra Collection. Box 30, Folder POCKETFUL OF MIRACLES, "Ride the Pink Cloud draft, notes" April 15, 1957.

Gallup, George. 1972. *The Gallup Poll: Public Opinion, 1935–1971.* Vol. 2. 3 vols. New York: Random House.

Harrison's Reports. "'The Lemon Drop Kid' with Bob Hope, Marilyn Maxwell and Lloyd Nolan", March 10, 1951.

Harrison's Reports. "'Susan Slept Here' with Dick Powell and Debbie Reynolds", July 3, 1954.

Harrison's Reports. "'Pocketful of Miracles' with Glenn Ford, Bette Davis, Hope Lange, Arthur O'Connell", December 1961.

"*Holiday Affair* Pressbook". 1949. RKO Radio Pictures. Reuben Library, British Film Institute. Microform.

Holmes, Susan Bennett. "Teen-Age Menace'" *Woman's Day*, May 1958.

House Committee on Un-American Activities. 1947. "Hearings Regarding the Communist Infiltration of the Motion Picture Industry Before the Committee on Un-American Activities, House of Representatives, Eightieth Congress, First Session". United States Congress.

Hudson, David. "Norman Lloyd's Long and Triumphant Run". The Criterion Collection. Accessed April 25, 2024. https://www.criterion.com/current/posts/7389-norman-lloyd-s-long-and-triumphant-run.

"*It's a Wonderful Life*, 1946". 1946. Motion Picture Association of America – Production Code Administration Records. Margaret Herrick Library Digital Collections. https://digitalcollections.os cars.org/digital/collection/p15759coll30/id/18576.

"*It's a Wonderful Life* Pressbook". 1946. Liberty Films. Reuben Library, British Film Institute. Microform.

Ladies' Home Journal. "Going Steady... A National Problem", July 1949. Women's Magazine Archive. ProQuest.

LIFE Magazine. "How to Bring Up a Young Daughter: Tips from a Teen-Ager's Smart Mama!", March 11, 1946. ProQuest.

LIFE Magazine. "Naked at Bergdorf's: A Shopper's Dream Takes Place in New York Store", March 11, 1946. ProQuest.

LIFE Magazine. "A&P Super Markets Advertisement", July 9, 1951. ProQuest.

"*Miracle on 34th Street* Pressbook". 1947. Twentieth Century Fox. Reuben Library, British Film Institute. Microform.

Office of the Historian, Foreign Service Institute. "Milestones: 1953–1960 – Office of the Historian". United States Department of State. Accessed July 10, 2023.

Perkins, Jeanne. "Dior". *LIFE*, March 1, 1948.

"Provisions of the Housing Act of 1949". 1949. *Monthly Labor Review* 69 (2): 155–159.

Pryor, Thomas M. "Academy Repeals Ruling on 'Oscars'; Anti-Communist Ban, Voted 2 Years Ago, Is Revoked as 'Unworkable,' 'Impractical'". *The New York Times*, January 14, 1959, sec. Archives.

Ramsaye, Terry. "What the Production Code Really Says". *Motion Picture Herald*, August 11, 1934.

Rand, Ayn. 1946. "Textbook of Americanism". The Motion Picture Alliance for Preservation of American Ideals. Foundation for Economic Education. https://fee.org/resources/textbook-of-americanism/.

Rand, Ayn. 1947. "Screen Guide for Americans". The Motion Picture Alliance for the Preservation of American Ideals.

Read Miller, Cynthia. "Walt Disney Visits Henry Ford's Greenfield Village". The Henry Ford Museum. February 22, 2014. https://web.archive.org/web/20140222100833/http://www.thehenryford.org/exhibits/pic/2005/september.asp#more.

Reading Eagle. "Amos 'n' Andy Look for Exit As They Plan New TV Show", June 17, 1951.

Slide, Anthony. "Hollywood's Fascist Follies". *Film Comment*, July 1991.

"*The Bishop's Wife* Pressbook". 1947. RKO Radio Pictures. Reuben Library, British Film Institute. Microform.

The Frank Capra Collection. The Ogden and Mary Louise Reid Cinema Archives, Wesleyan University.

Tiebout, Harry M. "The Pink Cloud and After". September 1955. https://www.aagrapevine.org/magazine/1955/sep/pink-cloud-and-after.

Truman, Harry S. "Special Message to the Congress Recommending a Comprehensive Health Program'" The Harry S. Truman Library and Museum. November 19, 1945. https://www.trumanlibrary.gov/library/public-papers/192/special-message-congress-recommending-comprehensive-health-program.

Variety. "Top Grossers of 1948", January 5, 1949. ProQuest.

Variety. "Pictures: Top Grossers of 1951", January 2, 1952. ProQuest.

Variety. "1954 Box Office Champs", January 5, 1955. ProQuest.

Variety. "*Babes in Toyland*", December 1, 1961. ProQuest.

Variety. "*Pocketful of Miracles*", October 13, 1961. ProQuest.

Variety. "Pictures: All-Time Top Grossers", January 6, 1965. ProQuest.

Weiler, A. H. 1961. "*Pocketful of Miracles*". *The New York Times Film Reviews*, December 15, 1961.

"*White Christmas* Pressbook". 1954. Paramount Pictures. Reuben Library, British Film Institute. Microform.

Wood, Abigail. "How To Let a Boy Know You're Alive". *Seventeen*, August 1958. ProQuest.

Wyler, William. "Open Forum". *The Hollywood Reporter*, November 7, 1947. The Hollywood Reporter (Archive: 1930–2015).

Secondary Source Materials

Books and Book Chapters

Ambrose, Stephen. E. 1984. *Eisenhower. Vol. 2, The President.* New York: Simon & Schuster.

Andersen, Thom. 2007. "Red Hollywood". In *"Un-American" Hollywood: Politics and Film in the Blacklist Era*, edited by Frank Krutnik, Steve Neale, Brian Neve, and Stanfield, 225–263. New Brunswick: Rutgers University Press.

Anderson, David. 1991. *Trapped by Success: The Eisenhower Administration and Vietnam 1953–1961.* New York: Columbia University Press.

Appy, Christian G. 2001. "'We'll Follow the Old Man': The Strains of Sentimental Militarism in Popular Films of the Fifties". In *Rethinking Cold War Culture*, edited by Peter J. Kuznick and James Burkhart Gilbert, 74–105. Washington DC: Smithsonian Institution Press.

Bailey, Beth L. 1989. *From Front Porch to Back Seat: Courtship in Twentieth-Century America.* Baltimore: Johns Hopkins University Press.

Barrier, J. Michael. 2007. *The Animated Man: A Life of Walt Disney.* Berkeley: University of California Press.

Basinger, Jeanine. 1986. *The "It's a Wonderful Life" Book.* New York: Knopf.

Bazin, André. 1997. *Bazin at Work: Major Essays & Reviews from the Forties & Fifties.* Translated by Alain Piette and Bert Cardullo. London: Routledge.

Blake, David Haven. 2016. *Liking Ike: Eisenhower, Advertising, and the Rise of Celebrity Politics.* Oxford: Oxford University Press.

Boorstin, Daniel J. 1973. *The Americans: The Democratic Experience.* New York: Random House.

Boyer, Paul S. 1994. *By the Bomb's Early Light: American Thought and Culture at the Dawn of the Atomic Age.* Chapel Hill: The University of North Carolina Press.

Branden, Barbara. 1987. *The Passion of Ayn Rand.* London: W.H. Allen.

Broadwater, Jeff. 1992. *Eisenhower & the Anti-Communist Crusade.* Chapel Hill: The University of North Carolina Press.

Buhle, Paul, and David Wagner. 2002. *Radical Hollywood: The Untold Story Behind America's Favorite Movies.* New York: New Press.

Burns, Jennifer. 2009. *Goddess of the Market: Ayn Rand and the American Right.* Oxford: Oxford University Press.

Burstein, Andrew. 2007. *The Original Knickerbocker: The Life of Washington Irving.* New York: Basic Books.

Calefato, Patrizia. 2004. *The Clothed Body.* Translated by Lisa Adams. Oxford: Berg.

Carman, Emily, and Philip Drake. 2019. "Doing the Deal: Talent Contracts in Hollywood". In *Hollywood and the Law,* edited by Paul McDonald, Emily Carman, Eric Hoyt, and Philip Drake, 309–352. London: Bloomsbury Publishing.

Carney, Raymond. 1986. *American Vision: The Films of Frank Capra.* Cambridge: Cambridge University Press.

Casey, Steven. 2017. "Confirming the Cold War Consensus: Eisenhower and the 1952 Election". In *US Presidential Elections and Foreign Policy: Candidates, Campaigns, and Global Politics from FDR to Bill Clinton,* edited by Andrew Johnstone and Andrew Priest, 82–104. Lexington: University Press of Kentucky.

Casty, Alan. 2009. *Communism in Hollywood: The Moral Paradoxes of Testimony, Silence, and Betrayal.* Lanham, MD: Scarecrow Press.

Chen, Yung-fa. 2023. *Making Revolution: The Communist Movement in Eastern and Central China, 1937–1945.* 1st ed. Vol. 26. Berkeley: University of California Press.

Chernus, Ira. 2008. *Apocalypse Management: Eisenhower and the Discourse of National Insecurity.* Stanford: Stanford University Press.

Cieutat, Michel. 1988. *Frank Capra.* Paris: Rivages.

Conant, Michael. 1960. *Antitrust in the Motion Picture Industry: Economic and Legal Analysis.* Los Angeles: University of California Press.

Connelly, Mark, ed. 2000a. *Christmas at the Movies: Images of Christmas in American, British and European Cinema.* Cinema and Society Series. London: I.B. Tauris Publishers.

Connelly, Mark. 2000b. "Santa Claus: The Movie". In *Christmas at the Movies: Images of Christmas in American, British and European Cinema,* edited by Mark Connelly. Cinema and Society Series. 115–135. London: I.B. Tauris Publishers.

Cripps, Thomas. 1993. *Making Movies Black: The Hollywood Message Movie from World War II to the Civil Rights Era.* Oxford: Oxford University Press.

Critchlow, Donald T. 2007. *The Conservative Ascendancy: How the GOP Right Made Political History.* Cambridge, MA: Harvard University Press.

Critchlow, Donald T. 2013. *When Hollywood Was Right: How Movie Stars, Studio Moguls, and Big Business Remade American Politics.* New York: Cambridge University Press.

Crosby, Donald F. 1978. *God, Church, and Flag: Senator Joseph R. McCarthy and the Catholic Church, 1950–1957.* Chapel Hill: The University of North Carolina Press.

Curti, Merle. 1946. *The Roots of American Loyalty.* New York: Columbia University Press.

Damms, Richard. V. 2002. *The Eisenhower Presidency, 1953–1961.* New York: Longman.

Davis, Amy M., ed. 2019. *Discussing Disney.* Bloomington: Indiana University Press.

Delton, Jennifer. 2018. "Politics of Liberal and Conservatism". In *The Routledge History of the Twentieth-Century United States,* edited by Jerald Podair and Darren Dochuk. 127–137. New York: Routledge.

Dixon, Wheeler W. 2012. *Death of the Moguls: The End of Classical Hollywood.* Techniques of the Moving Image. New Brunswick: Rutgers University Press.

Doherty, Thomas. 2002. *Teenagers and Teenpics: Juvenilization of American Movies.* Philadelphia: Temple University Press.

Doherty, Thomas. 2007. *Hollywood's Censor: Joseph I. Breen & the Production Code Administration.* New York: Columbia University Press.

Doherty, Thomas. 2018. *Show Trial: Hollywood, HUAC, and the Birth of the Blacklist.* New York: Columbia University Press.

Dominkova, Petra. 2008. "I Want That Mink! Film Noir and Fashion". In *If Looks Could Kill: Cinema's Images of Fashion, Crime and Violence*, edited by Marketa Uhlirova, 138–143. Fashion in Film. London: Koenig Books and Fashion in Film Festival.

Dunn, Charles W., and J. David Woodard. 2003. *The Conservative Tradition in America.* 2nd ed. Lanham, MD: Rowman & Littlefield.

Dylan, Huw, David V. Gioe, and Michael S. Goodman. 2020. "The CIA and Cuba: The Bay of Pigs and the Cuban Missile Crisis". In *The CIA and the Pursuit of Security: History, Documents and Contexts*, 112–126. Edinburgh: Edinburgh University Press.

Eckert, Charles. 1991. "The Carole Lombard in Macy's Window". In *Stardom: Industry of Desire*, edited by Christine Gledhill, 30–40. New York: Routledge.

"Evolution and Landscape of Nursing Home Care in the United States". 2022. In *The National Imperative to Improve Nursing Home Quality: Honoring Our Commitment to Residents, Families, and Staff.* National Academies Press.

Falk, Andrew Justin. 2010. *Upstaging the Cold War: American Dissent and Cultural Diplomacy, 1940–1960.* Culture, Politics, and the Cold War. Amherst: University of Massachusetts Press.

Forbes, Bruce David. 2007. *Christmas: A Candid History.* Berkeley: University of California Press.

Fried, Richard M. 1991. *Nightmare in Red: The McCarthy Era in Perspective.* Oxford: Oxford University Press.

Gehring, Wes D. 1995. *Populism and the Capra Legacy.* Westport, CT: Greenwood Press.

Golby, J. M., and A. W. Purdue. 1986. *The Making of the Modern Christmas.* Athens, GA: University of Georgia Press.

Goldman, Eric A. 2013. *The American Jewish Story through Cinema.* Austin: University of Texas Press.

Goodall, Alex. 2013. *Loyalty and Liberty – American Countersubversion from World War I to the McCarthy Era.* Chicago: University of Illinois Press.

Gordon, Robert J. 2016. *The Rise and Fall of American Growth: The U.S. Standard of Living since the Civil War.* Princeton: Princeton University Press.

Goudsouzian, Aram. 2004. *Sidney Poitier Man, Actor, Icon.* Chapel Hill: The University of North Carolina Press.

Gould, Lewis L. 2014. *The Republicans: A History of the Grand Old Party.* Oxford: Oxford University Press.

Grant, Matthew, and Benjamin Ziemann. 2016. *Understanding the Imaginary War: Culture, Thought, and Nuclear Conflict, 1945–90.* Manchester: Manchester University Press.

Griffith, Robert. 1987. *The Politics of Fear: Joseph R. McCarthy and the Senate.* 2nd ed. Amherst: University of Massachusetts Press.

Gunter, Matthew C. 2012. *The Capra Touch: A Study of the Director's Hollywood Classics and War Documentaries, 1934–1945.* London: McFarland & Co.

Hale, Nathan G. 1995. *The Rise and Crisis of Psychoanalysis in the United States: Freud and the Americans, 1917–1985.* Freud in America, v. 2. New York: Oxford University Press.

Heale, Michael J. 1990. *American Anticommunism: Combating the Enemy Within, 1830–1970.* Baltimore: Johns Hopkins University Press.

Hillman, Elizabeth Lutes. 2005. *Defending America: Military Culture and the Cold War Court-Martial.* Politics and Society in Twentieth-Century America. Princeton: Princeton University Press.

Hitchcock, William I. 2018. *The Age of Eisenhower: America and the World in the 1950s.* New York: Simon & Schuster.

Hollands, Joshua M. 2019. "Animating America's Anticommunism: Alice's Egg Plant (1925) and Disney's First Red Scare". In *Discussing Disney*, edited by Amy M. Davis, 35–52. Bloomington: Indiana University Press.

Hopper, Kim, and Jill Hamberg. 1984. *The Making of America's Homeless: From Skid Row to New Poor, 1945–1984*. New York: Community Service Society of New York.

Horsley, Richard. 2001. "Christmas: The Religion of Consumer Capitalism". In *Christmas Unwrapped: Consumerism, Christ, and Culture*, edited by Richard Horsley and James Tracy, 165–187. Pittsburgh: Trinity Press International.

Humphries, Reynold. 2010. *Hollywood's Blacklists: A Political and Cultural History*. Edinburgh: Edinburgh University Press.

Jeffreys-Jones, Rhodri. 2007. *The FBI: A History*. New Haven: Yale University Press.

Jian, Chen. 2001. *Mao's China and the Cold War*. Chapel Hill: The University of North Carolina Press.

Kaplan, James. 2019. "What Is a War Song?" In *Irving Berlin*, 190–202. New York Genius. New Haven: Yale University Press.

Kataoka, Tetsuya. 2023. *Resistance and Revolution in China: The Communists and the Second United Front*. 1st ed. Vol. 11. Berkeley: University of California Press.

Kazin, Michael. 2017. *The Populist Persuasion: An American History*. 2nd revised ed. New York: Cornell University Press.

Keppel, Ben. 2016. *Brown v. Board and the Transformation of American Culture: Education and the South in the Age of Desegregation*. Baton Rouge: Louisiana State University Press.

Kovel, Joel. 1994. *Red Hunting in the Promised Land: Anticommunism and the Making of America*. New York: Basic Books.

Krause Knight, Cher. 2014. *Power and Paradise in Walt Disney's World*. Gainesville, FL: University Press of Florida.

Kusmer, Kenneth L. 2002. *Down & Out, On the Road: The Homeless in American History*. Oxford: Oxford University Press.

Kuznick, Peter J., and James Burkhart Gilbert, eds. 2001. *Rethinking Cold War Culture*. Washington DC: Smithsonian Institution Press.

Ledbetter, James. 2011. *Unwarranted Influence: Dwight D. Eisenhower and the Military-Industrial Complex*. New Haven: Yale University Press.

Macor, Alison. 2022. *Making The Best Years of Our Lives: The Hollywood Classic That Inspired a Nation*. Austin: University of Texas Press.

Maravillas, Anthony Rama. 2016. "Overrated Pleasures and Underrated Treasures: Mamie Eisenhower, a Bridge between First Lady Archetypes". In *A Companion to First Ladies*, edited by Katherine A. S. Sibley, 492–502. Wiley Blackwell Companions to American History. Chichester, UK: Wiley Blackwell.

Marling, Karal Ann. 1994. *As Seen on TV: The Visual Culture of Everyday Life in the 1950s*. Cambridge, MA: Harvard University Press.

Marling, Karal Ann. 2001. *Merry Christmas!: Celebrating America's Greatest Holiday*. Cambridge, MA: Harvard University Press.

Mason, Robert. 2012. *The Republican Party and American Politics from Hoover to Reagan*. Cambridge: Cambridge University Press.

Mast, Gerald. 1982. *The Movies in Our Midst: Documents in the Cultural History of Film in America*. Chicago: University of Chicago Press.

Matusow, Allen J. 1984. *The Unraveling of America: A History of Liberalism in the 1960s*. 1st ed. The New American Nation Series. New York: Harper & Row.

May, Elaine Tyler. 2017. *Homeward Bound: American Families in the Cold War Era*. 3rd ed. New York: Basic Books.

McBride, Joseph. 1992. *Frank Capra: The Catastrophe of Success.* New York: Simon & Schuster.

McGirr, Lisa. 2001. *Suburban Warriors: The Origins of the New American Right.* Politics and Society in Twentieth-Century America. Princeton: Princeton University Press.

Millen, Raymond. 2016. "The Post–Korean War Drawdown under the Eisenhower Administration". In *Drawdown: The American Way of Postwar,* edited by Jason W. Warren, 190–207. New York: New York University Press.

Miller, Gabriel. 2013. *William Wyler: The Life and Films of Hollywood's Most Celebrated Director.* Screen Classics. Lexington: University Press of Kentucky.

Miller, Ron. 2016. "Bob Hope". In *Conversations with Classic Film Stars*, edited by James Bawden and Ron Miller, 357–372. Lexington: University Press of Kentucky.

Miller, William. 1962. "The Realm of Wealth". In *The Reconstruction of American History*, edited by John Higham, 137–156. London: Hutchinson.

Modell, John. 1991. *Into One's Own: From Youth to Adulthood in the United States, 1920–1975.* Berkeley: University of California Press.

Morgan, Iwan W. 2016. *Reagan: American Icon.* London: I.B. Tauris Publishers.

Myers, Max A. 2001. "Christmas on Celluloid: Hollywood Helps Construct the American Christmas". In *Christmas Unwrapped: Consumerism, Christ, and Culture*, edited by Richard Horsley, 39–54. Pittsburgh: Trinity Press International.

Nadel, Alan. 1995. *Containment Culture: American Narratives, Postmodernism, and the Atomic Age.* Durham, NC: Duke University Press.

Nash, George H. 2008. *The Conservative Intellectual Movement in America Since 1945.* 30th anniversary edition. Wilmington, DE: ISI Books.

Navasky, Victor. 1999. *Naming Names.* 1st ed. New York: Hill and Wang.

Nissenbaum, Stephen. 1996. *The Battle for Christmas: A Cultural History of America's Most Cherished Holiday.* 1st ed. New York: Vintage Books.

O'Reilly, Kenneth. 1983. *Hoover and the Un-Americans: The FBI, HUAC, and the Red Menace.* Philadelphia: Temple University Press.

Pach, Chester J., and Elmo Richardson. 1991. *The Presidency of Dwight D. Eisenhower.* Lawrence, KS: University Press of Kansas.

Palmer, A. 2015. *The Santa Claus Man: The Rise and Fall of a Jazz Age Con Man and the Invention of Christmas in New York.* Guilford, CT: Rowman & Littlefield.

Pelka, Fred. 2012. *What We Have Done: An Oral History of the Disability Rights Movement.* Amherst: University of Massachusetts Press.

Perlstein, Rick, ed. 2008. "The 'Checkers Speech' (September 23, 1952)". In *Richard Nixon*, 64–80. Speeches, Writings, Documents. Princeton: Princeton University Press.

Phillips-Fein, Kim. 2009. *Invisible Hands: The Making of the Conservative Movement from the New Deal to Reagan.* New York: W. W. Norton & Company.

Poague, Leland. 1994. *Another Frank Capra.* Cambridge Studies in Film. Cambridge: Cambridge University Press.

Porst, Jennifer. 2019. "The Preservation of Competition: Hollywood and Antitrust Law". In *Hollywood and the Law*, edited by Paul McDonald, Emily Carman, Eric Hoyt, and Philip Drake, 159–206. London: Bloomsbury Publishing.

Radosh, Ronald, and Allis Radosh. 2005. *Red Star Over Hollywood: The Film Colony's Long Romance with the Left.* San Francisco: Encounter Books.

Railton, Ben. 2021. *Of Thee I Sing: The Contested History of American Patriotism.* American Ways. Lanham, MD: Rowman & Littlefield.

Raymond, Emilie. 2015. *Stars for Freedom: Hollywood, Black Celebrities, and the Civil Rights Movement.* A Capell Family Book. Seattle: University of Washington Press.

Reichard, Gary W. 1988. *Politics as Usual: The Age of Truman and Eisenhower.* Arlington Heights, IL: Harlan Davidson.

Remini, Robert V. 1967. *Andrew Jackson and the Bank War: A Study in the Growth of Presidential Power.* New York: W. W. Norton.

Restad, Penne L. 1995. *Christmas in America: A History.* New York: Oxford University Press.

Richards, Jeffrey. 1973. *Visions of Yesterday.* London: Routledge.

Roffman, Peter, and Jim Purdy. 1981. *The Hollywood Social Problem Film: Madness, Despair, and Politics from the Depression to the Fifties.* Bloomington: Indiana University Press.

Russell, James, and Jim Whalley. 2017. *Hollywood and the Baby Boom: A Social History.* New York: Bloomsbury Academic.

Sbardellati, John. 2012. *J. Edgar Hoover Goes to the Movies: The FBI and the Origins of Hollywood's Cold War.* Ithaca, NY: Cornell University Press.

Schickel, Richard. 1968. *The Disney Version: The Life, Times, Art and Commerce of Walt Disney.* New York: Simon & Schuster.

Schmidt, Leigh Eric. 1995. *Consumer Rites: The Buying & Selling of American Holidays.* Princeton: Princeton University Press.

Schneider, Gregory L. 2009. *The Conservative Century: From Reaction to Revolution.* Lanham, MD: Rowman & Littlefield Publishers.

Schrecker, Ellen. 1998. *Many Are the Crimes: McCarthyism in America.* London: Little, Brown and Company.

Scott, Ian. 2021. *Robert Riskin: The Life and Times of a Hollywood Screenwriter.* 1st ed. Lexington: The University Press of Kentucky.

Scott, Kaia. 2018. "Managing the Trauma of Labor: Military Psychiatric Cinema in World War II". In *Cinema's Military Industrial Complex*, edited by Haidee Wasson and Lee Grieveson, 1st ed., 116–136. Berkeley: University of California Press.

Sklar, Robert. 1994. *Movie-Made America: A Cultural History of American Movies.* Rev. ed. New York: Vintage Books.

Smith, Jeff. 2014. *Film Criticism, the Cold War, and the Blacklist: Reading the Hollywood Reds.* Berkeley: University of California Press.

Staiger, Janet. 1985. "The Package-Unit System: Unit Management after 1955". In *The Classical Hollywood Cinema: Film Style & Mode of Production to 1960*, by David Bordwell, Janet Staiger, and Kristin Thompson, 330–337. New York: Columbia University Press.

Stone, Isidor F. 1989. *In a Time of Torment: 1961–1967.* A Nonconformist History of Our Times. Boston: Little, Brown and Company.

Thaxton, Ralph A. 2024. *Salt of the Earth: The Political Origins of Peasant Protest and Communist Revolution in China.* 1st ed. Berkeley: University of California Press.

Theoharis, Athan G. 2002. *Chasing Spies: How the FBI Failed in Counterintelligence But Promoted the Politics of McCarthyism in the Cold War Years.* Chicago: Ivan R. Dee.

Underhill, Stephen M. 2020. *The Manufacture of Consent: J. Edgar Hoover and the Rhetorical Rise of the FBI.* East Lansing, MI: Michigan State University Press.

Wagner, Steven. 2024. *Eisenhower for Our Time.* Ithaca, NY: Cornell University Press.

Waits, William B. 1993. *The Modern Christmas in America: A Cultural History of Gift Giving.* New York: New York University Press.

Wang, Zuoyue. 2008. *In Sputnik's Shadow: The President's Science Advisory Committee and Cold War America.* New Brunswick: Rutgers University Press.

Weart, Spencer R. 2012. *The Rise of Nuclear Fear.* Cambridge, MA: Harvard University Press.

Wills, Gary. 2010. *Bomb Power: The Modern Presidency and the National Security State.* New York: Penguin Books.

Wills, John. 2017. *Disney Culture.* New Brunswick: Rutgers University Press.

Winkler, Allan M. 1993. *Life under a Cloud: American Anxiety about the Atom.* Oxford: Oxford University Press.

Witham, Nick. 2023. *Popularizing the Past: Historians, Publishers, and Readers in Postwar America.* Chicago: University of Chicago Press.

Articles

Auerbach, Jonathan. 2006. "American Studies and Film, Blindness and Insight". *American Quarterly* 58 (1): 31–50.

Bailey, Beth. 2004. "From Front Porch to Back Seat: A History of the Date". *OAH Magazine of History* 18 (4): 23–26.

Chernus, Ira. 2005. "Operation Candor: Fear, Faith, and Flexibility". *Diplomatic History* 29 (5): 779–809.

Devitt, James. 1998. "Tokens of Deception in the 'Checkers' Speech". *Political Communication* 15 (1): 1–14.

Doepke, Matthias, Moshe Hazan, and Yishay D. Maoz. 2015. "The Baby Boom and World War II: A Macroeconomic Analysis". *The Review of Economic Studies* 82 (3 (292)): 1031–1073.

Fleming, Kevin C., Jonathan M. Evans, and Darryl S. Chutka. 2003. "A Cultural and Economic History of Old Age in America". *Mayo Clinic Proceedings* 78 (7): 914–921.

Gauger, Michael. 2005. "Flickering Images: Live Television Coverage and Viewership of the Army—McCarthy Hearings". *The Historian* 67 (4): 678–693.

Laughlin, Elizabeth A. 2012. "The Rise of American Industrial and Financial Corporations". *Gettysburg Economic Review* 6 (5): 42–57.

Madgwick, P. J. 1971. "The Politics of Urban Renewal". *Journal of American Studies* 5 (3): 265–280.

Malsberger, John W. 2011. "Dwight Eisenhower, Richard Nixon, and the Fund Crisis of 1952". *The Historian* 73 (3): 526–547.

Mangelsdorf, Philip. 1967. "When William Allen White and Ed Howe Covered the Republicans". *Journalism Quarterly* 44 (3): 454–460.

Noakes, John A. 1998. "Bankers and Common Men in Bedford Falls: How the FBI Determined That 'It's a Wonderful Life' Was a Subversive Movie". *Film History* 10 (3): 311–319.

Noakes, John A. 2000. "Official Frames in Social Movement Theory: The FBI, HUAC, and the Communist Threat in Hollywood". *The Sociological Quarterly* 41 (4): 657–680.

Oren, Laura. 2018. "No-Fault Divorce Reform in the 1950s: The Lost History of the 'Greatest Project' of the National Association of Women Lawyers". *Law and History Review* 36 (4): 847–890.

Poulson, Micah. 2023. "Heroes Abroad, Forgotten at Home: The Case for Reparation for Black WWII Veterans." *Georgetown Journal on Poverty Law & Policy* 31 (1): 151–169.

Richards, Jeffrey. 1972. "Frank Capra and the Cinema of Populism". *Cinema*, no. 5, 22–28.

Rodgers, Daniel T. 1982. "In Search of Progressivism". *Reviews in American History* 10 (4): 113 – 132.

Rollins, Peter C. 1974. "Film and American Studies: Questions, Activities, Guides". *American Quarterly* 26 (3): 245 – 265.

Sobchack, Vivian C. 1980. "Beyond Visual Aids: American Film as American Culture". *American Quarterly* 32 (3): 280 – 300.

Stein, Julie Solow. 2013. "Early to Wed: Teenage Marriage in Postwar America". *Journal of the History of Childhood and Youth* 6 (2): 359 – 382,406.

Stevenson, Charles A. 2008. "The Story Behind the National Security Act of 1947". *Military Review* 88 (3): 13 – 20.

Whaples, Robert M. 2020. "Why Didn't Galbraith Convince Us That America Is an Affluent Society?" *The Independent Review* 24 (4): 579 – 592.

Whiteley, Nigel. 1987. "Toward a Throw-Away Culture. Consumerism, 'Style Obsolescence' and Cultural Theory in the 1950s and 1960s". *Oxford Art Journal* 10 (2): 3 – 27.

Index

www.ingramcontent.com/pod-product-compliance
Lightning Source LLC
Chambersburg PA
CBHW030313100426
42812CB00002B/685